Adobe® Audition® 2.0

CLASSROOM IN A BOOK®

www.adobepress.com

Adobe

Adobe® Audition® 2.0 Classroom in a Book®

Adobe Systems Incorporated, 345 Park Avenue, San Jose, California 95110-2704, USA

Adobe Press books are published by Peachpit, Berkeley, CA. To report errors, please send a note to errata@peachpit.com.

Printed in the USA

ISBN 0-321-38550-0

9 8 7 6 5 4 3 2

Contents

Getting Started

1 A Quick Tour of Adobe Audition

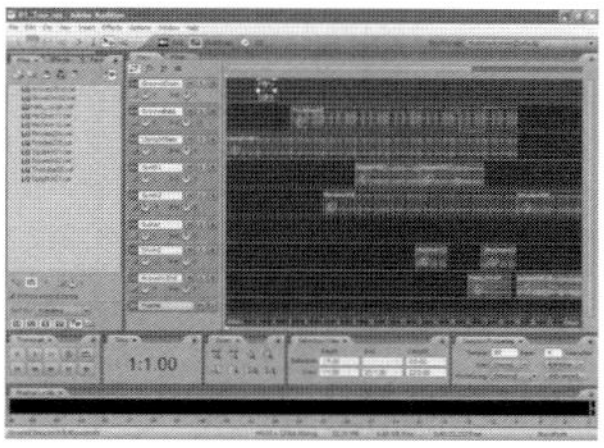

2 Audition Basics

3 Working in Edit View

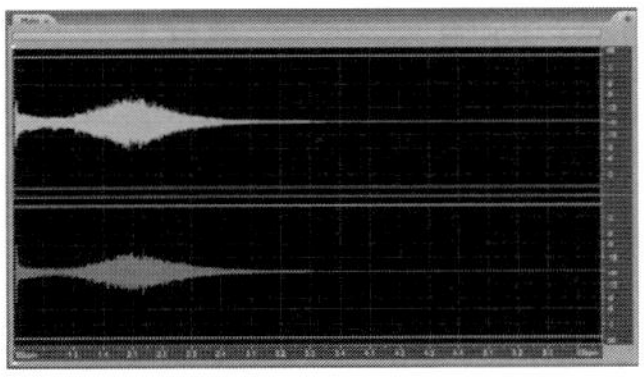

4 Working in Multitrack View

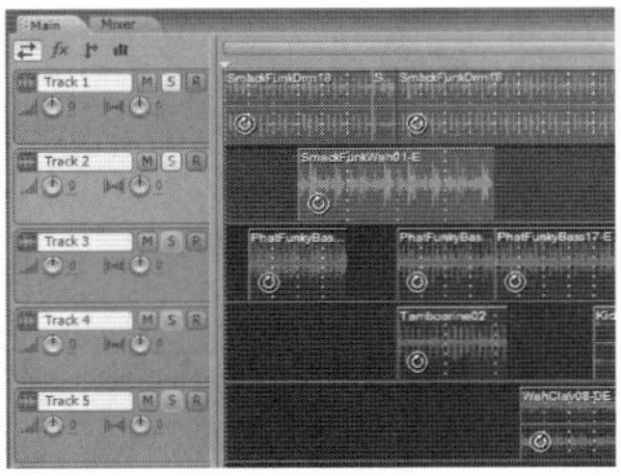

5 Working with Loops and Waves

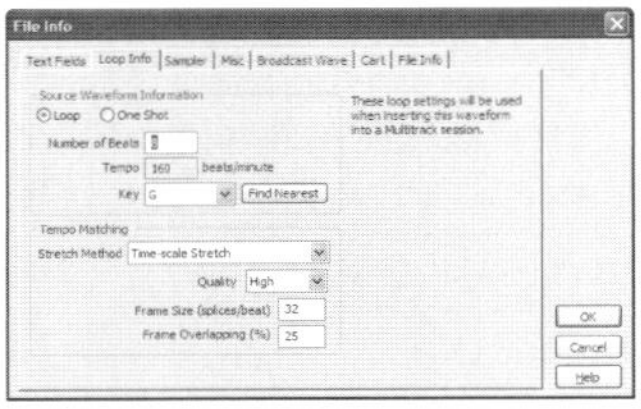

6 Noise Reduction

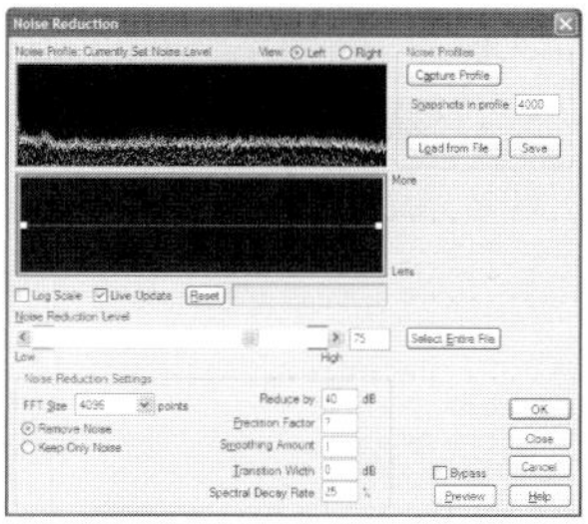

7 Editing Voices

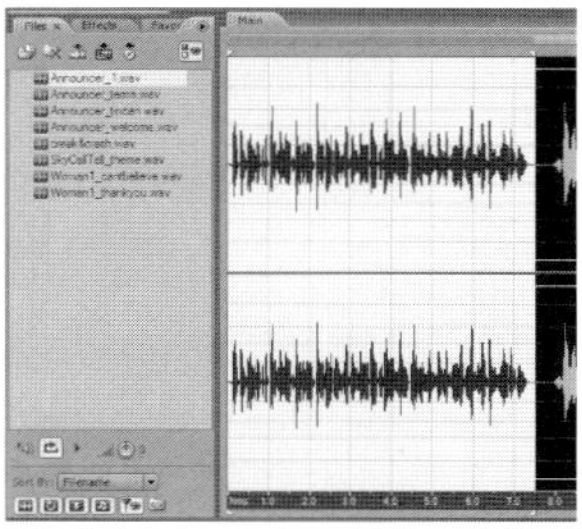

8 Mixing and Real-Time Effects

9 Using Audition's Equalization Tools

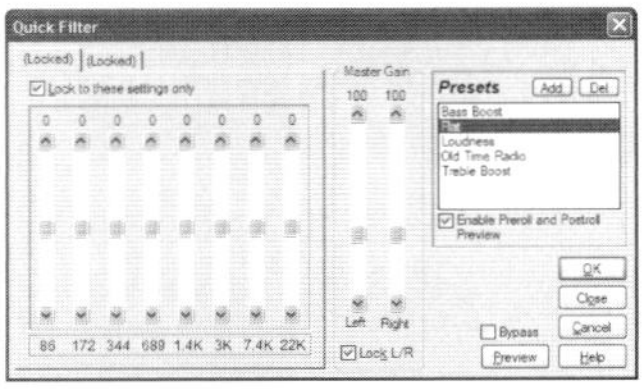

10 Using Audition's Automation Tools

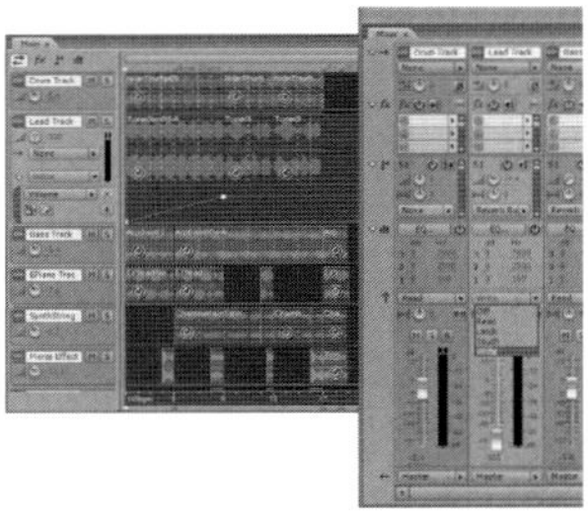

11 Optimizing Audio for the Internet

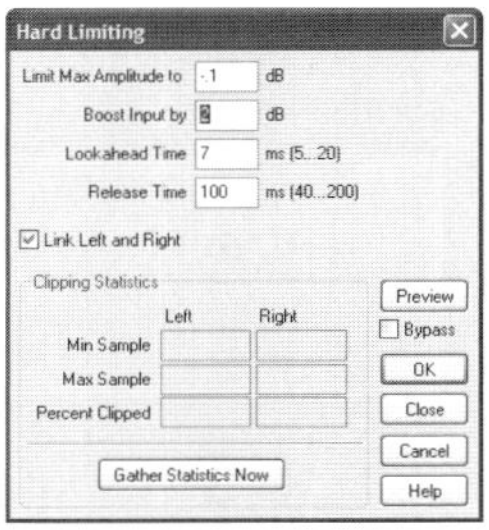

12 Using the CD View

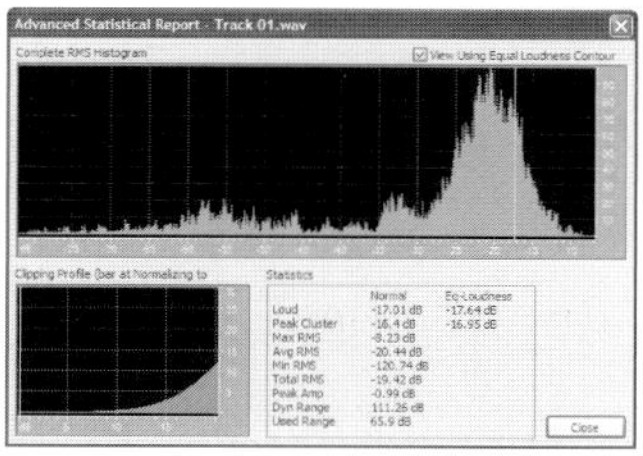

13 Integrating Adobe Audition and Adobe Premiere Pro

Getting Started

Welcome to Adobe® Audition. Audition is a powerful audio editing and production tool that offers precision, control, and seamless integration with other Adobe professional software, including Adobe Premiere Pro and Adobe After Effects. Using Audition, you can produce professional-quality sound files for distribution electronically, on CD or DVD, or for other recording purposes.

About Classroom in a Book

Adobe Audition 2.0 Classroom in a Book® is part of the official training series for Adobe audio and video software from Adobe Systems, Inc.

The lessons are designed so that you can learn at your own pace. If you're new to Adobe Audition, you'll learn the fundamentals you'll need to master in order to put the program to work. If you've already been using Adobe Audition, you'll find that Classroom in a Book teaches many advanced features, including tips and techniques for using this exciting audio tool.

Each lesson provides step-by-step instructions for creating a specific project. You can follow the book from start to finish, or study only the lessons that meet your interests and needs. The lessons concludes with a review section summarizing what you've covered.

Prerequisites

Before beginning to use *Adobe Audition 2.0 Classroom in a Book*, you should have a working knowledge of your computer and its operating system. Make sure you know how to use the mouse, and standard menus and commands, and also how to open, save, and close files. The lessons reference the file extensions when describing file names. You can set Windows to display or not display file extensions. If you need to review these techniques, see the printed or online documentation included with your Microsoft Windows documentation.

Installing Adobe Audition 2.0

You must purchase the Adobe Audition software separately. For complete instructions on installing the software, see the "How to Install" Readme file on the application CD.

Copying the Classroom in a Book files

The Classroom in a Book CD includes folders containing all the electronic files for the lessons. Each lesson has its own folder. You must copy these folders onto your hard disk to use the files for the lessons. To save room on your hard disk, you can copy the folders for each lesson as you need them.

1 Insert the *Adobe Audition 2.0 Classroom in a Book* CD into your CD-ROM drive.

Note: *The CD contains both data and music tracks. If your computer is set to automatically play music CDs, you may need to access the lesson folders using Windows, by closing any multimedia applications such as Windows Media Player or iTunes.*

2 From My Computer, right-click the drive containing the CD-ROM and choose Explore from the contextual menu that appears.

3 Create a folder on your hard disk and name it AA_CIB.

4 Do one of the following:

- Copy the individual lesson folders into the AA_CIB folder.
- Copy only the single lesson folder you need.

Additional resources

Adobe Audition 2.0 Classroom in a Book is not meant to replace documentation that comes with the program. Only the commands and options used in the lessons are explained in this book. For comprehensive information about program features, refer to these resources:

- Adobe Audition Help, which you can view by choosing Help > Adobe Audition Help.
- Training and support resources on the Adobe web site (www.adobe.com), which you can view by choosing Help > Online Support if you have a connection to the Internet.

Adobe Certification

The Adobe Training and Certification Programs are designed to help Adobe customers improve and promote their product-proficiency skills. The Adobe Certified Expert (ACE) program is designed to recognize the high-level skills of expert users. Adobe Certified Training Providers (ACTP) use only Adobe Certified Experts to teach Adobe software classes. Available in either ACTP classrooms or on site, the ACE program is the best way to master Adobe products. For Adobe Certified Training Programs information, visit the Partnering with Adobe Web site at http://partners.adobe.com.

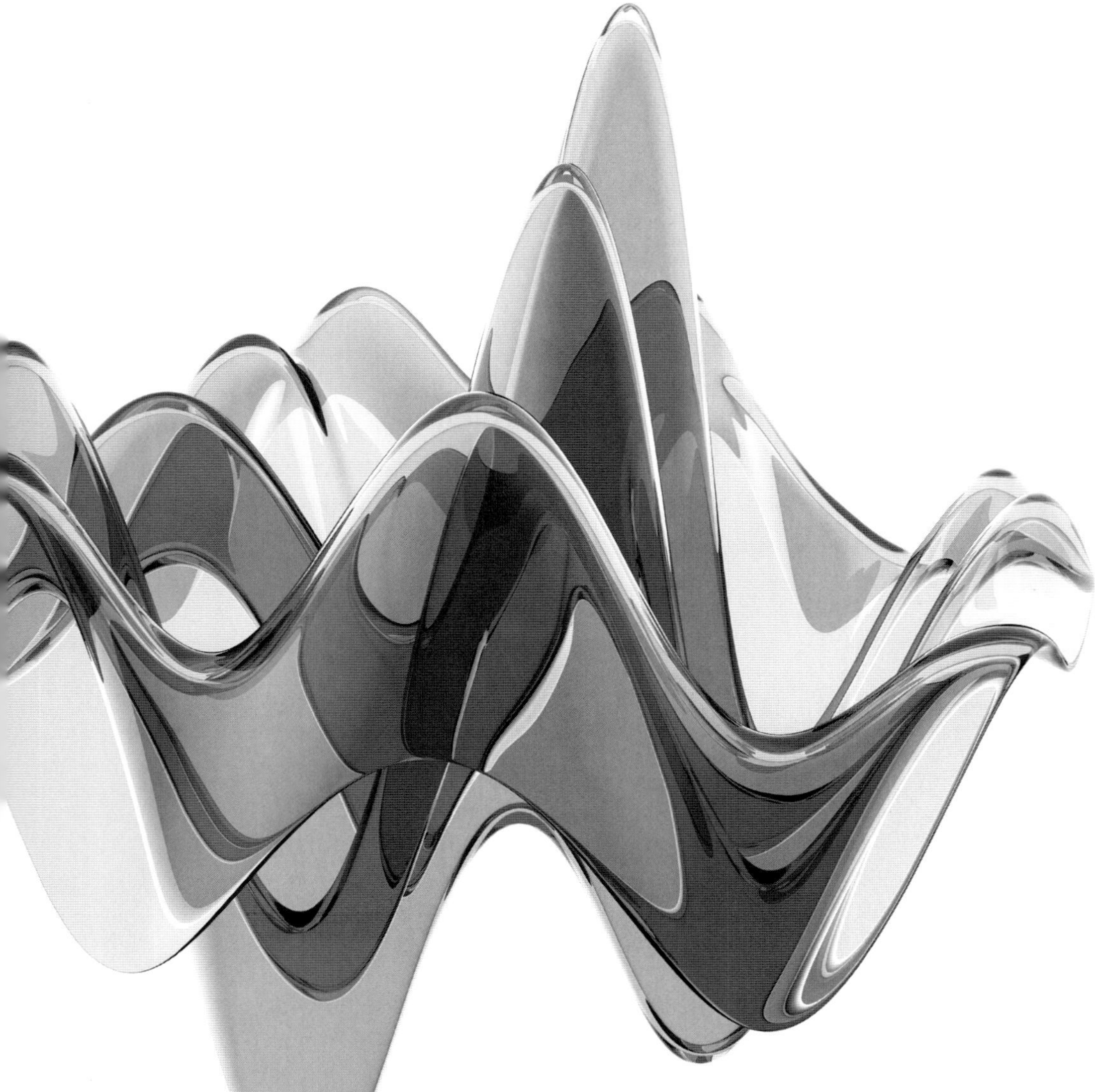

1 A Quick Tour of Adobe Audition

In this lesson, you will be introduced to the tools and interface of Adobe Audition 2.0. Future lessons provide more in-depth exercises and specific details of the tools and features. You'll start the tour by opening a partially completed Audition session where you'll add the finishing touches to a 60 second jazz song. In this Quick Tour, you will learn how to navigate within Audition, add music tracks, use loops, repair noisy audio, and then export the session to an .mp3 audio file.

The example files and resources that accompany this lesson are found on the *Adobe Audition 2.0 Classroom in a Book* CD. Before you proceed with the following steps, you need to copy these resources from the CD to your hard disk. If you have not already done so, see "Copying the Classroom in a Book files" on page 2.

1 Start Adobe Audition, and click on the Multitrack View button () near the top of your display.

2 Choose File > Open Session, and open the 01_start.ses file in the AA_01 folder, which you copied to your hard disk.

3 From the File menu found at the top left corner of your display, choose File > Save Session As. Enter the name **01_Tour.ses**, and save the file in the AA_01 folder on your hard disk.

Renaming the file keeps the original file untouched, in case you want to return to the original source file. Take a moment to look at the Audition interface and its various components. You should be able to see audio tracks, their controls, clips, Audition's toolbars, and buttons.

4 Play the currently open 01_Tour.ses session by clicking on the Play from Cursor to End of File button ( ) in the Transport panel, which is located in the lower left corner of the Audition window. Play from Cursor to End of File is the button's default behavior. Right-click on buttons in the Transport panel to change their default behavior. You can also press the spacebar on your computer keyboard as a shortcut to play the session.

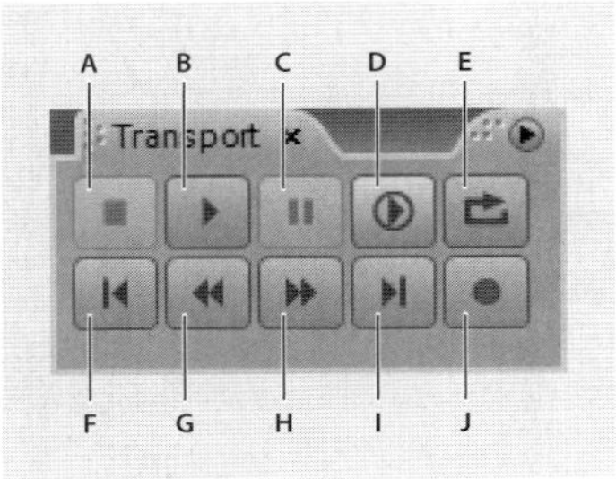

The Transport panel controls:
A. Stop.
B. Play from Cursor to End of File.
C. Pause.
D. Play from Cursor to End of View.
E. Play Looped (View or Sel).
F. Go To Beginning or Previous Marker.
G. Rewind.
H. Fast Forward.
I. Go To End or Next Marker.
J. Record.

Note: *You may need to maximize the window to see all controls available within Audition. When the window size is reduced, certain controls are not displayed. You can maximize the window by clicking the Maximize button (□) in the upper right corner of the window.*

5 Press the spacebar again to stop the playback of the session. To hear how the completed session will sound after you follow all the instructions in this lesson, choose File > Open Session, and open and play the 01_end.ses file in the AA_01 folder.

6 When you are ready to start working, close the 01_end.ses file by choosing File > Close All. Choose File > Open Session and select 01_Tour.ses.

The file 01_Tour.ses should be listed under your recently used files, which Audition displays at the bottom of the File menu.

Navigating the session

As the 01_Tour.ses session is displayed in Multitrack View, all the sound files used in the session are listed along the left portion of the window in the Files panel.

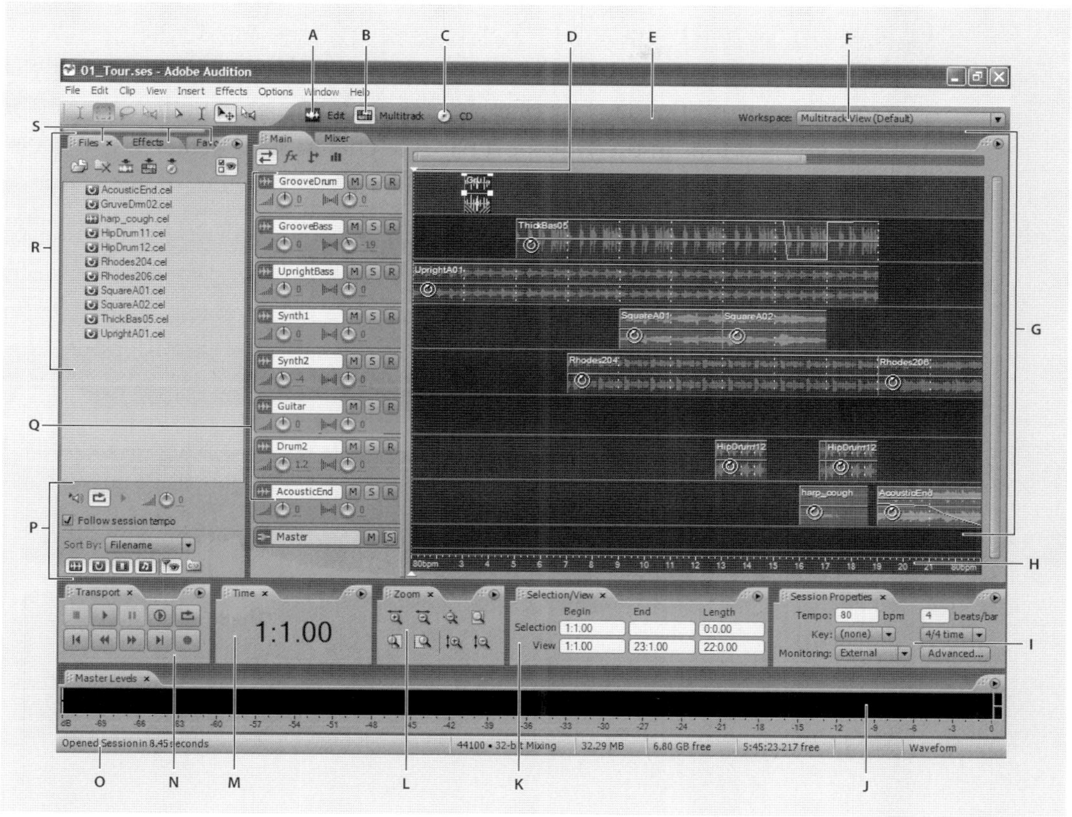

Adobe Audition work area:
A. *Edit View button.* ***B.*** *Multitrack View button.* ***C.*** *CD View button.* ***D.*** *Start-time indicator.*
E. *Toolbar area.* ***F.*** *Workspace menu.* ***G.*** *Display area.* ***H.*** *Timeline.* ***I.*** *Session Properties panel.*
J. *Master Levels panel.* ***K.*** *Selection/View panel.* ***L.*** *Zoom panel.* ***M.*** *Current Time display.*
N. *Transport panel.* ***O.*** *Status bar.* ***P.*** *Files panel options.* ***Q.*** *Track list.* ***R.*** *Files panel.*
S. *Tabbed panels.*

The Multitrack View consists of tracks, and each track can contain one or more clips within it. The multitrack is located near the center of the screen. In this session, each clip represents a recording of a musical instrument and each track has been labeled to identify the instrument used. You can navigate through a session using various methods.

1 Bring your cursor over the Play button ( ) in the Transport panel, which is located at the bottom left corner of the Audition window. If you keep your cursor over this button without clicking, a tooltip briefly appears mentioning the function of this button. The tooltip displays, Play from Cursor to End of File, which is the default function of this button. Click this button to begin playback of the session.

As the session begins to play, the playback cursor, which is a white vertical line, begins to move across the timeline of the multitrack. As this cursor moves over a clip, the contents of the clip are played. If various tracks contain clips whose contents occur simultaneously, all the tracks are played in synchronization.

Notice the arrangement of the clips inside the multitrack. The first instrument to start is the UprightBass, which begins playing immediately. As the playback cursor hits the GruveDrm02 clip, you hear this component. The GrooveBass track represents yet another track. Each instrument is on a different track, yet the overall result is multiple instruments playing together in synchronization.

2 Press the Pause button ( ) to pause the session. The playback cursor stops and the current time is displayed at the bottom of the window. Since the timeline is currently showing time in Bars and Beats, the location is displayed in this form of measurement. We paused our session when the playback cursor reached Bar 15 beat 1, tick 1.

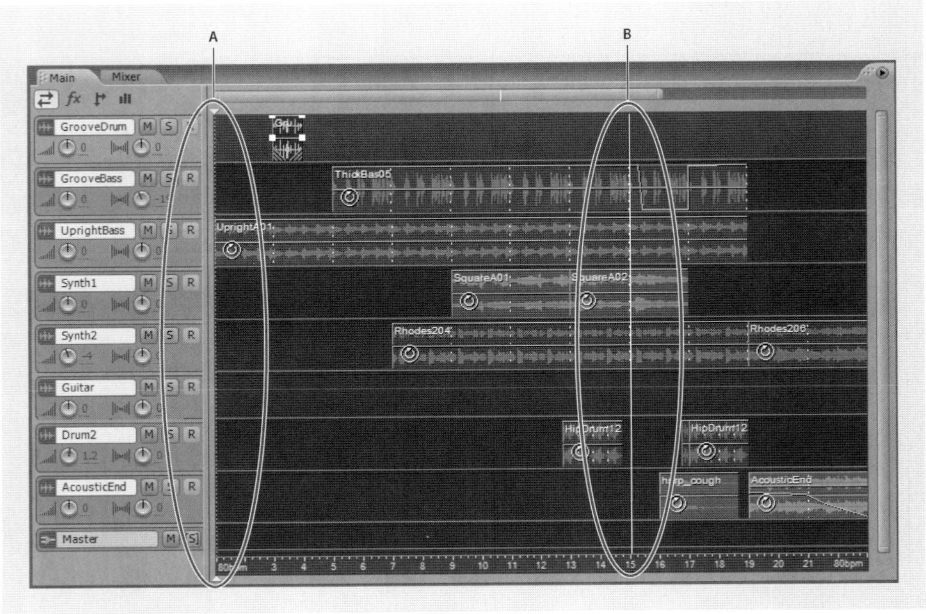

A. Start-time indicator (yellow). B. Playback cursor (white).

3 Click the Play button ( ) in the Transport panel and note that the session begins at the start rather than resuming from the pause point. This is because the Play button starts to play from the location of the start-time indicator, which is represented by a dotted yellow line ending in yellow triangles on both the top and bottom. It is located at the beginning of the session right now. This indicator can be relocated to establish a different starting point for playback. To resume playback from a paused location, click the Pause button again.

4 If necessary, press the spacebar on your keyboard to stop the playback. In addition to using the Transport panel controls, Audition offers many keyboard shortcuts to perform common commands.

5 Right-click on the timeline ruler that is found at the bottom of the multitrack display, and choose Display Time Format > Decimal (mm:ss.ddd) from the context menu. This changes the time format in this session from Bars and Beats to minutes and seconds.

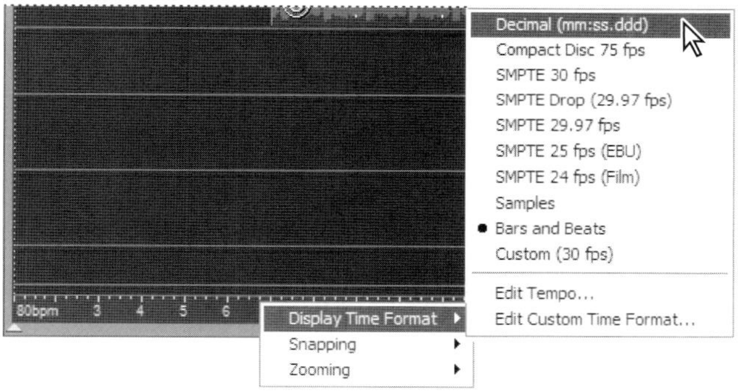

6 Place the cursor over one of the yellow triangles of the start-time indicator. The cursor changes to a pointing finger ( ), allowing you to move the start-time indicator to a specific point in the multitrack. Click and drag to the right.

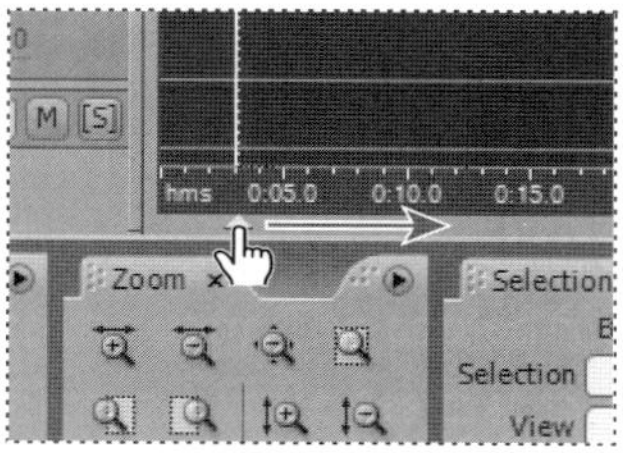

Start-time indicator being dragged to a new location.

As you drag to the right, the contents of the session are scrubbed to help you find a new location for the start-time indicator. Release your mouse button to let go of the start-time indicator. It gets relocated at the point you release. Additionally, you can use the left and right arrow keys on your computer keyboard to accurately relocate the start-time indicator. When using the arrow keys, the session is not scrubbed.

7 Click and drag the start-time indicator slowly across the multitrack to approximately the 24 second mark. This location is also the beginning of the audio clip named SquareA01. Keep an eye on the Time Display panel to know your location as you drag the start-time indicator.

8 Click the Play button in the Transport panel controls, the session begins to play from near the 24 second mark, where you just relocated your start-time indicator. The start-time indicator is frequently used to navigate and play specific sections within a session. Press the spacebar to stop playing the session.

9 Right-click on the timeline ruler, and using the context menu, choose Display Time Format > Bars and Beats. This changes the ruler back from the decimal format to Bars and Beats. This is a more traditional time display for working with loop-based files. Note that this context menu also lets you set the Snapping options for the start-time indicator and the Zoom level. This session was originally displaying time in Bars and Beats format. You then changed it to the decimal format of minutes, and seconds, and then changed it back to Bars and Beats. You can therefore change the units of measurement based upon your needs and the type of session you are creating.

10 Click the Go to Beginning or Previous Marker button (⏮) in the Transport panel to place the start-time indicator at the beginning of the session. When the start-time indicator is at the start of the session, the time display shows 1:1.00. This is read as Bar 1 beat 1.

Working with loops

To better understand the concept of Bars and Beats, look in the Files panel and notice, but don't select, the drum loop entitled GruveDrm02.cel. A file having the .cel or .wav and the loop icon (🔁) next to it signifies that it is an Audition file capable of being looped in the multitrack. This clip has already been inserted into the first track.

1 Press the spacebar to begin playing the session file. Since the start-time indicator is located at the beginning of the session (Bar 1 beat 1), this is where the playback begins. At Bar 3 beat 1, the GruveDrm02 clip plays for exactly one bar and then ends. When the drumbeat stops playing, press the spacebar again to stop the playback cursor.

In this session, each bar consists of exactly four beats, as confirmed by the Session Properties panel found at the bottom right of your display. Also note that the tempo of your session has been set at 80 bpm in this panel. Press the spacebar again and when the drum begins, count the four beats in the drum loop. When the bar is over, press the spacebar to stop playing the session.

2 Click to select the GruveDrm02 clip in the Multitrack View. Place your cursor over the diagonal lines visible at the bottom right corner of the GruveDrm02 clip. Your cursor changes to the loop editing icon (), a double arrow with a small loop.

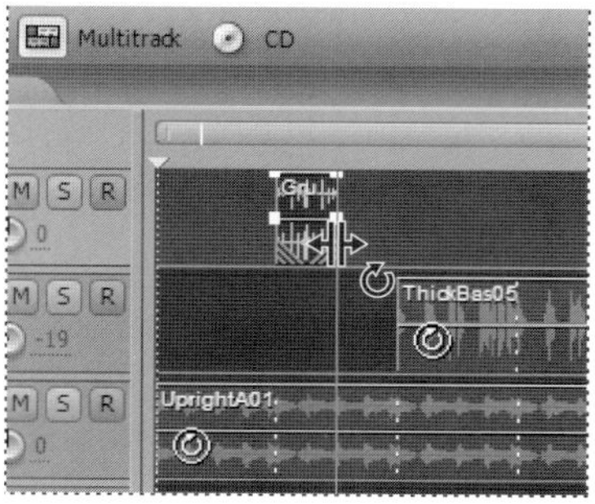

3 Click and drag to the right, extending the loop so it ends at the same time as the clips in both Track 2 and Track 3, ThickBas05 and UprightA01 respectively. As you extend the loop, a dashed white line is created within the clip for every new bar, helping you keep track of the number of bars, and ensuring that the clip ends precisely on a beat.

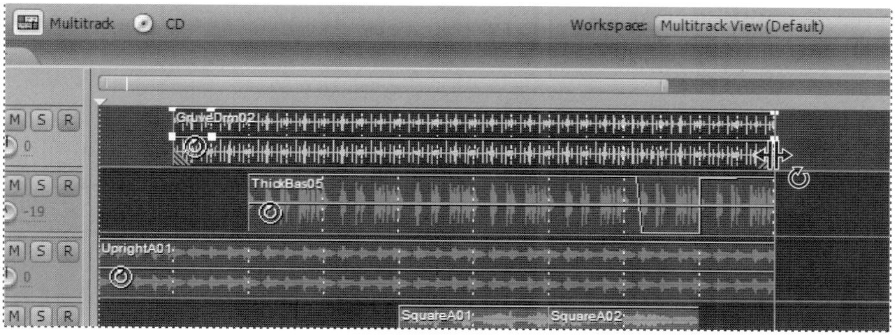

4 Press the Home key on your keyboard to place the start-time indicator at the beginning of the session. Press the spacebar to play the session. The drum track loops seamlessly for 16 bars. The original drum clip was one bar in length. You were able to extend the clip because this clip was designed to be looped. Press the spacebar to stop playback after you have reviewed the file.

Note: *Adobe Audition 2.0 ships with a Loopology DVD of nearly 5,000 individual music loops sampled from a variety of musical sources. It is also possible to create your own loops in Audition's Edit View. You will explore this feature in Lesson 3.*

5 At the top of the Files panel, click on the Import File button ( ) and select the file GuitLick02.cel in the AA_01 folder on your hard disk. Click the Open button to import this file into the Files panel. This file is now displayed in the Files panel.

Note: *Audition lets you easily preview the files before importing them into the Files panel, as well as after they have been imported into it. Check the Auto Play option in the Import window, or after importing a file, click the Auto Play button ( ) in the Files panel. Selected files are then played.*

6 Click and drag the file GuitLick02.cel into the empty track named Guitar. Place it near the beginning of the track and release the mouse.

Click and drag GuitLick02.cel to the empty Guitar track.

7 From the toolbar, select the Move/Copy Clip tool () and then click on the GuitLick02 clip. Without releasing your mouse button, drag the clip to the right.

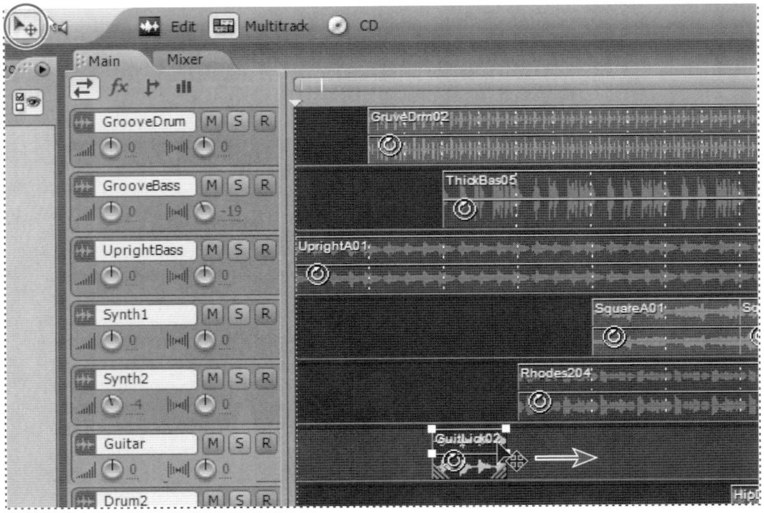

The Move/Copy Clip tool is found in the toolbar.

As you drag the clip into the multitrack, notice that the beginning and the end of the clip can snap to the individual beats on the ruler. Drag the clip so the beginning aligns with the Bar 11 beat 1 (11:1.00) mark. A vertical gray line appears when the clip is aligned to this position. Make sure the gray line is aligning at the beginning of the clip, not the end.

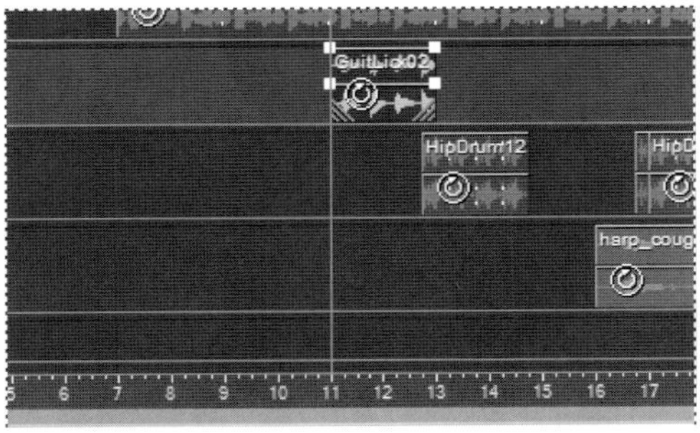

***Note:** It is useful to refer to the status bar at the bottom of the window. As you move clips through the multitrack, the status bar reflects the location of the start of the clip.*

8 Place your cursor on the triangular handle at the bottom right of the GuitLick02 clip. The cursor changes to the loop editing icon (). Click and drag toward the right to extend the clip to Bar 15 beat 1 (15:1.00).

9 Click and drag the start-time indicator to Bar 8 beat 1 (8:1.00) and then press the spacebar on your keyboard to play the session from this point.

Muting and soloing tracks

Audition provides tools to make it easier to work with multiple tracks. To separate specific tracks from the others, you can use Audition's solo and mute options.

1 Click and drag the start-time indicator to approximately Bar 9 beat 1 (9:1.00). This is the point where the clip SquareA01 in the Synth1 track begins.

2 Press the spacebar on your keyboard to play the session. In the Synth1 track, click the Solo button (S). This button lights up when selected. All clips except the ones contained in the Synth1 track become grayed-out to visually identify that they will not be audible during playback. Press the spacebar to stop the playback cursor. Click the Solo button for Synth1 track once more to turn it off. Other tracks are now audible during playback.

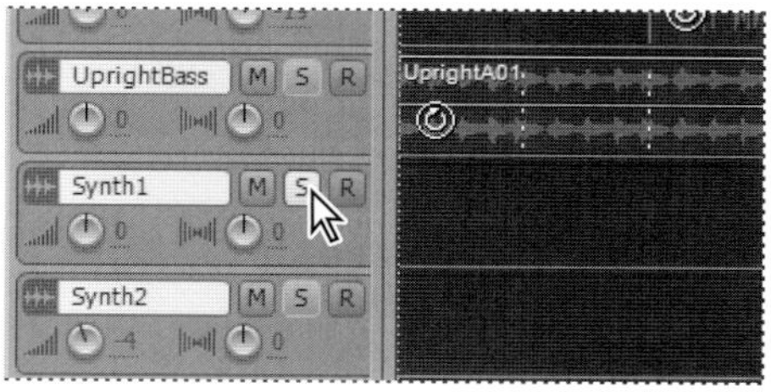

3 Mute the Synth1 track by clicking the Mute button (M). This button lights up when selected. This causes the contents of Synth1 track to become grayed-out, indicating that they will not be audible during playback. The Mute button is the functional opposite of the Solo button.

4 Press the spacebar to begin playing the session. Since you had positioned the start-time indicator at Bar 9 beat 1 in step 1, that's where the playback begins.

After a few seconds of playback, click the Mute button for the Synth1 track again to make its contents audible. Press the spacebar to stop playing the session. The Mute and Solo buttons can be used as a session is playing, and when playback has been stopped.

5 Press the Esc key, then use the left and right arrows on your computer keyboard and relocate the start-time indicator to approximately Bar 7 beat 1 (7:1.00). Click the Solo button for the GrooveDrum track. Now click on the Solo button for the Synth2 track. Press the spacebar to begin playback. You will hear the GrooveDrum track and the Synth2 tracks only.

Clicking the Solo buttons on two or more tracks allows you to play selected tracks together. Other tracks will be inaudible as shown by their grayed-out contents.

6 Press the spacebar to stop playing the session. Turn off the Solo buttons for the GrooveDrum track and the Synth2 track to re-enable the playback of remaining tracks.

Changing track volume and pan

You can modify the volume and pan position of each track in a multitrack session. All clips located within the track are affected by these changes.

1 Click on the Solo button in the Synth1 track to isolate this track from the others. In the Synth1 track properties, just below the Mute and Solo buttons, you will find two knobs. The one on the left controls the volume of this track, measured in decibels. The knob on the right controls the panning (stereo placement) of this track, where -100 represents hard left and +100 represents hard right locations in the stereo field. Currently, both these knobs are set to their default values of 0.

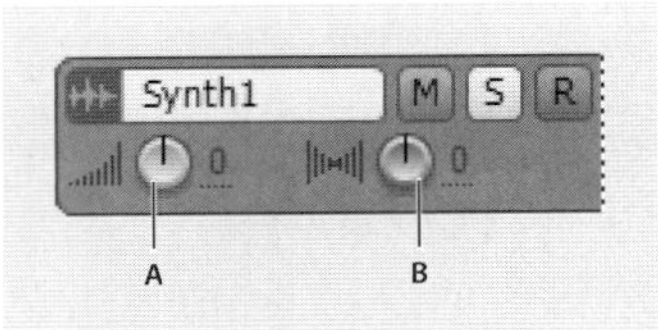

A. *Track Volume knob.*
B. *Track Pan knob.*

Note: *Depending on the level of detail at which you want to work, Audition lets you view your session at different vertical and horizontal zoom levels. If you zoom out too much vertically, the Volume and Pan knobs for each track will become hidden. You can make these two knobs visible by clicking a few times on the Zoom In Vertically button ( ) found in the Zoom panel. If you zoom in far enough, you can also see the various other controls for each track below these knobs. The extra settings you will see—Input/Output, Effects, Sends, or Equalization (EQ)—depend on which of these settings has been chosen to be viewed using the four buttons that appear above the first track in the multitrack.*

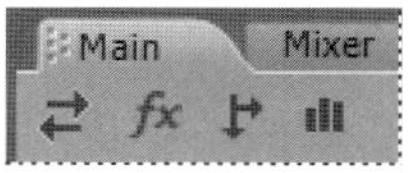

2 Move the start-time indicator to approximately Bar 9 beat 1. Press the spacebar to begin playback to hear the soloed Synth1 track. As this track plays, click on the Volume knob and drag your cursor to the right, raising the volume of the Synth1 track to 10 dB. You will immediately hear this change as the Synth1 track becomes louder. Release your mouse button and press the spacebar to stop playback.

3 Press the spacebar again to start playback from Bar 9 beat 1. Click on the Volume knob and this time drag to the left, continuing past 0 to -7 dB. As you change the values to a negative number, the volume is lower than the original setting. Drag the knob back to the right to return it to its default value of 0 dB. Click on the Solo button for the Synth1 track to enable the remaining tracks. Press the spacebar to stop playback.

4 Press the Esc key once on your keyboard to shift the focus from track controls back to the multitrack. Press the Home key to return the start-time indicator to the beginning of the multitrack, and then press the spacebar again to play the session from the beginning. In the UprightBass track, click on the Pan knob and drag to the left to set it at -50. As you do so, you can hear the bass shifting to the left. Now drag this knob to the right to set it at +50. This causes the bass track to seem like it's emanating from the right channel. Click once on the blue number that appears to the right of the Pan knob, type in **0**, and press Enter on your computer keyboard. This returns the Pan knob back to its default position of 0. Press the spacebar to stop playback.

Note: *Depending on the speaker setup of your computer system, changes to Pan settings may be more apparent when listening to the audio using headphones. The stereo speakers on a laptop or the built-in speakers of a computer may not provide sufficient distance between left and right channels to make Pan effects immediately noticeable.*

Applying non-destructive effects

Audition 2.0 offers a wide variety of real-time effects that you can add to any track to enhance its impact. For example, you might want to add a reverb to a vocal track to make it seem like it is taking place in a spacious hall. Or you might wish to process a guitar track with an effect, just like a guitar player processes a guitar's sound with a pedal or a stomp-box for chorus, flanger, or wah-wah.

When you add such effects to a track in the Multitrack View, they are heard for all the clips contained within that track. An advantage of real-time effects in the Multitrack View is that they do not alter the original clips at all. As the session plays, Audition performs all computations required to make you hear the effects. Nothing is actually changed in the source waveform files, which is why these effects are called non-destructive real-time effects. In the following steps, you will add a real-time Flanger effect to the Guitar track.

1 Solo the Guitar track in the Multitrack View by clicking on the Solo button (S) in its track properties. Move the start-time indicator to Bar 11 beat 1 (11:1.00) by clicking and dragging or by using the left and right arrow keys on your computer keyboard. This location in time is where the GuitarLick02.cel clip starts to play for four bars. Press the spacebar to begin playback and hear the soloed guitar track. When the playback cursor reaches Bar 15 beat 1 (15:1.00), press the spacebar again to stop playback.

2 Click on the Mixer tab found at the top left corner of the Main panel.

Switching to the Mixer panel in the Multitrack View.

The Mixer panel opens up, showing a channel strip corresponding to each track in your session. Looking from the top to bottom for each track, you'll find controls for track Input, Effects (or FX), Sends, Equalization (or EQ), Automation, Panning, Track Status, Volume, and Output Destination.

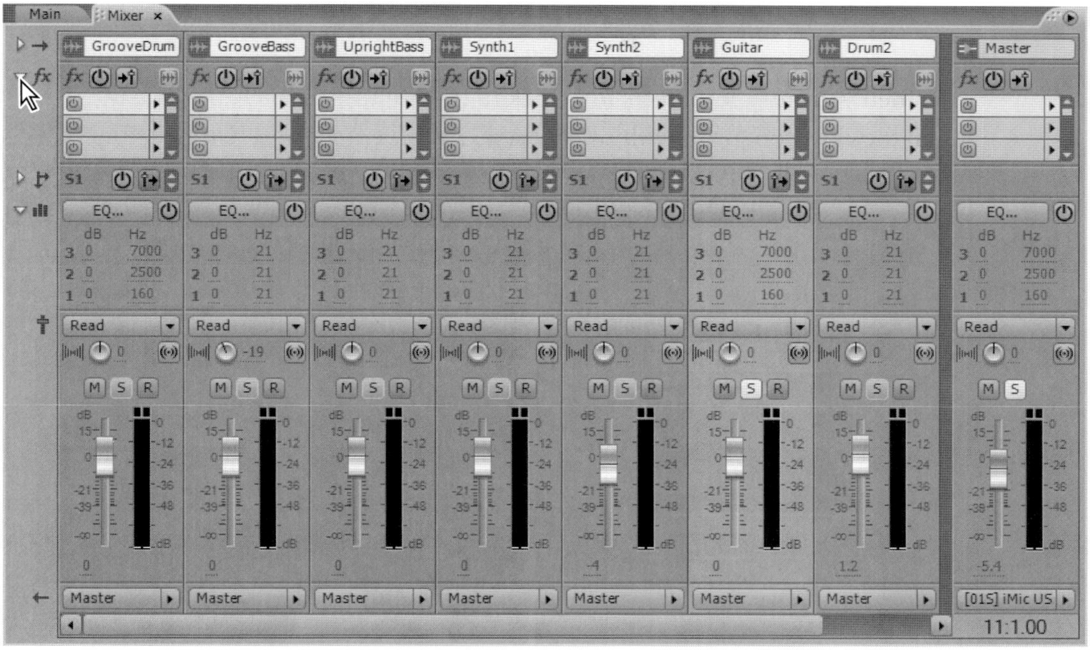

The Mixer panel with collapsible sections.

The Mixer panel is a complementary interface to the Main panel of the Multitrack View. Changes made in one window are reflected in the other. The solo status of the Guitar track is also reflected in the Mixer panel. The volume and pan settings you accessed via the track properties in the previous exercise are easily accessible in the Mixer panel as well.

3 Confirm that you can see the three effect slots in the FX section for your tracks. If not, click on the Show/Hide Effects Controls triangle (▷) that appears on the left edge of the Mixer panel to expand the FX section.

You might have to collapse some of the other sections of the Mixer or expand the Audition window to display the effect slots.

4 In the mixer strip for the Guitar track, click on the black triangle in the first effect slot. From the context menu that opens up when you click, choose Delay Effects > Flanger.

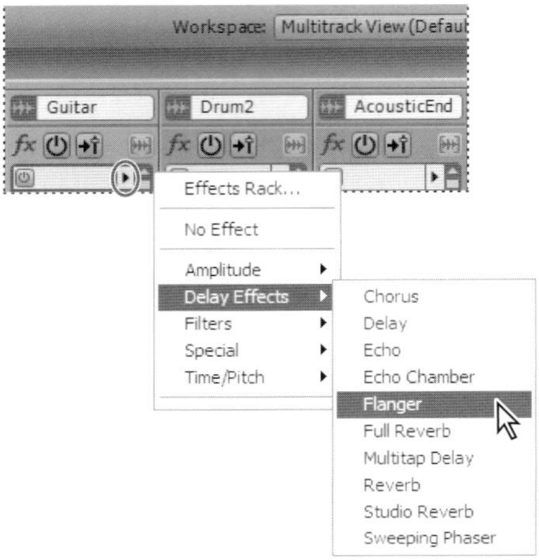

A window called "Effects Rack: Guitar" opens and displays the Effects Rack on the left, in which the Flanger effect has been inserted. On the right, the settings pertaining to this effect are displayed. A Flanger adds a short, periodically varying delay to the track.

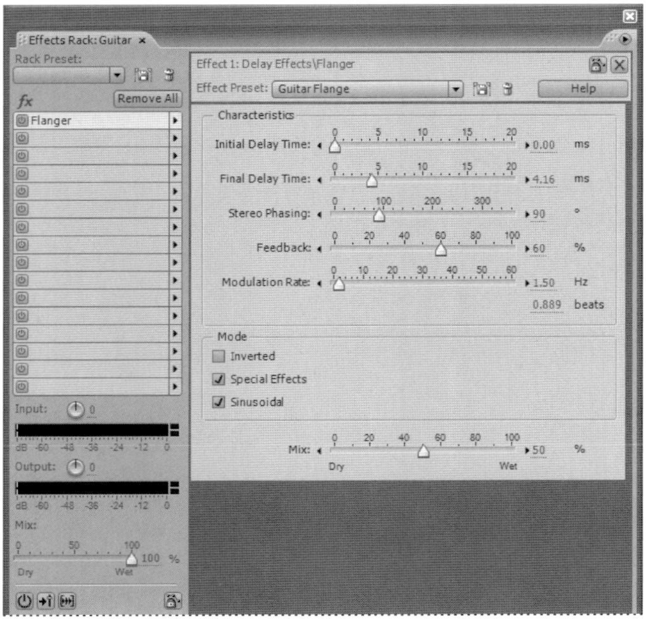

5 In the settings for the Flanger effect that appear on the right, click on the Effect Preset menu at the top and choose the Guitar Flange preset from the drop-down menu. Press the spacebar to hear the guitar with the Flanger effect. The Guitar Flange effect causes the guitar to sound warbled. Stop the playback by pressing the spacebar.

6 Click on the Power button ( ) in the slot where the Flanger effect has been inserted. This turns off the power to the Flanger effect. Press the spacebar to hear the original sound of the guitar without any effect applied to it. While the playback is still in progress, click on this Power button again to bring back the Flanger effect. Do this several times to get an idea of how the addition of an effect can drastically change the resulting sound of a track.

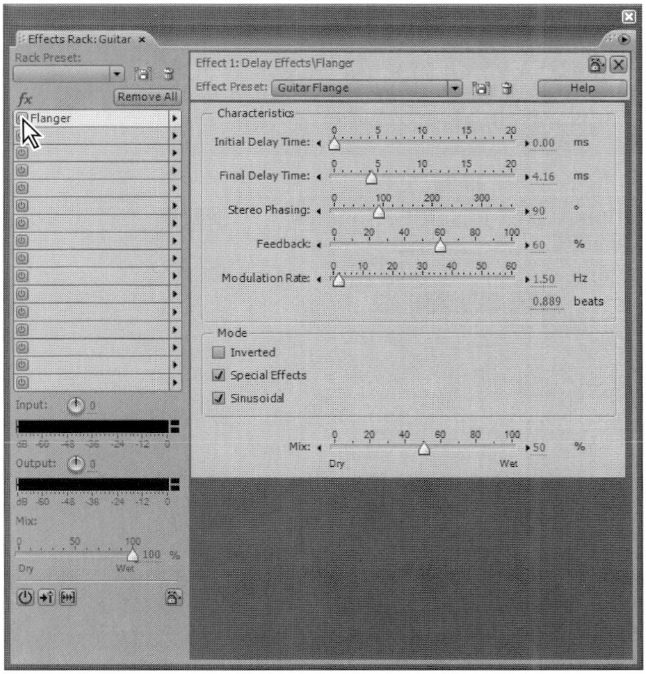

Bypassing the Flanger effect slot for the Guitar track.

7 Stop the playback. Confirm that power to the Flanger slot is back on. Close the Effects Rack window for the Guitar track by clicking the Close button ( ) at its top right. When you do so, you return to the Mixer panel.

8 In the mixer strip for Guitar track, click the Solo button (S) to turn it off, thereby enabling all the other tracks for playback.

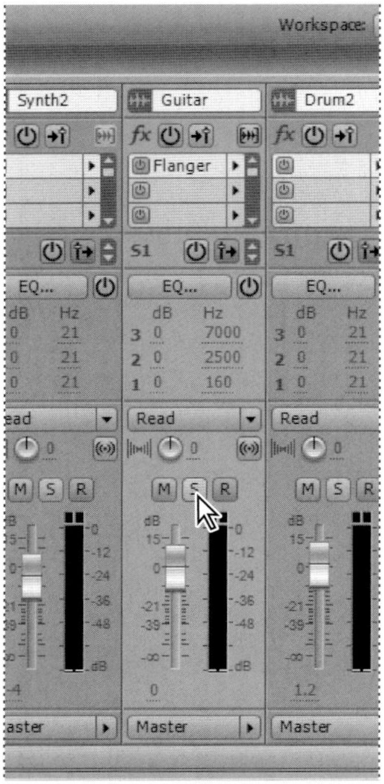

Mixer strip for Guitar track with the Flanger effect inserted into its Effects Rack.

9 Press the Home key, then press the spacebar to begin playback and hear how the entire session sounds after having added an effect to the Guitar track. Click the Main tab at the top left of the Mixer panel to return to the main interface of the Multitrack View.

Note: *You can 'chain' several effects into the successive slots of the Effects Rack and quickly see or edit their respective settings by simply clicking on each slot.*

Using Hiss Reduction

Working non-destructively with effects is a powerful way to work with digital audio. In addition, Audition also can perform destructive edits that change the original source files when you work in the Edit View. Some features of Audition are only available in the Edit View, such as Noise, and Hiss Reduction, along with the Spectral View.

1 In the Multitrack View, within the track named AcousticEnd, double-click on the clip harp_cough.cel to enter the Edit View. This clip is displayed as an audio waveform in the Edit View.

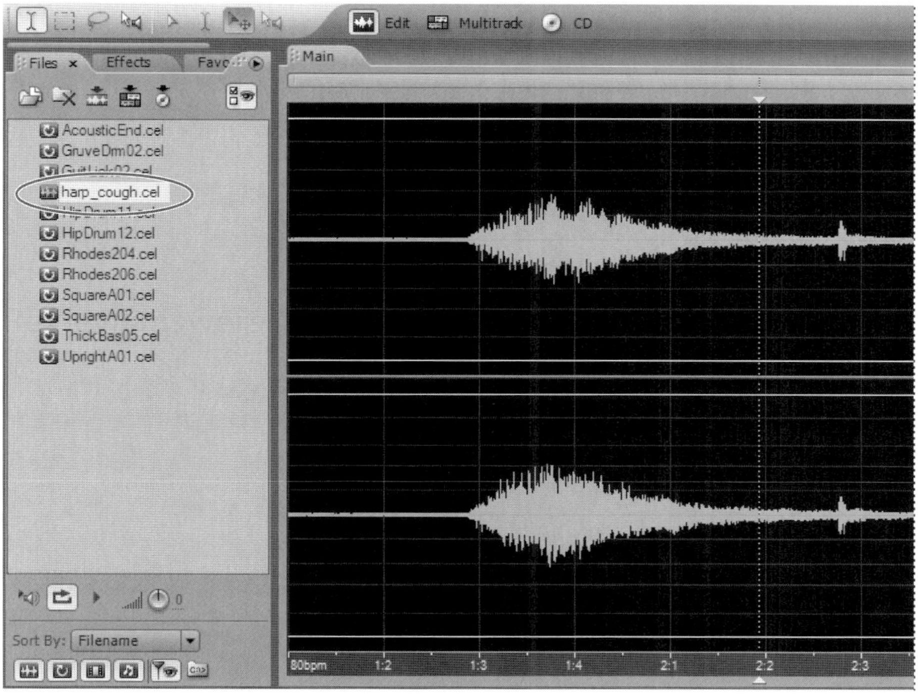

Note: *Certain commands and features are available only in the Edit View and not in the Multitrack View. You can always switch between views by clicking on the Edit View button ( ) or Multitrack View button ( ) located near the top of the window. Changes you make to a file in the Edit View are updated in the Multitrack View.*

2 Press the Home key on your keyboard to place the start-time indicator at the beginning of the waveform, and then press the spacebar to play the file from beginning to end. The source for this file was a live performance. This recording includes a slight hiss along with a cough at the end of the harp phrase, which impacts the quality of the final file. You will remove these deficiencies in the file using powerful noise restoration tools available in the Edit View.

3 Choose Edit > Select Entire Wave to select the entire waveform of the harp_cough clip. You can also use the Ctrl+A keyboard shortcut for this purpose. The entire waveform gets highlighted in white.

4 Choose Effects > Restoration > Hiss Reduction (process) to open the Hiss Reduction window.

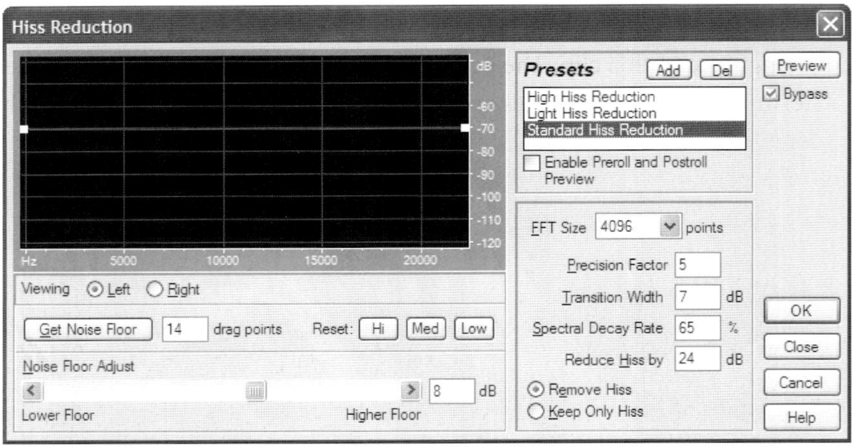

5 In the Hiss Reduction window, select Standard Hiss Reduction from the list of presets, and then click Preview. The hiss decreases dramatically after applying this effect. To hear the difference, with the Preview button still on, check the Bypass option and the hiss returns. Uncheck the Bypass option to hear the effect of hiss reduction again. Click the OK button to apply hiss reduction on the waveform.

This is a destructive edit because the original waveform was modified. You can see that the waveform changes slightly after the application of this effect.

6 Press the spacebar to play the modified file. Although the hiss has been reduced, the cough still remains. You are going to remove the cough in the following steps.

7 Click the Multitrack View button ( ), then move the start-time indicator to Bar 15 beat 1 (15:1.00). Press the spacebar to play the session. You will notice that the hiss is reduced for the harp clip because changes made to a file in Edit View are automatically reflected in the Multitrack View.

Using the Spectral View

Adobe Audition is able to display and edit sound files in a unique Spectral View.

1 In the Multitrack View, double-click the Harp_cough.cel clip in the Acoustic End track to display the waveform in the Edit View.

2 Choose View > Spectral Frequency Display to view the spectrum of this waveform. The Spectral Frequency Display opens. In this display, the horizontal ruler is displaying the total playing time of this clip. The vertical ruler measures frequency. This view lets you determine which frequencies are most prevalent in a waveform. It also helps you to understand how the spectral contents of a clip change over time. For any given frequency, brighter colors signify greater amplitude, and dull colors signify lesser amplitude.

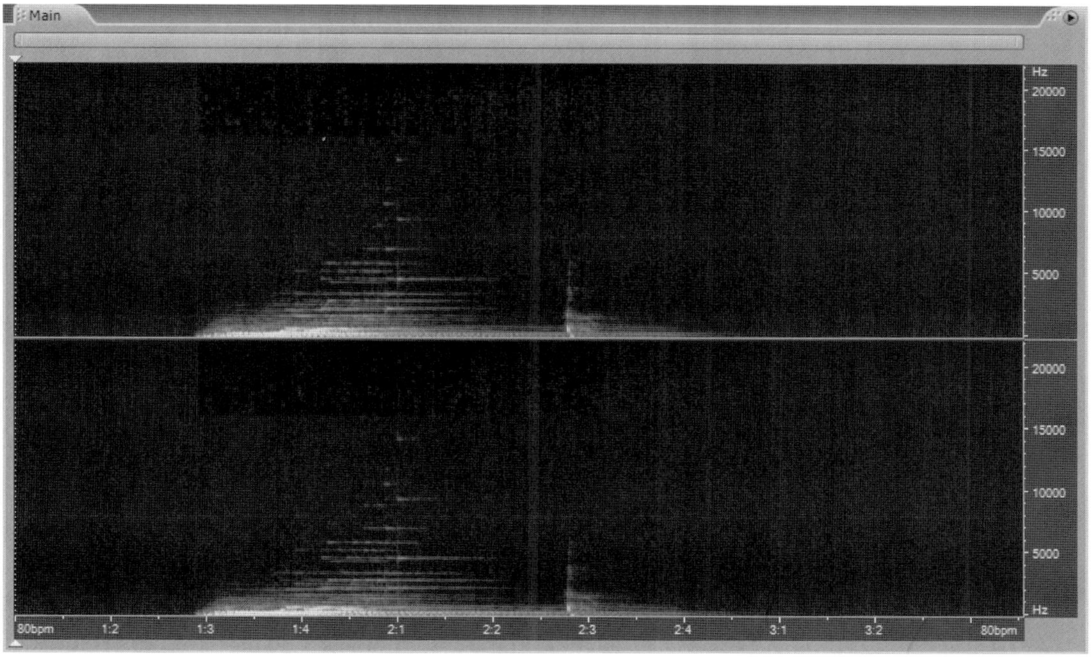

3 While still in the Spectral Frequency Display, press the Home key on your keyboard to place the start-time indicator at the beginning of time ruler, and then press the spacebar to play the file. It is very easy to note the cough at the end of the file, as it can be seen as a sudden spike in the spectrum.

4 Choose the Marquee Selection tool ( ) from the toolbar located at the top left of your display. Click and drag a marquee selection around the spectral representation of the cough as shown below. Press the spacebar to play just the selection. Listen carefully and you should hear the cough along with the diminishing sound of the harp. Be careful to not select too large of an area beyond the cough.

Note: *While in the Spectral Frequency Display, in addition to the Marquee Selection tool, you can also choose the Lasso Selection tool ( ) and the Time Selection tool ( ) to best suit the type of selection you need to make in the spectrum. Audition also includes a Scrub tool which can assist you in finding exact locations within the spectrum.*

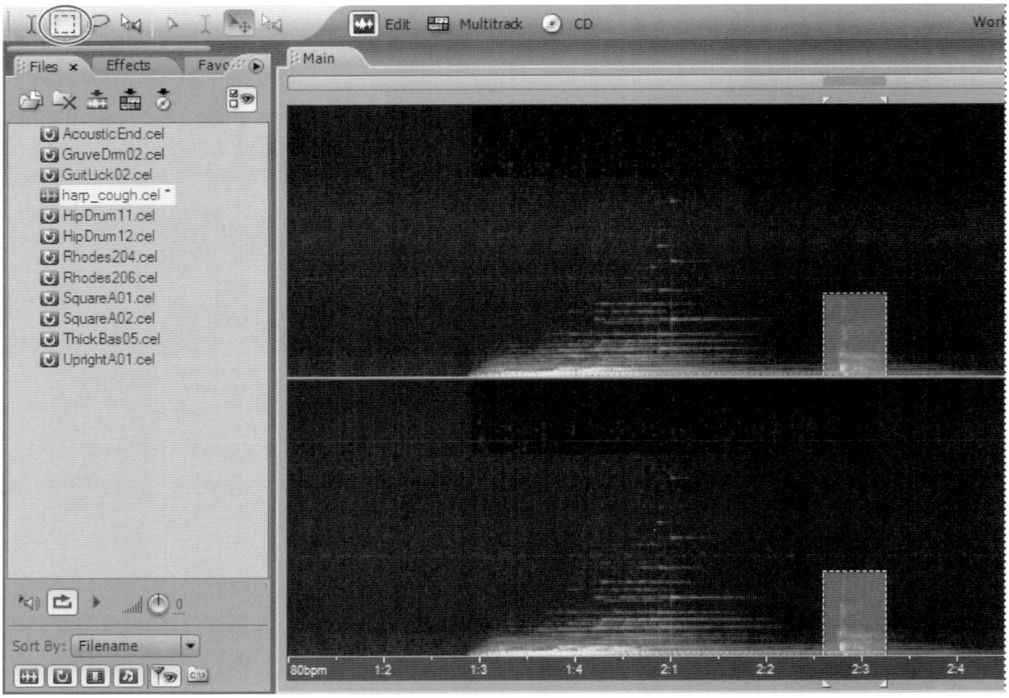

5 Choose Effects > Restoration > Click/Pop Eliminator (process) to open the Click/Pop Eliminator window. This effect will be applied only to the selection you made with the Marquee tool.

6 Click the Fill Single Click Now button at the bottom of the Click/Pop Eliminator window. Audition processes the file and applies the effect. If the selected area is too large, this option is not available.

***Note:** This is one of many methods available for repairing audio. As you learn more about Adobe Audition, you will discover the Favorites panel and will be able to use the Repair Transient favorite to remove similar imperfections.*

7 Press the spacebar again. The cough has been removed, yet the diminishing tones of the harp have been preserved. Press the Home key to return the start-time indicator to the beginning of the clip and listen to the entire clip. When you switch back to the Multitrack View in the next step, you'll notice that the changes you've just made have been updated in the multitrack.

Changing the tempo of an entire session

Once you have created a final version of a song, you have the flexibility in Audition to change the tempo; to make a session faster or slower.

1 Click the Multitrack View button to return to the session. Press the Home key to return the start-time indicator to the beginning of the session. Press the spacebar to begin playing. Listen to the session for three or four bars to get a sense of the tempo and then press the spacebar to stop playing.

2 In the Session Properties panel found at the lower right corner of the display, click in the Tempo field, which is currently set to 80 bpm. Bpm represents beats per minute and determines the speed at which the song plays.

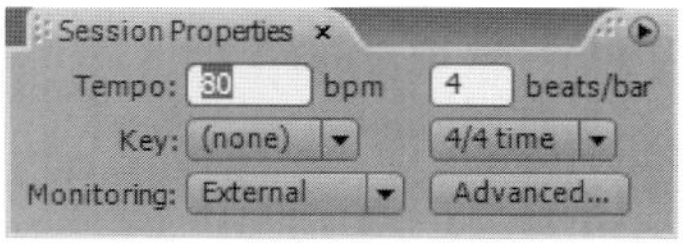

3 Type in **100** as the new tempo in the Tempo field. Press the Enter key and Audition will update the session, which may take a few moments. All the tracks are time-stretched to match the session's new tempo.

4 Press the Home key on your keyboard to place the start-time indicator at the beginning of your session. Press the spacebar to play. The updated session has a faster tempo of 100 beats per minute, yet the original pitch of the instruments has not changed.

***Note:** You cannot use the Edit > Undo/Redo commands after changing the tempo of the session. You'll have to manually type in the previous tempo if you don't like the new one.*

Exporting a session to mp3 audio format

Audition can export audio files in many different file formats, including the mp3 format.

1 Choose File > Save Session As. Navigate to the AA_01 folder on your hard disk and enter the name **01_Final.ses**. Press the Save button.

Note: *Audition may alert you to save the edited harp_cough.cel. If so, click Yes to save the edited file, and click OK if Audition alerts you that you may be saving to a lower fidelity file format.*

2 Choose File > Export > Audio Mix Down. In the Export Audio Mix Down window, click the Save as type drop-down menu and choose mp3PRO®.

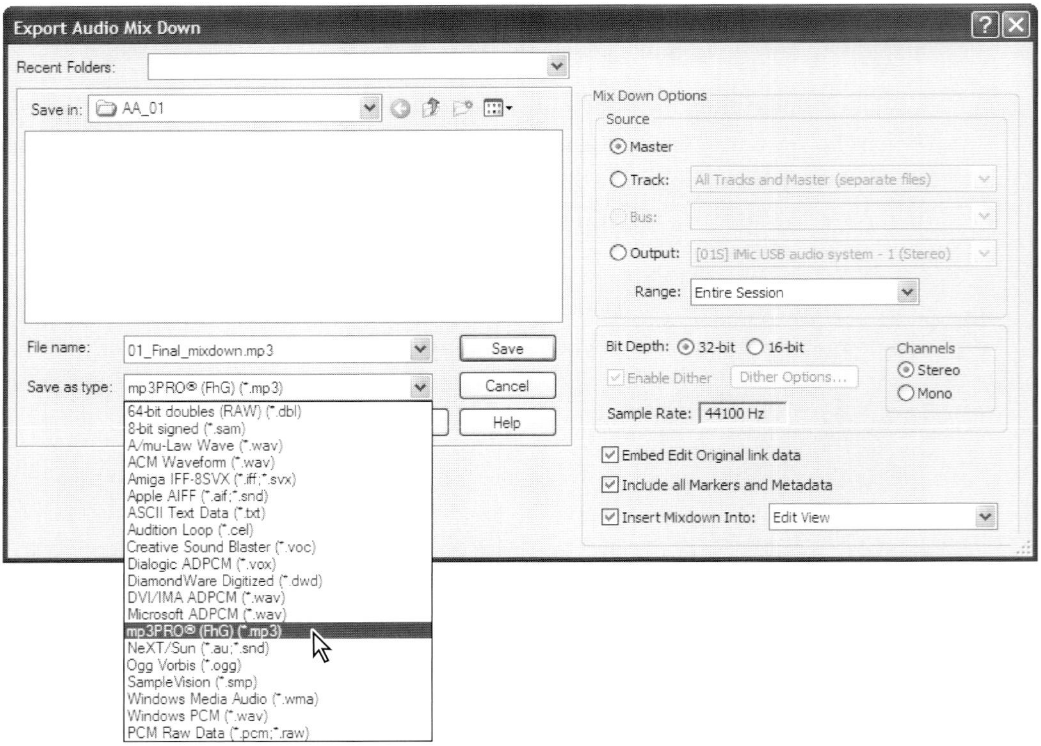

3 Click the Options button and the MP3/mp3PRO® Encoder Options window opens.

4 In the MP3/mp3PRO® Encoder Options window, click the Presets menu in the upper left corner and select 192 Kbps Stereo, then click OK. Click Save to export the .mp3. The .mp3 file is mixed down and saved to your hard disk, and can be opened in Audition or using any hardware or software capable of playing .mp3 audio files.

5 Choose File > Close All.

Congratulations! You have completed your tour of Adobe Audition 2.0.

2 Audition Basics

Audition's editing tools allow you to quickly and easily manipulate audio clips. You can select portions of audio clips for editing, and preview files before placing them into a session. You can take advantage of Audition's customizable working environment, and use three separate views to efficiently navigate through sessions and files.

In this lesson, you'll learn how to do the following:

- Use the Multitrack and Edit Views.
- Work with the Selection/View controls.
- Use the Transport controls.
- Use the Zoom controls.
- Work with toolbars, panels, and workspaces.

Adobe Audition displays your work using three views: the Edit View, the Multitrack View, and the CD View. This lesson is focused on the common features among the three views. Each view is also discussed specifically in Lessons 3, 4, and 12. When you open an Audition session, the Multitrack View is displayed. Adobe Audition sessions are project files which, in turn, point to sound or music files. The session files do not contain any sound or music files—rather, the files used by Audition are referenced by the session file.

1 Start Adobe Audition and select the Multitrack View button ( ).

Note: *If you have not already copied the resource files for this lesson onto your hard disk from the* Adobe Audition 2.0 Classroom in a Book *CD, do so now. See "Copying the Classroom in a Book files" on page 2.*

2 To review the finished session file, choose File > Open Session. Navigate to the AA_CIB folder you created on your hard disk, and open the file 02_end.ses in the AA_02 folder.

3 Click the Play from Cursor to End of File button (▶) in the Transport panel. The complete file is played for you.

The Play from Cursor to End of File button in the Transport panel.

4 Close the 02_end.ses file by choosing File > Close All after you have reviewed the completed session.

5 Choose File > Open Session, and open the 02_start.ses file in the AA_02 folder, which is also located in the AA_CIB folder on your hard disk.

When you open an existing session in Audition, the program takes a few moments to load the existing sound files into the session window.

At the bottom of the application window is a status bar, displaying useful information about the session. Move your cursor over the various clips in the multitrack session. The names of the loops used in the session are displayed in the status bar. The sample rate is 44,100 Hz, which is the sample rate for compact discs, and the size of the complete file is approximately 145 megabytes. The last number displays the amount of free space available for storage in your hard disk. While this is the default layout for the status bar, right-clicking the status bar lets you add or remove information about the session, therefore your status bar may look different.

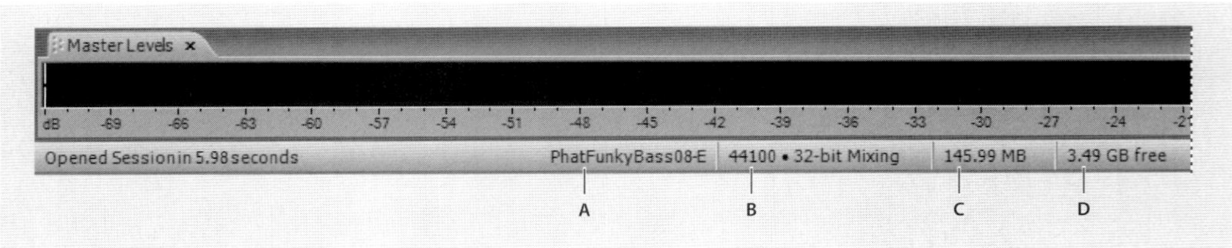

A. *Clip name.* ***B.*** *Sample rate.* ***C.*** *Size of file.* ***D.*** *Free space on your hard disk.*

Audition session files

It is important to remember that Adobe Audition's session files, which are identified by their .ses file extension, contain no audio data themselves. Each session file 'points' to other audio files on your computer or network. The Audition session file keeps track of where the audio files are stored on your computer, each file's duration and location within the session, and the envelopes and effects that are applied to the tracks.

A session file is dependent upon the audio files to which it points, so it's important to keep your files organized. As you are getting started with Audition, it is a good idea to keep all files related to a session in the same folder. Adobe Audition provides an option to save a copy of all files used in a session, including the session file, into the same folder. To access this option, choose File > Save Session As and select the Save copies of all associated files option.

Sample rates

Sample rate indicates the number of digital snapshots taken of an audio signal each second. This rate determines the frequency range of an audio file. The higher the sample rate, the closer the shape of the digital waveform will be to that of the original analog waveform. Low sample rates limit the range of frequencies that can be recorded, which can result in a recording that poorly represents the original sound.

To reproduce a given frequency, the sample rate must be at least twice that frequency. For example, CDs have a sample rate of 44,100 samples per second, so they can reproduce frequencies up to 22,050 Hz, which is beyond the limit of human hearing, 20,000 Hz.

The most common sample rates for digital audio are as follows:

- 11,025 Hz—Poor AM Radio Quality/Speech (low-end multimedia)—0-5,512 Hz frequency range.
- 22,050 Hz—Near FM Radio Quality (high-end multimedia)—0-11,025 Hz frequency range.
- 32,000 Hz—Better than FM Radio Quality (standard broadcast rate)—0-16,000 Hz frequency range.
- 44,100 Hz—CD Quality—0-22,050 Hz frequency range.
- 48,000 Hz—DAT Quality—0-24,000 Hz frequency range.
- 96,000 Hz—DVD Quality—0-48,000 Hz frequency range.

—From Adobe Audition Help

6 To view the entire session from beginning to end, click the Zoom Out Full Both Axes button ( ) located in the Zoom panel controls, along the bottom of the window. This is a convenient way to view all the tracks in your session.

7 If your Selection/View panel is not currently open, choose Window > Selection/View Controls. The View fields in this window display the beginning, ending, and length of the viewable part of the session. The length of your view should now be 1:22:708, which is also the duration of the session.

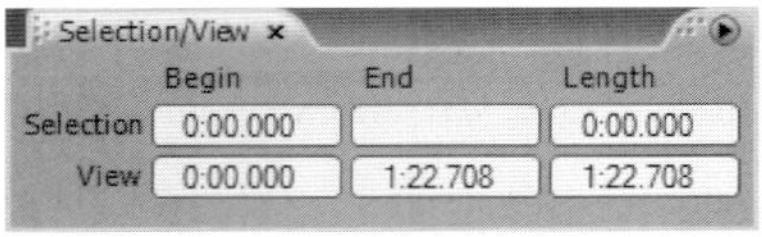

8 Choose View > Display Time Format > Bars and Beats. The units in the timeline ruler at the bottom of the screen are now bars and beats, as are the units in the Selection/View panel. The length of the session in bars and beats should be 32:2.15.

Audition can be used for different types of projects, which require different time displays. This session opened with a time display of minutes, seconds, and milliseconds, and you changed it to bars and beats. Working with loops is often easier with a time display in bars and beats.

9 Choose the Move/Copy Clip tool ( ) and click the last clip in Track 1, which is the drum track. Drag the clip to the right to move it, then choose Ctrl+Z to undo the move, thereby returning the clip to its original position. This tool allows you to change the location of clips in a session.

Note: *There are three tools in Audition for moving and selecting clips: the Move/Copy Clip tool ( ), the Time Selection tool ( ), and the Hybrid tool ( ).*

10 Click the Time Selection tool ( ) and place your cursor approximately halfway into the first clip located in the first track. Click and drag to the left, selecting the first half of the clip.

Notice the selection covers all five tracks of the session, not just the first track. Adobe Audition's Multitrack View allows you to add audio files to different tracks of a session in order to create a multi-layered sound composition. For example, while playing a session, you can adjust the volume of any track in real time. Final sessions are then mixed down for use in a CD or as a sound file such as a .wav or .mp3. In Lesson 4, you will explore the mixing capabilities in the Multitrack View.

Note: *The Hybrid tool combines the functionality of both the Move/Copy Clip tool and the Time Selection tool. When using this tool, the left-click on a two-button mouse functions as the Time Selection tool, while the right-click functions as the Move/Copy Clip tool.*

11 Click the Zoom to Selection button in the Zoom panel. Click the Play from Cursor to End of View button and only the view within the display window is played. When the playback cursor reaches the end of the display window, it stops. Use this method to preview certain sections of your tracks. Click once in the multitrack to deselect the current selection.

12 Click the Play from Cursor to End of File button and the entire session plays. When the playback cursor reaches the end of the display window, it continues playing until it reaches the end of the session.

13 Click the Stop button at any point.

14 Place your cursor over the green horizontal scroll bar, directly above Track 1. The hand icon appears; click and drag to the right or left, scrolling through the session.

15 Place your cursor on the right edge of the green horizontal scroll bar. The cursor changes to a magnifying glass with arrows. Click and drag to the right to zoom out horizontally. Click and drag to the left to zoom in horizontally. Do this three times to get a sense of how this tool works.

Note: *This method of zooming also works for vertical zooming by using the green vertical scroll bar found at the right edge of the Main panel.*

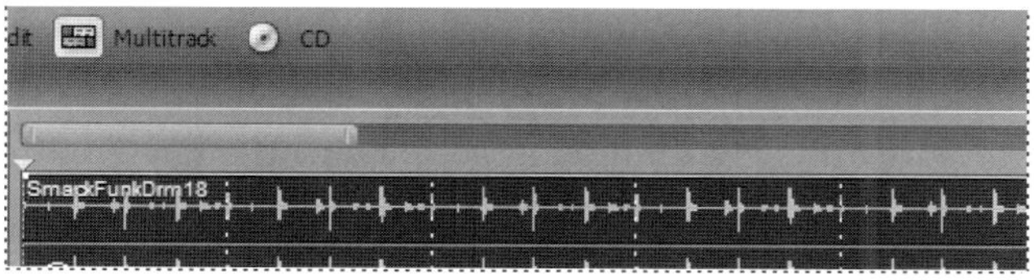

16 Click the Zoom Out Vertically button ( ) to expand the view and see all the tracks in the session.

Audition also makes use of a mouse with a scroll wheel. Place your cursor over the horizontal scroll bar and scroll the mouse wheel down to zoom out. Place your cursor over the time display and scroll the mouse wheel up to zoom in. Place your cursor over a track name and scroll the mouse wheel down to zoom out vertically.

While Audition can use an unlimited number of tracks per session, the number of concurrently visible tracks is dependent upon the display resolution of your monitor. Changing your view allows you to see more tracks or to focus on a portion of a specific track. Click the Zoom Out Full Both Axes button ( ) to see all your tracks fit into one screen vertically and horizontally.

17 Click to select the Hybrid tool ( ). Left-click at the start of the multitrack session and drag to the right, selecting the first eight bars of the session. Press either Play button to play these eight bars.

18 Click the right range indicator, which is the yellow flag at the top and bottom of the selection end, and drag it to Bar 11 beat 1. Then click and drag the left range indicator, which is also a yellow flag, to the Bar 7 beat 1 position. All 4 bars in this region are selected. Press the Play button to play the selection. If necessary, use the Selection/View panel controls, located in the bottom right corner of the window, to help you make the selection.

Note: *You can expand or reduce the range of your selection by moving either of the yellow range indicators to the left or the right. When you drag, the session is automatically scrubbed to help you find a new location easily. If the scrubbing distracts you, you can disable it by choosing Edit > Preferences > Multitrack > Play audio while scrubbing with the Start Time Indicator. Disabling scrubbing also makes it easier to snap the start-time indicator to a specific location.*

Using the Files panel

The loops and files used in the current session are listed in the Files panel. By default, Audition lists the current samples by their file name.

1 If not already selected, click the Show Options icon ( ) in the upper right of the Files panel and ensure that you can see various options below the file names.

2 If your sort order is not already set to Filename, select it now by clicking on the Sort By drop-down menu at the bottom of the Files panel, and choosing Filename.

Your files are now in alphabetical order. The first two files are Kick&Sizzle.cel and KickCymbalRoll01.cel. Notice the audio icon ( ) next to the file names. This marks files as audio file types that do not contain looping information.

3 If it is not already selected, select the Loop Play button ( ) at the bottom of the Files panel and then select the PhatFunkyBass08-E.cel loop by clicking on it once. Press the Play button ( ) next to the Loop Play button at the bottom of the Files panel. The sound loops continuously from beginning to end until you press the Stop button ( ). Notice that these buttons and the volume control are in the Files panel, not the Transport panel.

Note: *If you accidentally double-click on the files in the Files panel, they open in the Edit View for editing. Return to the Multitrack View by clicking the Multitrack View button ( ) at the top of the window, or choose View > Multitrack View.*

4 If it is not already selected, click the AutoPlay button ( ) at the bottom of the Files panel, and then click on each file to play it automatically. You do not have to wait for a file to end before previewing the next file. Use the Down Arrow key on your keyboard to navigate through your list of files one at a time. You can also adjust the Preview Volume knob to raise or lower the volume of the files. Press the Stop button when you are done previewing the files.

Working with views and toolbars

Much of your work in Audition will involve switching between the Edit View and the Multitrack View.

1 Click on the Edit View button ( ) in the View Toggle toolbar. The workspace changes from the Multitrack View to the Edit View.

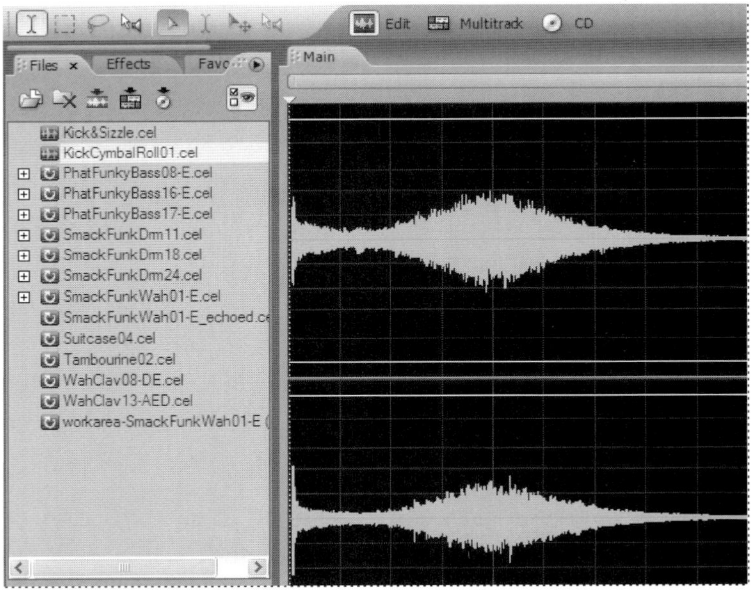

The Edit View is used to modify a single audio waveform; examples might include adding an effect or deleting part of a clip. Changes made to files in the Edit View are destructive—adding an effect or trimming a loop changes the original file once it is saved. Edits made in the Multitrack View are non-destructive, meaning the original files remain untouched.

2 Click on the Multitrack View button ( ) to return to the multitrack.

3 Click on the CD View button ( ) to display this view. The Files panel stays consistent between the three views, but the menu commands are different in each of the views.

4 Click on the Multitrack View button.

5 Double-click on the first clip in Track 1, SmackFunkDrm18.cel, to enter the Edit View. The waveform of the selected clip is displayed. Click the Multitrack View button to return to Multitrack View.

6 In the Files panel, right-click the loop file Suitcase04.cel and choose Edit File. This is another method to enter the Edit View. Return to the Multitrack View by pressing the number 9 on your keyboard.

Note: *Audition uses a variety of keyboard commands, including numbers, letters, and function keys. You can customize keyboard shortcuts, MIDI Triggers, and assigning or modifying keys to access specific commands or effects by choosing Edit > Keyboard Shortcuts and MIDI Triggers.*

7 Choose View > Shortcut Bar > Show. Choose View > Shortcut Bar > View Toggles. Toolbars which are currently open have a check mark beside them. If View Toggles does not have a check mark, select it now, adding the View Toggles shortcut to your Shortcut Bar.

8 Right-click anywhere on the Shortcut Bar, which you made visible in the last step, revealing a context menu with a list of shortcut groups that can be displayed. As with the list displayed under the View menu, shortcuts with a check mark beside them are currently open, while unchecked shortcuts are hidden. Select the View Toggles option to remove the shortcut.

Note: *You can right-click on a shortcut in the Shortcut Bar to access its context menu, and then select View Toggles to display this shortcut within the Shortcut Bar.*

9 Place your cursor over the CD button in the toolbar. A tooltip appears, describing the function of the button. Tooltips also display the keyboard shortcut in brackets. Close the Shortcut Bar by choosing View > Shortcut Bar > Show and unchecking the option.

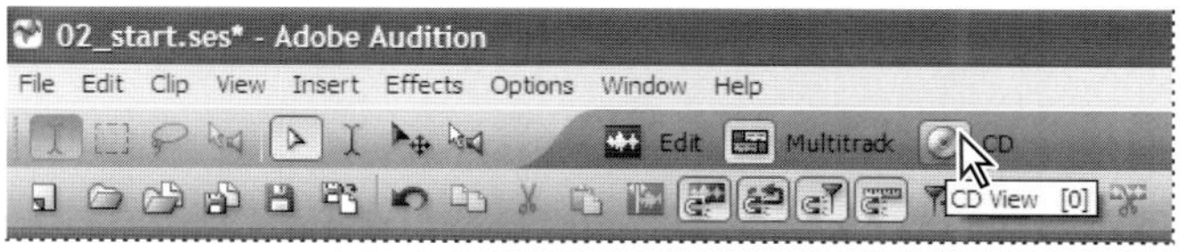

Working with panels and workspaces

Panels in Adobe Audition can be viewed either as docked panels or as independent floating windows. You can customize how you want to view different panels and windows to suit your working style and requirements. This is especially useful if you are working with multiple monitors. Your custom screen layouts can be saved as workspaces and can be recalled later at the click of a button.

1 If necessary, switch to the Multitrack View by choosing Window > Workspace > Multitrack View (Default).

2 Below the Main panel, find the docked Time panel, and increase its length by clicking and dragging its right edge to the right when the cursor shape has changed to two vertical lines with arrows (↤|↦). The neighboring Zoom panel is adjusted automatically to make room.

The Time panel as a docked panel.

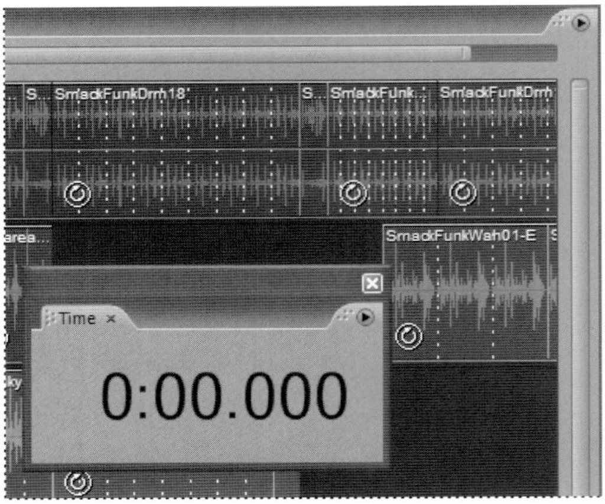

The Time panel as a floating window.

3 Click on the Palette menu button (◉) on the top right of the docked Time panel and choose Undock Panel.

4 Resize the floating Time window by clicking and dragging the lower right corner when the shape of the cursor changes to a double sided arrow (↘). You can resize a floating window by clicking any side or corner.

5 Choose > Window > Workspace > New Workspace. In the dialog box that appears, type **Centered Floating Time** as the name, and press OK.

The current arrangement of panels and windows on your screen has been saved as a new workspace. This workspace will remember the location and sizes of all your docked panels.

6 Click on the (☒) icon in the tab of the floating Time window to close it.

7 Choose Window > Time to make the floating Time window reappear in the last place you put it. In general, docked panels are preferable to floating windows because they do not interfere with your view of the tracks and track controls. You will now learn to dock the Time panel.

8 Bring your cursor over the tab of the floating Time window and when this area becomes brighter, click and drag toward the bottom left.

The shape of your cursor changes to (↖▭) to signify that you are trying to find a new place to dock this window. As you drag your cursor to various areas of the screen, Audition prompts you about available docking targets by highlighting blue drop zones near your cursor.

9 With the mouse button still pressed, drag toward the bottom left of the screen until you reach the left edge of Transport panel. When its left drop zone becomes highlighted, release your mouse.

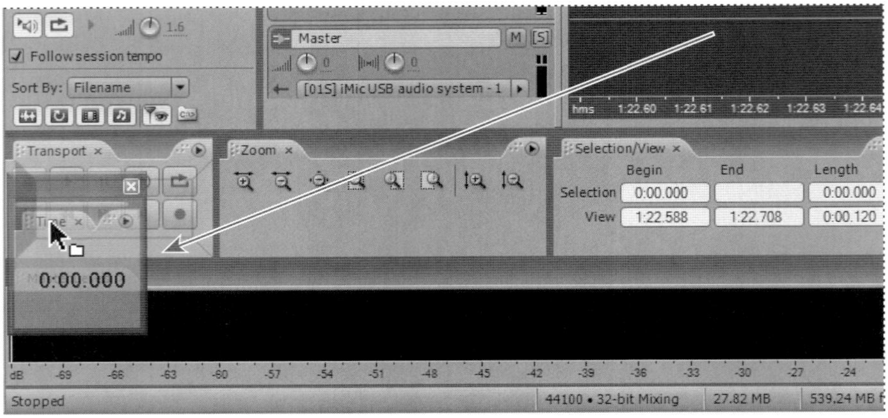

The drop zone of the Transport panel gets highlighted when you drag near it.

The Time panel docks to the left of Transport panel.

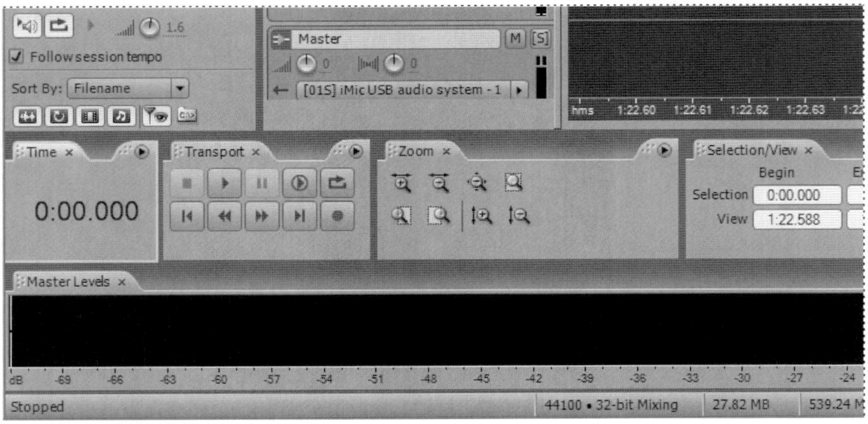

Note: *If you accidentally dock the Time panel somewhere else, click the Palette menu button (⯈) for the Time panel and choose Undock panel, just as you did in step 3.*

10 Grab the docked Time panel by its tab, and drag it toward the right of the Transport panel. When the right drop zone for the Transport panel gets highlighted, release your mouse button. The Time panel moves to the right of the Transport panel.

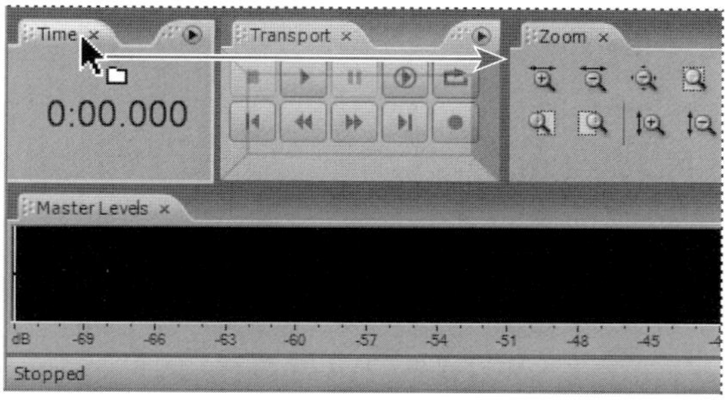

Right drop zone for the Transport panel gets highlighted when you drag a panel near it.

You can dock a panel on the left, right, top, or bottom of a target panel, depending on which drop zone is highlighted when you release the mouse. If you release when the target's middle drop zone is highlighted, the two panels get grouped together. To the left of the Main panel are two such grouped panels: Files and Effects. You will undock the Effects panel from the group and then dock it so that it becomes grouped with the Files panel again.

11 Hold down the Ctrl key and click on the Effects tab of the grouped panels. Drag toward the center of your screen. The Effects panel breaks loose from the group and becomes an independent floating window. Drag this floating window near the center of your screen. Release the mouse button.

As you drag, Audition does not prompt you about the available docking spaces because you are holding down the Ctrl key. This is the second method to create a floating window from a docked panel.

12 Grab the floating Effects window by its tab and drag it back to the Files panel. When the middle drop zone of the grouped panels gets highlighted, release the mouse button. The Effects panel is re-grouped with the Files panel.

Note: *If you don't see the Favorites panel grouped with the Files panel as shown in this screenshot, choose Window > Favorites to make the Favorites panel visible.*

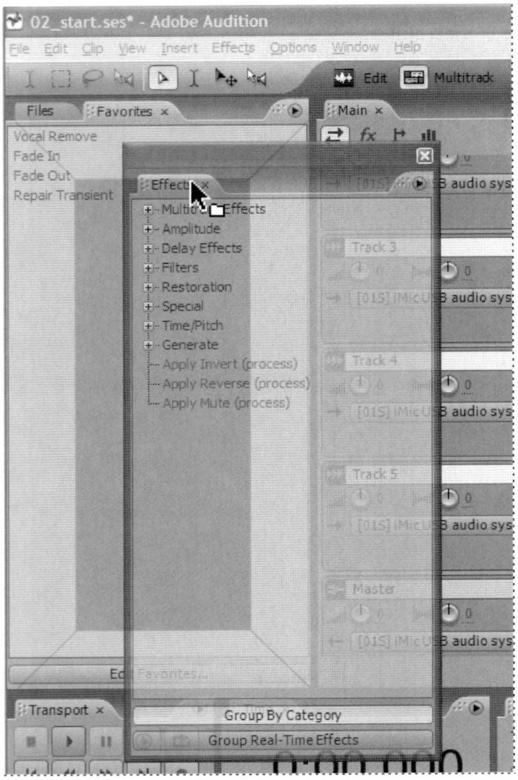

Middle drop zone highlighted.

13 Choose Window > Mixer to open the Mixer panel, if it is not already open.

14 Grab the tab for the Mixer panel and drag it to the right. At the right edge of your screen, a light green highlight appears. Release the mouse at this point. The Mixer gets docked along the right edge of the screen.

The Mixer docked at the right edge of the work area.

15 Choose > Window > Workspace > New Workspace. In the dialog box that follows, type **Right Docked Mixer** as the name and press OK to save the workspace.

16 Click on the Workspace drop-down menu located in the top right of the Main panel and choose Centered Floating Time to switch to the screen layout you had saved in step 5.

The panels on the screen instantly change to the way you had saved them while saving this workspace. Creating such workspaces is a great time-saving feature. As you become more familiar with Audition, you'll find that you like to have your panels arranged in different ways for different tasks. Saving a workspace for each task can boost your efficiency and speed.

17 Switch back to the Right Docked Mixer workspace by choosing it from the Workspace menu. Reduce the size of the Mixer panel so that you only see the Master track in the mixer, as demonstrated in the screenshot above.

18 If your timeline is not set to display bars and beats, choose View > Display Time Format > Bars and Beats. Using the Hybrid tool ( ) in the upper left of the Main panel, click and drag in Track 5, making a selection starting at Bar 8 beat 1 and ending at the Bar 12 beat 1 mark. You may have to adjust the range boundaries, represented by the yellow flags at the corners of the selected area, to make the selection. Use your Selection/View panel below the multitrack to confirm the length of the selection. You should have a total selection of 4 bars.

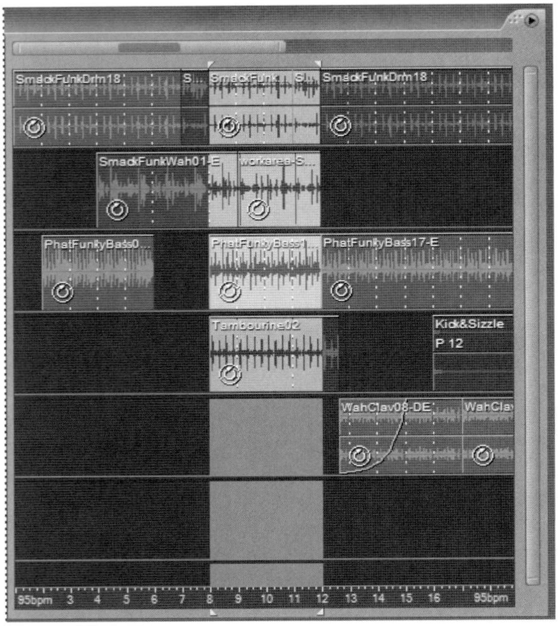

19 Click the Play Looped button ( ) in the Transport panel. This loops the selection continuously, until you click the Stop button. Playing a looped selection is a useful way to preview changes to your session in real time.

20 As the session is playing, move the master volume fader in the Mixer panel toward the top to increase the overall volume and then toward the bottom to decrease it. Keep an eye on the Master Levels panel at the bottom, and notice how it changes as you move the slider. Press the spacebar to stop playing the session.

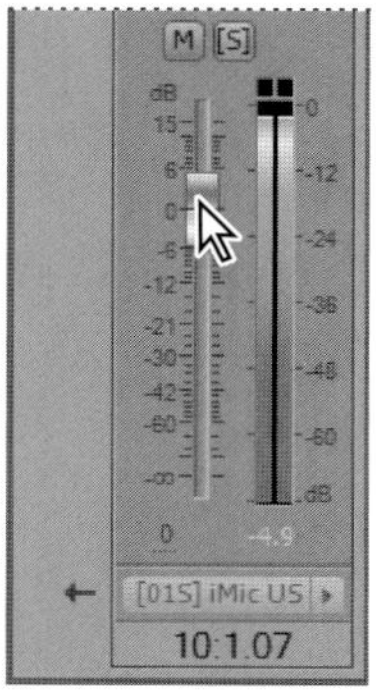

Level meters

To monitor the amplitude of incoming and outgoing signals during recording and playback, you use level meters. Edit View provides these meters in the Levels panel. Multitrack View provides them in the Master Levels panel, which shows the amplitude of an entire session, and track meters, which show the amplitude of individual tracks.

You can dock the Levels and Master Levels panels horizontally or vertically. When a panel is docked horizontally, the upper meter represents the left channel, and the lower meter represents the right channel.

—From Adobe Audition Help

Note: *As you begin to add more tracks to a session, you will generally need to lower your master mixer volume to prevent clipping. If your clip indicators are red, click on them to clear them.*

Naming your tracks

Audition is capable of handling an unlimited number of audio tracks per session. Currently, there are five tracks in this session.

1 To make sure you are seeing all the tracks in your session, click the Zoom Out Full Both Axes button ().

2 In the track controls for Track 1, click once on the name Track 1 and enter **Drums** in the name text box.

In the track controls for Track 2, click once on the name Track 2 and enter **Guitar** in the name text box. Repeat these steps for Tracks 3, 4, and 5, entering **Bass**, **Percussion**, and **Clav** respectively. It is useful to rename your tracks based on their content.

3 Change the color of the first SmackFunkDRm18 clip in the drum track by right-clicking it and choosing Clip Color from the context menu. In the Clip Color window, choose the first red shade in the upper left and click OK.

Modifying the color of individual sound clips in Audition is useful for visually identifying different instruments or loops. We have color-coded the session for you but have left the first clip as the default green.

4 Choose File > Save Session to update the 02_start.ses file.

5 Choose File > Close All.

Exploring on your own

1 Become more familiar with Audition's extended right-click functionality. Right-click on an empty portion of the multitrack, and experiment with using the Mute and Solo commands from the context menu, rather than the Main panel controls.

2 Grab the Mixer panel, which you docked on the right edge of the screen. If the Mixer panel is not currently open, choose Window > Mixer. Practice docking the Mixer panel into different sections of the interface.

3 Use the Time Selection tool to make a selection in your multitrack session. Use the Zoom to Selection tool, the Zoom In to Left Edge of Selection tool, and the Zoom In to Right Edge of Selection tool to view the results of each tool.

Review

Review questions

1 What is the difference between the Edit View and Multitrack View?

2 What is the quickest way to view all the tracks from beginning to end in your Multitrack View?

3 Where are the Move/Copy Clip tool, the Time Selection tool, and the Hybrid tool located, and how are these tools different?

4 What is the advantage of using workspaces?

Review answers

1 Edit View uses a destructive method of editing, which permanently alters a waveform when the file is saved. Permanent changes are preferable when converting sample rate and bit depth, mastering, or batch processing. Multitrack View uses a non-destructive method, which is not permanent, but requires more processing power. The flexibility of the Multitrack View is preferable when working with multi-layered musical compositions or video soundtracks.

2 The Zoom Out Full Both Axes button automatically scales your timeline to show every track in your session, as well as all clips within each track.

3 The Move/Copy Clip tool, the Time Selection tool, and the Hybrid tool are all located in the Shortcut Bar. Left-clicking with the Move/Copy Clip tool moves a clip from one area of the multitrack to another; right-clicking reveals a menu allowing you to create a copy of the clip. Left-clicking with the Time Selection tool selects a portion or all of a waveform; right-clicking displays a context menu but does not allow for making selections. Left-clicking with the Hybrid tool makes a selection for editing, while right-clicking moves a clip from one area of the multitrack to another.

4 Workspaces allow you to store and recall your favorite arrangements of windows and panels on the screen. Once you have your screen arranged the way you like it, you can save the arrangement as a custom workspace. You can create different workspaces for different tasks, and quickly switch between them.

3 Working in Edit View

The Edit View allows you to view and edit audio files in a waveform display. Editing is simple with Audition's selection tools, allowing you to cut, copy, mix and trim audio clips with precision. Effects such as Normalize, Reverb, and Stereo Field Rotate can easily be applied and also saved as favorites. The Preroll and Postroll Preview makes working with effects easier than ever.

In this lesson, you'll learn how to do the following:

- Use the Edit View.
- Select and edit waveforms.
- Combine audio clips.
- Apply effects and save them as favorites.

Getting started

In this lesson, you'll work with a series of files in the Edit View. If you have not already copied the resource files for this lesson onto your hard disk from the *Adobe Audition 2.0 Classroom in a Book* CD, do so now. See "Copying the Classroom in a Book files" on page 2.

1 Start Adobe Audition. Click the Multitrack View button if it is not already selected.

2 Choose File > Open Session, and open the 03_start.ses file located in the AA_03 folder, in the AA_CIB folder on your hard disk. Click the Zoom Out Full Both Axes tool ( ) to view all tracks in the session.

3 Choose File > Save Session As, and name the file **03_EditView.ses**, and save it in the AA_03 folder on your hard disk.

This session is the same one you worked with in Lesson 2. In this lesson, you will be working primarily in the Edit View.

4 To review the finished session file for this lesson, choose File > Open Session. Open the 03_end.ses file in the AA_03 folder, which is located within the AA_CIB folder on your hard disk.

5 Press the Home key on your keyboard and then play the session file by either clicking the Play button ( ) in the Transport panel or pressing the spacebar on your keyboard.

6 When you are ready to start working, close the 03_end.ses file by choosing File > Close All. Then, choose File > Open Session to re-open the 03_EditView.ses file.

Using the Edit View

By default, the session opens in the Multitrack View. To change to the Edit View, press the Edit View button ( ). The loops and files used in the session are displayed in the Files panel along the left side of the display under the Files tab. They are listed in the order specified by the Sort By field at the bottom of the Files panel.

You can also use the keyboard shortcut F12 to switch between the Edit View and the Multitrack View when either of these views is the active window.

1 In the Edit View, if the Loop Play button ( ) at the bottom of the Files panel is currently highlighted, click on it to deselect it. If the Auto Play button ( ) is highlighted, click it to disable it. Click once on the PhatFunkyBass08-E.cel file in the Files panel and then click the Play button ( ) in the Files panel. The clip plays once from beginning to end.

2 Click on the Loop Play button ( ) at the bottom of the Files panel to highlight it, and click the Play button.

The sound plays repeatedly until you click the Stop button ( ).

3 Double-click the file Tambourine02.cel in the Files panel to view its waveform. Click the Play button ( ) in the Transport panel—not the Play button in the Files panel.

The peaks of the visual waveform represent the loudest sections of the loop. Only a single waveform is displayed because this is a mono file.

4 To play the tambourine sample in a loop, click the Play Looped button ( ) in the Transport panel. Wait until it loops once, then press the spacebar to stop playing the file.

5 Double-click the loop file called KickCymbalRoll01.cel in the Files panel.

Two waveforms are displayed in this file because it is a stereo file. The waveform for the left channel appears at the top and the waveform for the right channel appears at the bottom.

6 Place the cursor on the white line just above the top waveform display. When the letter "L" appears, click to isolate the left channel of the loop. The bottom waveform is grayed out, indicating that it is not audible. Press the spacebar to listen to the left channel only.

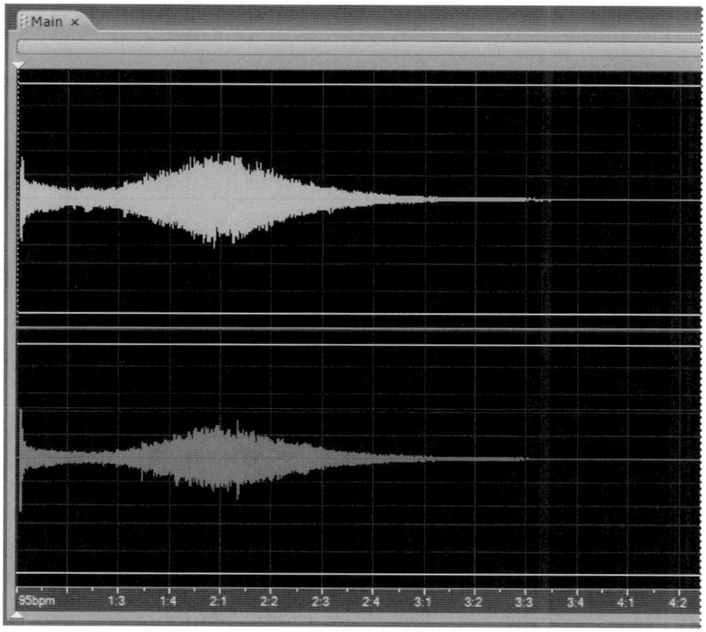

Depending on the audio setup of your computer, the stereo effect may be more noticeable with a pair of headphones. If you hear the audio in the right channel and not the left, be sure your speakers or headphones are properly connected.

Note: *Clicking on the white line at the bottom of the display will isolate the right channel only. Click in the middle of the display to restore the clip to its default stereo state.*

Sound fundamentals

Sound is created by vibrations in the air, like those produced by a guitar string, vocal cords, or a speaker cone. These vibrations force air molecules together, raising the air pressure slightly. The air molecules under pressure then push on the air molecules surrounding them, which push on the next set of molecules, and so on, causing a wave of high pressure to move through the air. As high pressure areas move through the air, they leave low pressure areas behind them. When these pressure highs and lows—or waves—reach us, they vibrate the receptors in our ears, and we hear the vibrations as sound.

When you see a visual waveform that represents audio, it reflects these waves of air pressure. The zero line in the waveform is the pressure of air at rest. When the line swings up, it represents higher pressure, and when the line swings low, it represents lower pressure.

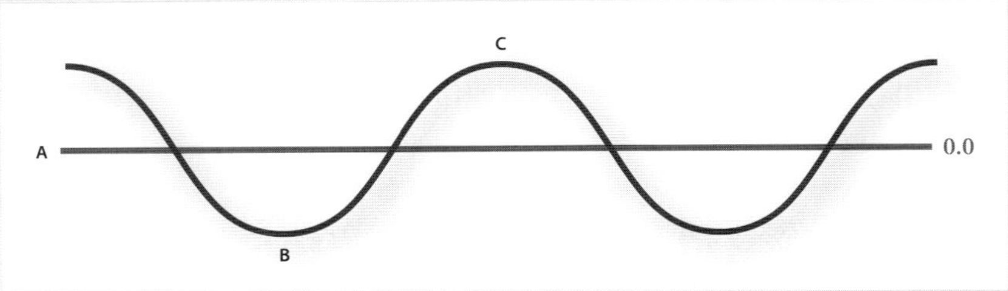

A sound wave represented as a visual waveform.
***A**. Zero line. **B**. Low pressure area. **C**. High pressure area.*

—From Adobe Audition Help

Selecting and editing waveforms

You may need to isolate a section of a waveform to apply an effect, listen to a section of sound more carefully, or trim an unwanted section of sound. In this section, you will select and edit a section of a waveform.

1 Double-click in an empty area of the Files panel below the file list, or choose File > Open, to import a new file into the Edit View.

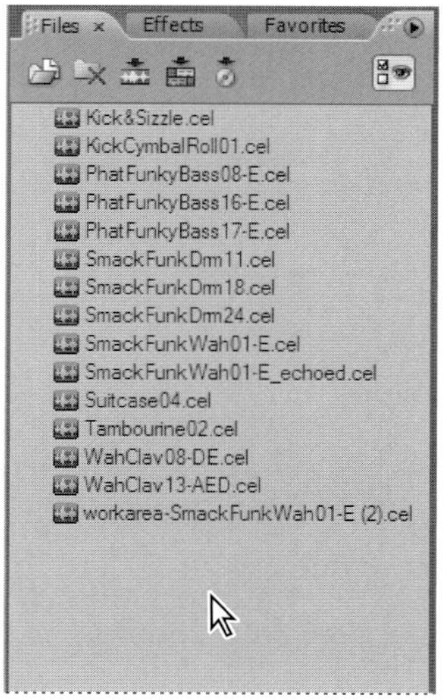

Double-click in an empty area to import a new file.

2 In the Import window, navigate to the AA_03 folder on your hard disk and select the ZildjianSizzle.cel file, then click Open. The file is imported into your Files panel.

3 From the Sort By drop-down menu in the Files panel, choose Filename, if it is not already selected. The ZildjianSizzle.cel file appears at the bottom of the file list. Double-click this file to display the waveform. The name of the waveform is displayed at the top of the Audition window. Press the spacebar to play the file. Press the spacebar again to stop playback.

4 Choose Edit > Copy to New to make a new copy of this sound file. When you are working in the Edit View, all changes you make to a sound file are destructive. Making a copy of your file ensures you have an unedited copy of the original sound file. Close the original ZildjianSizzle.cel file by right-clicking the file name in the Files panel, then choose Close Files from the context menu.

This removes the original file from the Files panel and you can now make modifications to the copy. The copied file is named ZildjianSizzle (2)*. The asterisk at the end of the filename indicates that this file is unsaved or that you have made changes to the file that require the file to be re-saved. This is a useful indicator to inform you that you need to save to retain any changes made.

5 Choose File > Save As from the File menu. In the Save As window, name the file **ZildjianSizzle_edited.cel** and click the Save button.

Note: *You may receive a warning message regarding saving files to a compressed file format. The .cel files which are the native file format for Audition loops are similar to .mp3 files in that audio data is compressed in order to reduce file size. However, the default compression rate for .cel files is 320 Kbps, which is extremely high and causes next to no detectable loss of quality. The .cel files can be saved at any compression rate used by .mp3 files, but unlike .mp3 files, .cel files do not add silence to the start and end of files. Click OK to close the alert window, if necessary.*

6 Double-click the ZildjianSizzle_edited file to view its waveform. This audio file has a few seconds of silence at the end of the sample, which you will remove. If your time display is not in Decimal format (minutes, seconds, milliseconds), change it now by choosing View > Display Time Format > Decimal (mm:ss.ddd).

7 Place your cursor at the beginning of the waveform, then click and drag to the right, ending the selection at the 9 second mark. Make sure you are selecting both channels of the file by confirming that both channels are highlighted in white as you are selecting them.

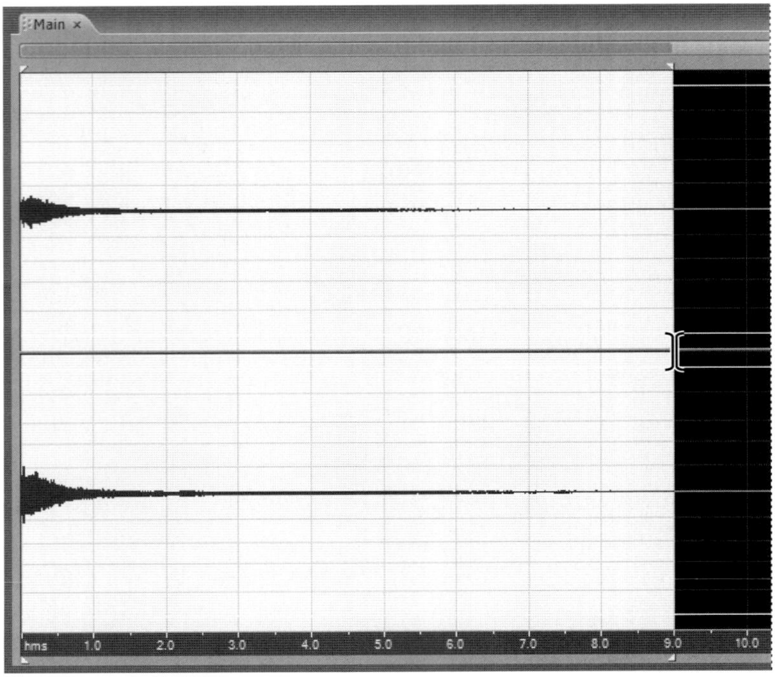

The Selection/View panel controls (located in the bottom right corner) show the beginning and ending points, as well as the total length of both the selection and the section of the waveform that's currently visible.

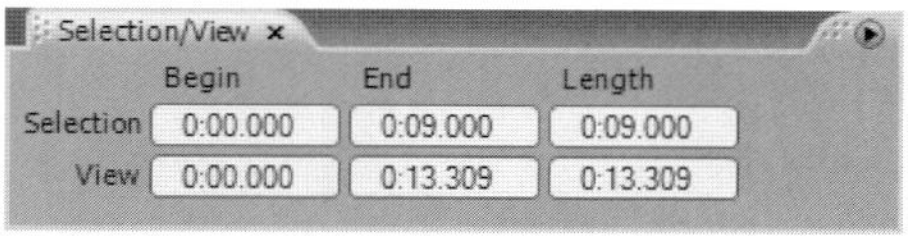

8 The Selection/View panel displays the length of your selection along with the total length of the waveform. The total length should be approximately 13.3 seconds, and the selection should be approximately 9 seconds, which is located in the End field. If necessary, adjust the length of your selection by grabbing either of the two yellow range boundaries, and slide them to the left or the right.

9 Click and drag the right range boundary, represented by the yellow triangles at the top or bottom of the timeline. Drag to the left to shorten the selection to approximately the 6 second mark.

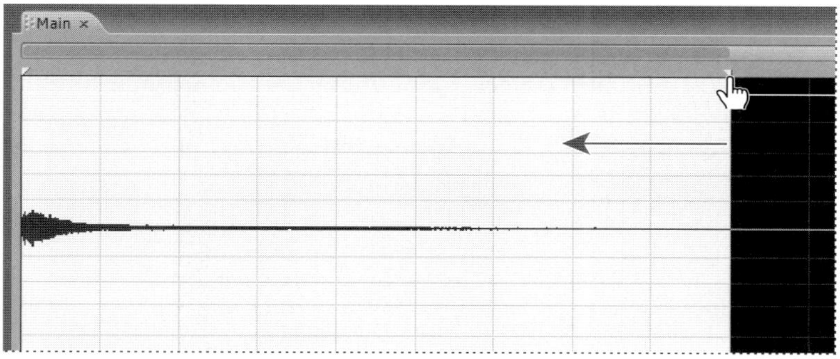

10 Press and hold the Shift key on your keyboard and click near the 4.5 second mark in the waveform to shorten the selection further. This is another method to modify a selection.

11 Choose Edit > Trim to keep the main crash of the cymbal and delete the silence. Trimming retains the information within a selection.

You can also delete the information within a selection.

12 Place your cursor at the 3 second mark; click and drag to the right to select the last 1.5 seconds of the waveform. Press the Delete key on your keyboard to remove this section.

13 Press the Home key on your keyboard to return the start-time indicator to the start of the audio file, and press the spacebar to play the shortened clip. Although the sound fades out, it does not completely fade to silence. You can confirm this visually by clicking the Zoom In Vertically button ( ) three consecutive times.

The height of the waveform increases so that you can view it in greater detail. Note that the decibel readings on the vertical ruler along the right side changes as you zoom in.

14 Using the Selection/View panel controls as a guide, select the waveform from approximately the 2.5 second mark to the end of the clip. Choose Effects > Amplitude > Amplify/Fade (process). The Amplify/Fade window is displayed.

15 Click the Fade tab within this window. From the list of presets, choose the Fade Out option. You may have to scroll down through the list of available presets to locate the Fade Out preset. Below the Presets section, make sure that the Enable Preroll and Postroll Preview check box is selected and then click the Preview button. Audition plays the selection as a loop, allowing you to listen carefully to the result of the effect. You should now hear the end of the cymbal as it fades out to silence. Uncheck the Enable Preroll and Postroll Preview check box and hear the difference in the sound. Preroll and Postroll Preview plays one second before the beginning of the selection (Preroll) and one second after (Postroll), and is useful for comparing the original sound with the edited version.

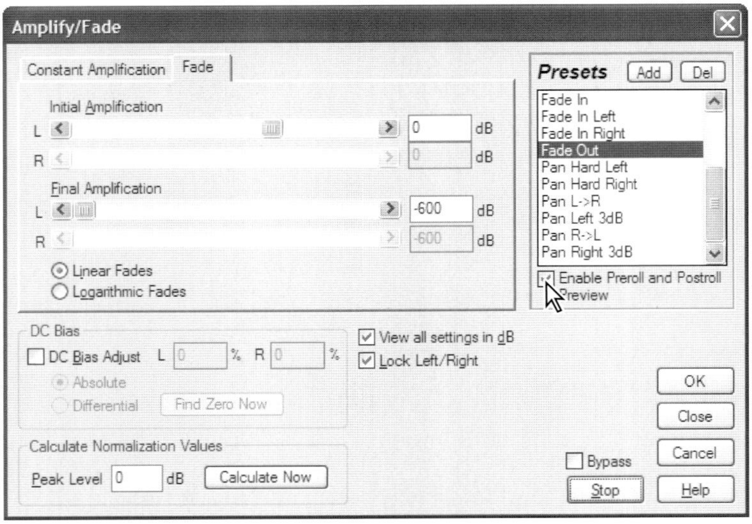

You can change the length of the preroll and postroll duration by right-clicking on the Play button ( ) in the Transport panel, and choosing Preroll and Postroll options.

16 Click OK to commit the Fade Out effect. The waveform fades to silence. Press F2 or choose Edit > Repeat Last Command to access the Amplify/Fade window again. The previous settings of the fade out should still be intact. Click OK to apply the effect again. Applying the Fade Out effect twice creates a faster fade out.

Preroll and Postroll can also be used in the Edit View. For example, if you would like to hear how the sample leads up to the fade out, you can do so by changing the behavior of the Play button.

17 If necessary, select the last 1.5 seconds of the waveform which have been faded. Right-click on the Play button ( ) in the Transport panel and choose Play Preroll and Selection. Click the Play button and Audition plays one second of the sound before the beginning of the selection.

This is an extremely useful technique for previewing effects because it allows you to maintain the original selection. If you need to make changes or add another effect, you can do so.

18 Right-click the Play button and select the default behavior, Play from Cursor to End of File. Press the Home key to send the start-time indicator to the beginning of the session.

19 Choose File > Save. Because you created this file as a copy at the start of this exercise, the original cymbal crash (ZildjianSizzle.cel) remains untouched.

Combining audio clips in Edit View

You can combine two or more clips in the Edit View using the Append Command. For example, you can add a drum roll at the end of the loop.

1 If the last clip you worked on, ZildjianSizzle_edited.cel, is not already displayed, double-click on the file name in the Files panel to view the waveform. If you exited Audition after the last exercise, you will need to re-import the ZildjianSizzle_edited.cel file into the Files panel.

2 Choose File > Open Append. The Open Append window appears. Select the file KickSnareEnding01(mono).cel from the AA_03 folder on your hard disk.

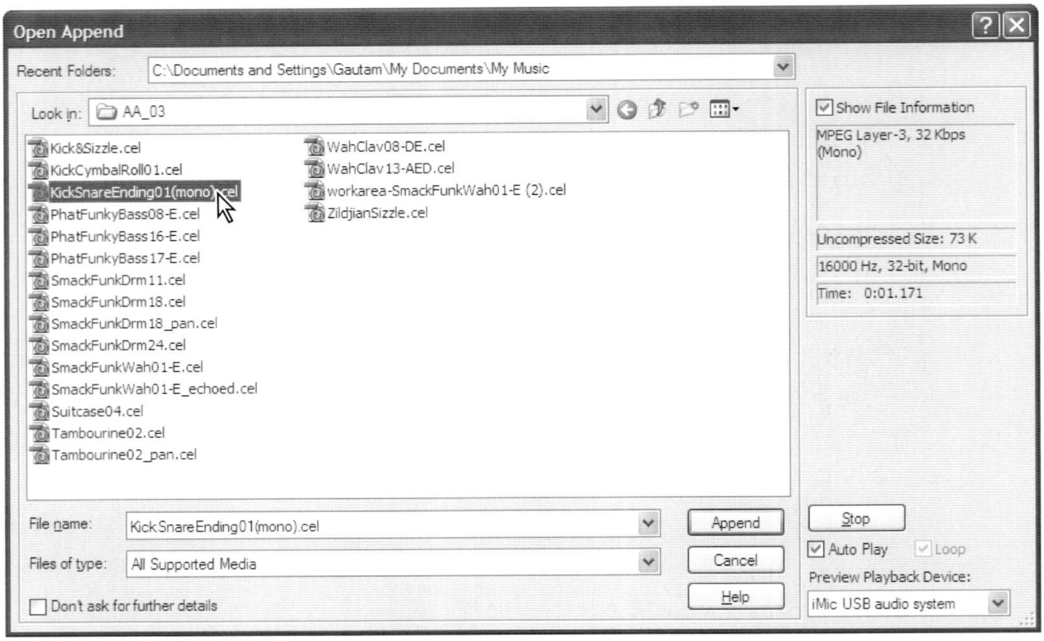

3 Inside the Open Append window, be certain that the Show File Information check box is checked. Along with other statistics, the file information indicates that this file is monaural, as it only has one channel. The file to which we are appending this mono file is a stereo file, with two channels. Audition will automatically convert the mono file to stereo.

4 Click the Append button and the kick snare is added to the end of the cymbal crash. Press the Home key and then press the spacebar to hear the new audio clip. You should be able to hear a difference between the stereo effect of the cymbal crash and the kick snare ending.

The kick snare may have come from a separate recording and does not have the same stereo presence as the cymbal crash. You will add a Reverb effect to the kick snare to make it sound more spacious and make it more compatible with the cymbal crash.

5 When you appended the KicksnareEnding01(mono).cel file to the cymbal crash file, Audition added a marker in the display window, marking the insertion point of the file. The marker is red in color and uses the title of the inserted file. Markers offer an excellent way to separate sections of a single waveform. You will work extensively with markers in Lesson 5, "Working with Loops and Waves."

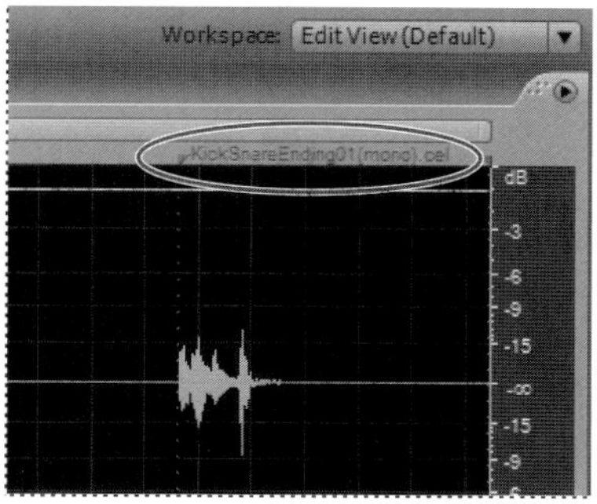

About markers

Markers are locations that you define in a waveform. Markers make it easy to navigate within a waveform to make a selection, perform edits, or play back audio.

In Adobe Audition, a marker can be either a point or a range. A point refers to a specific time position within a waveform (for instance, 1:08.566 from the start of the file). A range has both a start time and an end time (for example, all of the waveform from 1:08.566 to 3:07.379). You can drag start and end markers for a range to different times.

Markers have triangular handles that appear at the top and bottom of the Main panel. You use marker handles to select and adjust markers. You can also right-click a marker handle to access commands for working with markers.

—From Adobe Audition Help

6 If the Show Markers button () at the bottom of the Files panel is not already selected, click it now. A small plus sign appears to the left of the file ZildjianSizzle_edited.cel. Click on this plus sign (+), and the file name expands and the marker KickSnareEnding01(mono) is displayed as a sublevel.

7 Double-click on the marker name KickSnareEnding(mono), and note the section of the waveform matching the original KickSnareEnding01 is automatically highlighted.

8 Press the spacebar to hear the kick snare. Click the Effects tab to bring the Effects panel in front of the Files panel, and then click the plus sign (+) next to Delay Effects. Double-click the Studio Reverb effect to open the Studio Reverb window.

9 Be sure that the Preroll/Postroll Preview check box, located at the bottom left of the window, is checked. From the available list of presets, choose Room Ambience 1 and press the Preview Play button. You should hear the kick drum sound with the Studio Reverb added as it loops over and over. To hear the original sound, click the Power button (⏻) to turn it off. Click again to turn it back on and hear the Studio Reverb effect again.

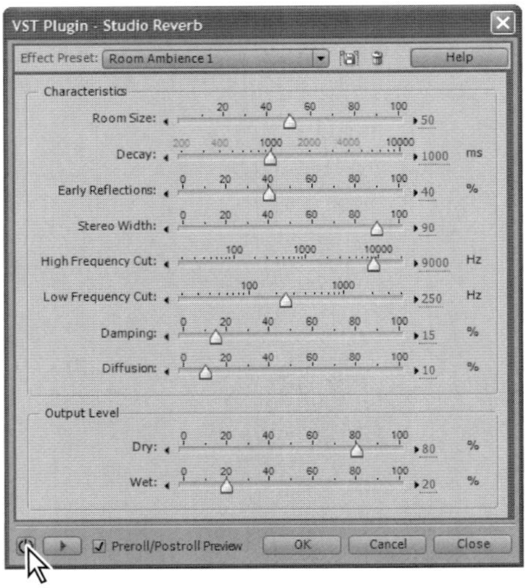

10 Click OK to apply the effect. Press the Home key to place the start-time indicator at the beginning of the clip and then press the spacebar to hear the changes. The new clip begins with the sound of a cymbal crash and ends with the sound of a snare drum.

11 Choose File > Save.

Applying the Stereo Field Rotate effect

In the Edit View, all changes you make to a waveform are permanent once you save the file. This is referred to as destructive editing. Non-destructive editing takes place in the Multitrack View, which you will explore in the next lesson. In addition to destructively editing a clip, changes made to files in the Edit View affect all instances of the file if it is used in the Multitrack View. If the same file is used many times in a session, one change in the Edit View will update it throughout the entire session.

1 Click the Files tab to bring the Files panel forward, and then double-click the Tambourine02.cel to display the waveform. This is a mono file. Click the Effects tab and then click on the plus sign (+) next to the Amplitude category. Certain effects are grayed-out and are unavailable because they can only be applied to a stereo waveform. You will convert this file to a stereo file.

2 Choose Edit > Convert Sample Type. The Convert Sample Type window appears. In the Channels section, click on the Stereo radio button. Make sure Left Mix and Right Mix are both at 100%. In the Bit Depth section, set **32** as the bit depth and click OK to apply the conversion.

The tambourine waveform now has a left and a right channel. The Amplitude effects, which were previously unavailable in the Effects tab, are now available.

3 Double-click the Stereo Field Rotate (process) effect to open the Stereo Field Rotate window.

4 From the list of presets, choose Pan Left to Right and click the Preview button. You should hear the tambourine begin on the left side of your speakers/headphones and pan to the right.

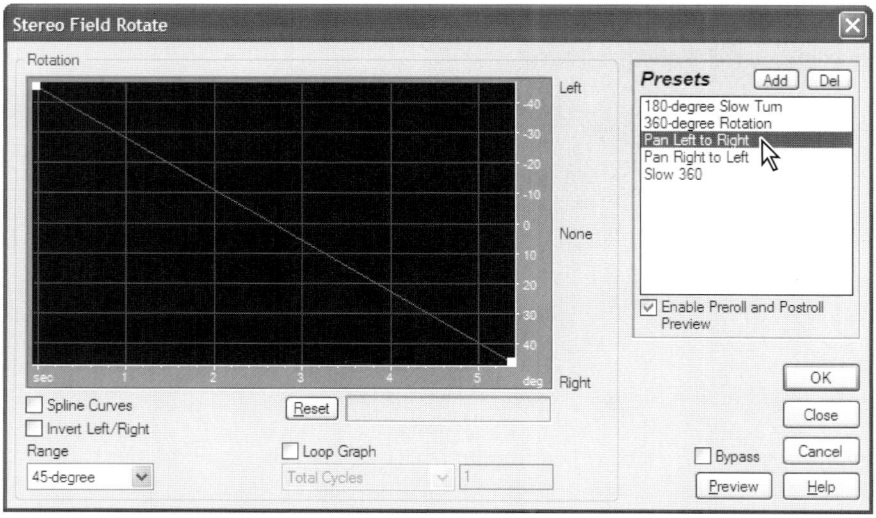

Default presets are often a good place to start when adding effects. You will often want to modify the default characteristics of the effect to meet your particular needs. Before you begin modifying this effect, note the x-axis and y-axis in the Stereo Field Rotate window. The x-axis represents the entire timeline, and starts at 0 seconds and ends at 5.3 seconds. The y-axis represents the number of degrees off stereo center for both the left and right channel.

The Pan Left to Right preset pans in a linear fashion from the left to the right over a period of 5.3 seconds. Halfway through the selection, the stereo effect is in the center. You will change the pan so that the transition from left to right takes place at a later point.

5 Click on the blue line at approximately the 3 second mark. An anchor point appears. Move the anchor point up the graph to the -30 degrees mark in the left channel. You can use the readout field beneath the graph to determine the anchor point's position in time and stereo space. Drag the anchor point to the point representing approximately 3.5 seconds and -30 degrees.

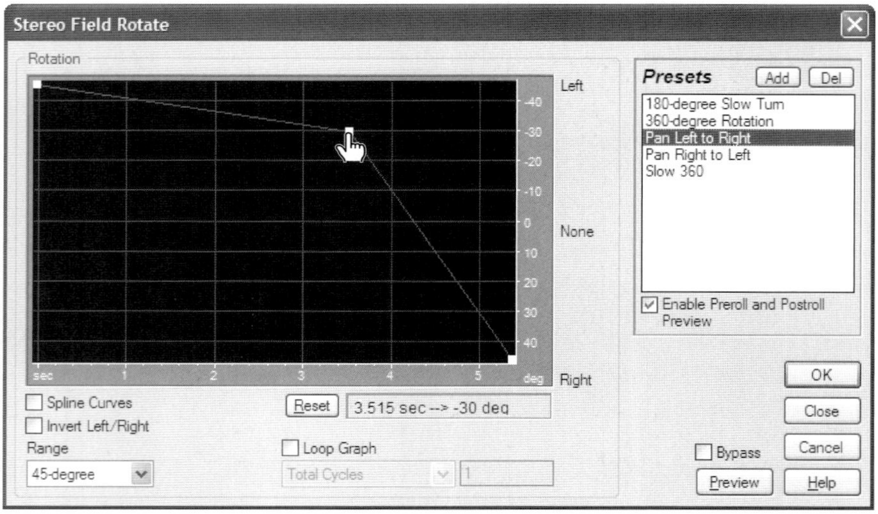

6 Preview the sound by clicking the Preview button.

The tambourine stays in the left channel for a longer period of time and then quickly shifts to the right channel. When previewing the sound, note where the blue line crosses the 0 axis. This is this point that the effect is at stereo center.

You can clear one point on a graph by left-clicking the point and dragging up or down off of the graph. If you have many anchor points on a line, you can clear all points by clicking the Reset button. This is also an excellent place to start when creating your own effects. Do not do this to the current lesson file, however.

7 Click on the Spline Curves check box. The line changes from two straight lines to a curved line. This creates a smoother transition from stereo left to stereo right. Click and drag the anchor point to the right, the values should be approximately 4.5 seconds and -30 degrees. Press Preview to hear the results. Do not apply the effect yet.

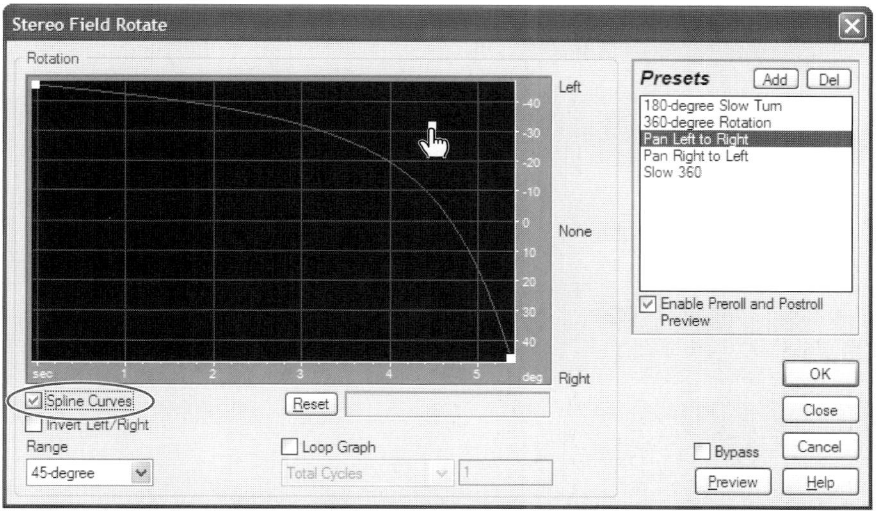

8 Before you apply the effect, click the Add button in the preset section. In the Add Preset window, type **Pan Left to Right Smooth** and click OK. Your new Stereo Field effect is added to the Presets and can be easily applied to other waveforms. Click OK again to close the Stereo Field Rotate dialog box and apply the effect.

Your waveform has now been modified to reflect the edits from this lesson. Because you started the stereo effect in the left channel, the waveform is higher than it is in the right. There is little information in the right channel at the beginning of the loop, and toward the end of the loop, the waveform increases in the right channel.

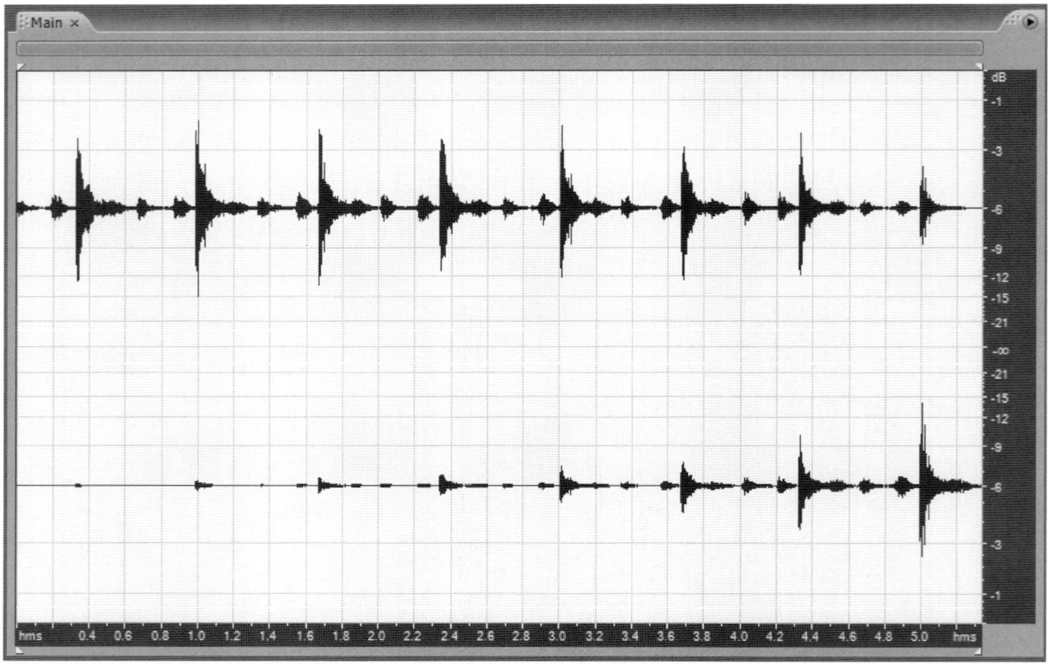

9 Choose File > Save As. Navigate to the AA_03 folder on your hard disk. Name the file **Tambourine02_pan.cel** and click Save.

Note: *If an alert message appears confirming that you are overwriting an existing file, click Yes.*

Adding a favorite

As you begin to work more with Audition, you may find yourself applying the same effects repeatedly. Saving effects as favorites allows you to name and access your effects in a central location. You can even assign keyboard shortcuts to access commonly used effects.

1 In the Edit View, click on the Favorites tab to bring the Favorites panel forward. If the Favorites tab is not visible, choose Window > Favorites to make it visible. Click the Edit Favorites button at the bottom of the Favorites panel. The Favorites window appears. Audition comes installed with certain favorites, such as Fade In and Fade Out.

2 Click the New button, and in the Name field, enter **Pan Left to Right Smooth**. In the Press New Shortcut Key field type the letter **D**.

3 In the Function tab, click the Audition Effect drop-down menu. A list of the effects available in Edit View appears. Choose Amplitude\Stereo Field Rotate (process).

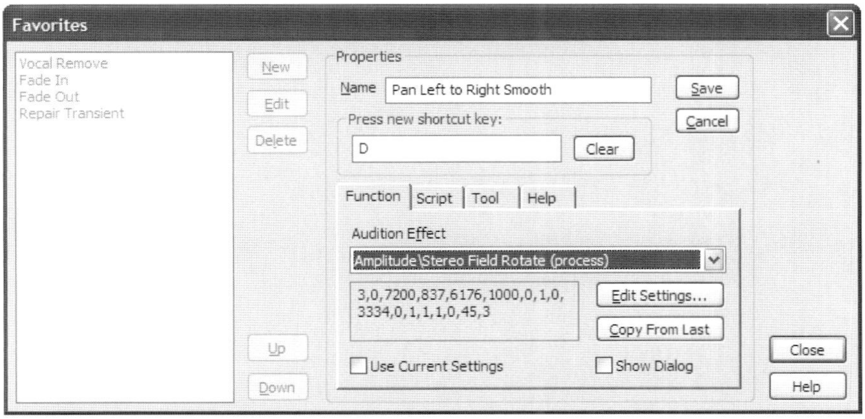

4 To ensure that the effect you are saving is the one you want, click the Edit Settings button. The Stereo Field Rotate window appears. Click to select the Pan Left to Right Smooth preset that you saved in the previous section, and click OK. Click the Save button and the favorite appears at the bottom of the Favorites list.

5 In the Favorites window, click the Up button to move your favorite to the top of the list of favorites. Click the Close button.

6 Click the Files tab to access your list of files. Double-click on the SmackFunkDrm18 .cel file to display the waveform. Click to select the waveform, then press the letter D to apply the Stereo Field Rotate effect. You may need to wait a few moments as Audition calculates and applies the changes. When the waveform changes, the effect has been applied. Press the spacebar to hear the effect.

Note: *You can also click the Favorites tab, then double-click the Pan Left to Right Smooth favorite to apply the effect.*

7 Choose File > Save As. If necessary, navigate to the AA_03 folder on your hard disk. Rename this file SmackFunkDrm_pan.cel and click Save.

Note: *If an alert message appears confirming that you want to overwrite an existing file, click Yes.*

8 Press F12 to enter Multitrack View. When working in Edit View, the Multitrack View is also open and all edits made in Edit View are automatically updated. Press the Home key and then press the Play button to hear the session. Pay particular attention to the stereo effect of the first drum clip, as well as when the tambourine begins. The stereo field changes you made have been incorporated into the main mix.

9 Choose File > Save Session and then choose File > Close All.

Exploring on your own

1 If you have not already previewed the Loopology collection of music clips which ships with Audition, create a new session in the Multitrack View and import two or three clips. Enter the Edit View and experiment with some of the different effects in the Effects panel.

2 Try adding one of the Studio Reverb presets to a drum track. Certain effects work better on certain classes of instruments. Chorus effects work well with single instruments or voices by enriching the presence of the track. To learn more about the behavior of certain effects, use the Help button in any effects window.

3 To change the length of the Preroll and Postroll, right-click on the Play button and choose Preroll and Postroll Options.

4 Use the Fade Out favorite to modify a waveform. Compare this process to the Amplify/Fade effect you used earlier in this lesson.

Review

Review questions

1 How do you make a new copy of a file in the Edit View? Why is this something you would want to do?

2 What is the Preroll and Postroll Preview, and where are the options for changing them?

3 What are markers?

Review answers

1 To make a copy of a file, it must be loaded into the Edit View display window and then copied by choosing Edit > Copy to New. Creating copies of your original files is useful when you want to preserve the original sound file or create multiple versions from the same source.

2 When you apply an effect to a selection, you often need to hear the original sound before and after the selection takes place. The Preroll and Postroll Preview provides additional preview of the waveform before and after your current selection. It can be enabled when you add an effect or, alternatively, when you press the Play from Cursor to End of File or Play from Cursor to End of View buttons in the Edit View. To change the Preroll and/or Postroll options of the Play buttons, right-click the button and choose the desired command from the menu.

3 Markers represent a specific point, or a range with a specific starting and ending point, within a waveform. Efficient use of markers can considerably speed up the editing and navigation process.

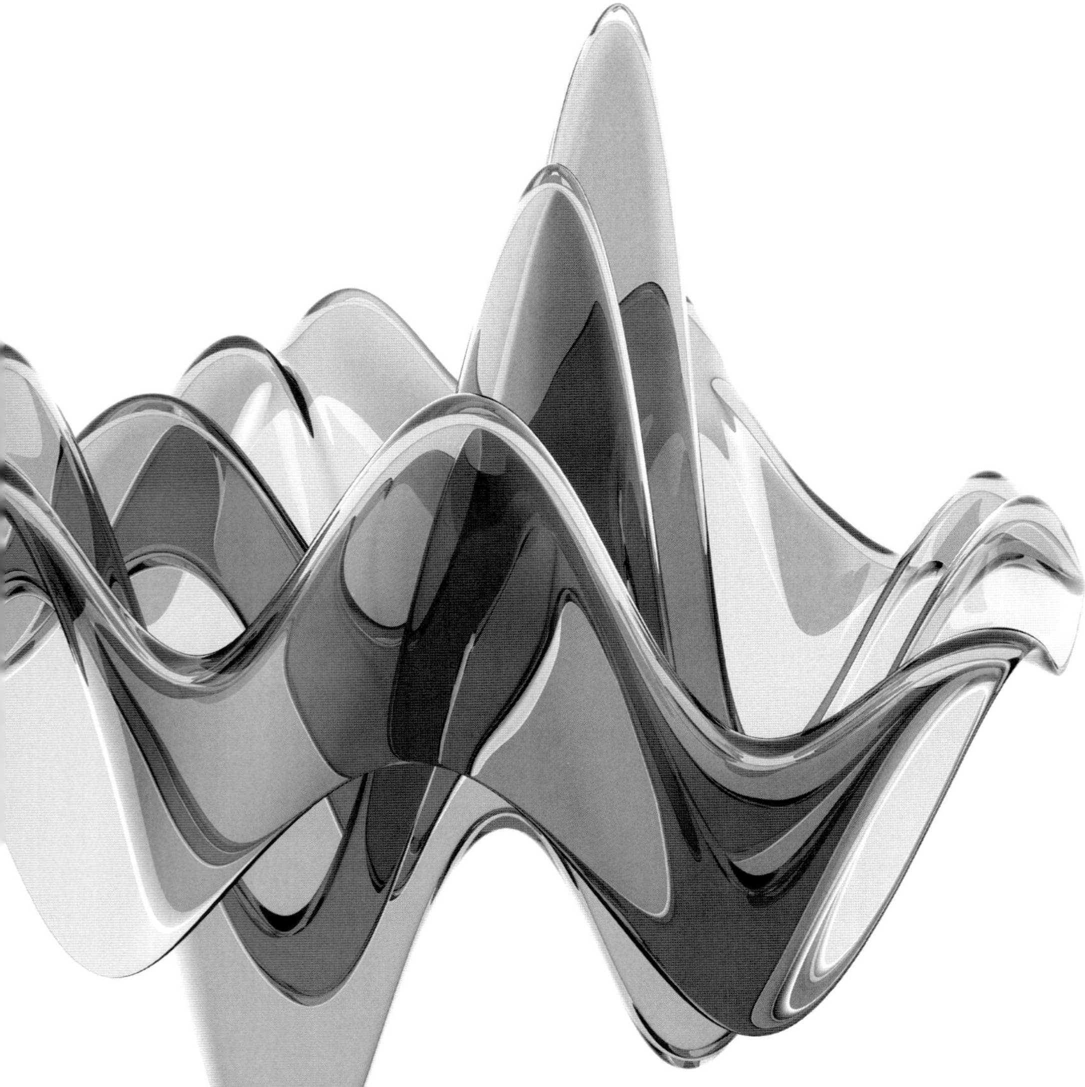

4 Working in Multitrack View

You can create multi-layered musical compositions using the audio clips supplied with Adobe Audition's extensive Loopology loop library. With real-time mixing, you control properties such as volume and pan. You can quickly add and edit Audition's non-destructive effects, such as Echo, Reverb, or equalization, allowing you to focus on the creative aspects of making music.

In this lesson, you'll learn how to do the following:

- Position clips within the Multitrack View.
- Use scrubbing to find important locations within your tracks and files.
- Control pan and volume envelopes.
- Add non-destructive effects to your multitrack session.

Getting started

In this lesson, you'll work with a series of files in the Multitrack View.

1 Start Adobe Audition. If necessary, click the Multitrack View button (▦).

2 If you have not already copied the resource files for this lesson onto your hard disk from the *Adobe Audition 2.0 Classroom in a Book* CD, do so now. See "Copying the Classroom in a Book files" on page 2.

3 To play the finished session file, choose File > Open Session, and open the 04_end.ses file in the AA_04 folder, which is located within the AA_CIB folder on your hard disk. Press the Home key, then play the session file by either clicking on the Play button (▶) in the Transport panel or pressing the spacebar on your keyboard.

4 When you are ready to start working, close the 04_end.ses file by choosing File > Close All.

5 Choose File > New Session. Choose 44100 from the list of sample rates and click OK. From the File menu, choose File > Save Session As and enter the name **04_multitrack.ses**. Navigate to the AA_04 folder, located in the AA_CIB folder on your hard disk and click Save.

6 Choose File > Import. Locate and open the AA_04 folder, then click on the file SmackFunkDrm18.cel. Click the Play button on the right side of the window to hear the file before you import it. Click Open and this file is placed into the Files panel.

Note: *Be certain to navigate to the AA_04 folder when importing the files for this lesson. Some of the file names are shared with files used in Lessons 2 and 3.*

About multitrack sessions

In Multitrack View, you can mix together multiple audio and MIDI clips to create layered soundtracks and elaborate musical compositions. You can record and mix unlimited tracks, and each track can contain as many clips as you need—the only limits are hard disk space and processing power. When you're happy with a mix, you can export a mixdown file for use on CD, the Web, and more.

Multitrack View is an extremely flexible, real-time editing environment, so you can change settings during playback and immediately hear the results. While listening to a session, for example, you can adjust track volume to properly blend tracks together. Any changes you make are impermanent, or nondestructive. If a mix doesn't sound good next week, or even next year, you can simply remix the original source files, freely applying and removing effects to create different sonic textures.

Adobe Audition saves information about source files and mix settings in session (.ses) files. Session files are relatively small because they contain only pathnames to source files and references to mix parameters (such as volume, pan, and effect settings). To more easily manage session files, save them in a unique folder with the source files they reference. If you later need to move the session to another computer, you can simply move the unique session folder.

—From Adobe Audition Help

Positioning clips within the Multitrack View

By default, when you start Adobe Audition, a new session opens in the Multitrack View. You will be working primarily in this view for this lesson.

1 Choose View > Display Time Format > Bars and Beats. Or, right-click the time display ruler that runs along the bottom of the Main panel in the Multitrack View. From the contextual menu that appears, choose Display Time Format. From the list of time displays, choose Bars and Beats, if it is not already selected.

2 If necessary, select the Files tab to bring the Files panel forward. Double-click the SmackFunkDrm18.cel file to open it in the Edit View, or right-click on the file name and choose Edit File. Choose File > File Info. The File Info window appears. Click on the Loop Info tab to access information about the source waveform. The Loop option is selected, indicating that this waveform was saved as a loop rather than an individual sound sample. The original tempo of this loop, which is 98.1 beats per minute, is also displayed. Click OK to close the File Info window.

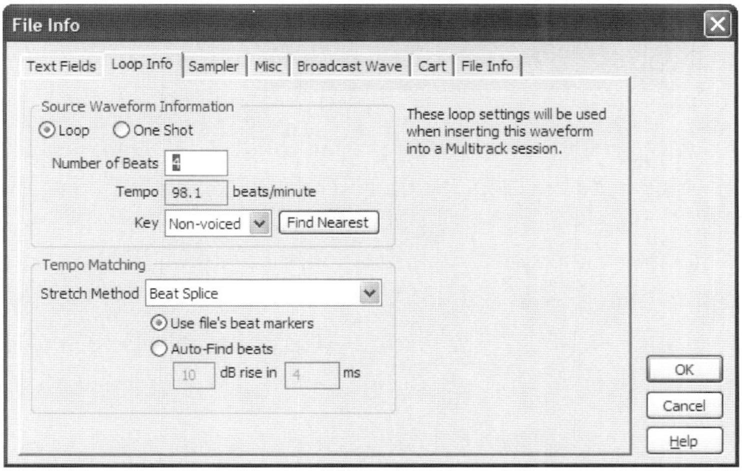

3 To hear the drum loop, click the Play Looped button ( ) in the Transport panel, and the drum loops continuously. After listening to the loop a few times, press the Stop button ( ) to stop playing the loop.

4 Click on the Multitrack View button () to return to the Multitrack View. Click in Track 1 to select it and then press the Home key to move the start-time indicator to the beginning. Click on the SmackFunkDrm18.cel file in the Files panel, then click the Insert Into Multitrack Session button () and the loop loads into the currently selected track. Press the spacebar to hear the session containing the newly placed drum sample. Press the spacebar again to stop the play cursor.

5 Select the Move/Copy Clip tool (). Click the right edge of the drum loop to select it. When your cursor changes to the loop editing icon (), click and drag the loop to the right. As the end of the loop approaches a new bar, notice that a thin white line appears, stretching from the top to the bottom of your display window. This line ensures that the loop is playing for a full bar. When you reach Bar 7 beat 1 (7:1.00), release the mouse.

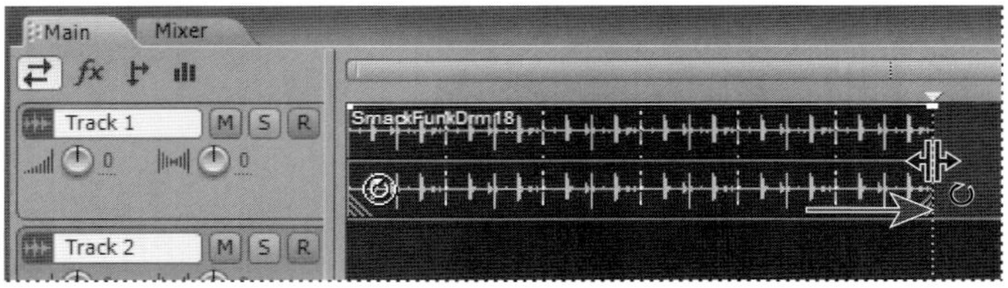

6 Click and drag on the right edge of the loop again to extend the loop to Bar 30 beat 1 (30:1.00). As you extend the loop, the timeline scrolls to accommodate the new length of the drum loop. When you reach Bar 30, look for the white line to snap to the end of the clip, ensuring that it is properly aligned. Click the Zoom Out Full Both Axes button () to view the entire timeline. Because music sessions begin at Bar 1 beat 1 (1:1.00), the length of your View will be 29 bars (29:0.00). This will also be the length of your final song; the equivalent of 29 bars in decimal format is approximately one minute and ten seconds.

7 You will now load the remaining files into the Files panel. Click on the Import File button () and the Import window appears. Confirm that you are viewing the AA_04 folder and click on Kick&Sizzle.cel, which should be the first file in the list. Shift+click on the last file in the list, WahClav13-AED.cel. This selects the entire range of files. Ctrl+click on SmackFunkDrm18.cel to deselect it because you have already imported this file into the session. Click the Open button.

Depending upon the speed of your computer, Audition may take a few moments to load files. When it is done, all the selected files are imported into the session and are listed in the Files panel.

8 You will now load the guitar clip into Track 2. Click the SmackFunkWah01-E.cel loop. If necessary, press the Play button (▶) in the Files panel to hear the guitar loop. If the Auto Play button (🔊) is selected, the clip will play automatically. Click and hold down on the SmackFunkWah01-E.cel loop in the Files panel, then drag it anywhere into Track 2. You can load loops into a specific track by dragging and dropping them from the Files panel.

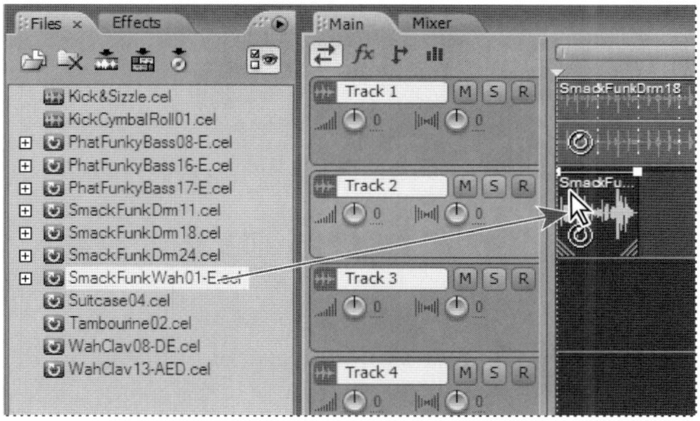

9 Click the SmackFunkWah01-E.cel clip to select it. Click again and drag the entire waveform from left to right to see how you can position a clip in time within a session. Position your guitar clip so the beginning starts at exactly Bar 4 beat 1. Use the status bar at the bottom of the display to help you locate the exact bar and beat.

10 Right-click on the time ruler along the bottom of the multitrack and choose Snapping from the context menu. Confirm that Snap to Ruler (Fine) has a check mark next to it. If not, select it now.

11 Click the handle on the bottom right corner of the guitar loop in Track 2 and extend it to the right. Drag the guitar clip until the end of the loop snaps to Bar 12 beat 1 (12:1.00). Notice that if you have zoomed-in enough horizontally, the white line appears at every beat, not just the end of a clip. Press the Home key on your keyboard, which moves the yellow start-time indicator to the beginning of the session. Press the spacebar to play the session. When the guitar begins to play, it is perfectly in time with the other clip. Press the spacebar to stop playing the session.

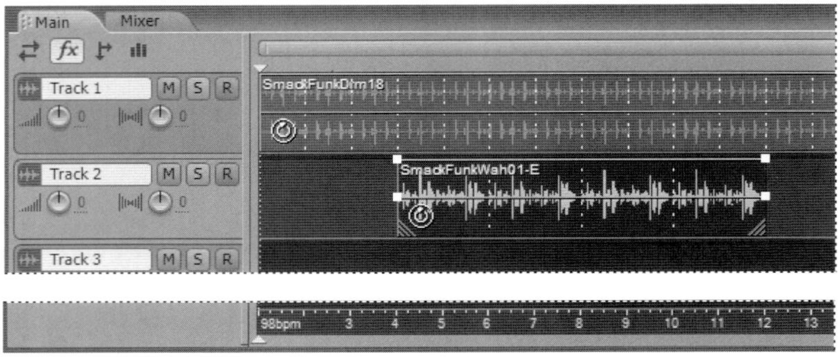

12 To add the same guitar loop to the end of your song, click and drag the SmackFunkWah01-E.cel loop from the Files panel into Track 2, and then position the beginning of the clip at Bar 24 beat 1 (24:1.00). Place your cursor on the bottom right corner of the clip and click and drag to extend the clip. Align the end of the guitar clip with the end of the drum clip in Track 1 at Bar 30 beat 1 (30:1.00).

Creating a bass track

You will now add three different bass clips to create a bass track.

1 Click and drag the loop PhatFunkyBass08-E.cel into Track 3 from the Files panel. Using the Move/Copy Clip tool, click and drag the entire clip so that it begins at the Bar 2 beat 1 (2:1.00) and then click and drag the lower right corner and extend the clip to the Bar 6 beat 1 (6:1.00). Remember to use the white lines to help align the clip to bars and beats, and the status bar to see the location of the clip being moved.

2 From the Files panel, click and drag the clip PhatFunkyBass16-E.cel into Track 3 and position the beginning of the clip at Bar 8 beat 1 (8:1.00). Click and drag the handle on the bottom right of the clip and extend the loop until it ends at Bar 12 beat 1 (12:1.00).

3 Drag the clip PhatFunkyBass17-E.cel into Track 3 from the Files panel. Position the beginning of the clip at Bar 12 beat 1 (12:1.00). Click and drag the handle on the bottom right of the clip to extend the loop so it ends at Bar 20 beat 1 (20:1.00).

4 Drag another instance of PhatFunkybass08-E.cel into your bass track. Place the beginning at Bar 20 beat 1 (20:1.00). Do not extend this clip.

Adding more tracks

To place your clips precisely on the timeline, you can also use the start-time indicator to align your clips. You will now align the end of a clip to the start-time indicator.

1 Press the Home key to ensure the start-time indicator is at the beginning of the session. It is represented as yellow triangles at the top and bottom of the multitrack. Place your cursor over one of the yellow triangles until it turns into a pointing finger (☝). Click and drag the start-time indicator until the time reads 12:3.00. If necessary, use the Selection/View window to specify the exact location of the start-time indicator.

2 Drag the Tambourine02.cel into Track 4 and position the clip so it begins at Bar 8 beat 1 (8:1.00). Click and drag the handle on the bottom right of the clip until it aligns with the start-time indicator at Bar 12 beat 3 (12:3.00). The start-time indicator is useful as a guide for clips.

Note: *When you drag the start-time indicator, Audition scrubs the session to help you hear where you are in the session. If, however, you find this behavior distracting, you can turn it off by choosing Edit > Preferences > Multitrack > Play audio while scrubbing with the Start Time Indicator. Audition 2.0 also offers a dedicated and flexible tool for scrubbing. The next section discusses scrubbing techniques in detail.*

3 Using the Move/Copy Clip tool (), right-click on the tambourine clip and drag your mouse slightly to the right. A new clip appears and moves with your cursor. The cursor itself has changed its shape to (). Drag to place the beginning of the newly created clip at Bar 22 beat 1 (22:1.00) and release your mouse button. A small context menu appears, choose Copy Reference Here.

Note: *A reference copy takes up no additional space on your hard disk. Changes made to the original file also modify all reference copies based on that file. Creating a unique copy creates a separate file that is unaffected by any changes made to the original file. Creating a unique copy increases the overall size of your session, as it creates a duplicate sound file on your hard disk.*

4 Drag the Kick&Sizzle.cel clip from the Files panel into Track 4, and then position the clip to start at 16 bars 1 beat (16:1.00). Note in the Files panel that the icon for this clip is marked as audio (). This indicates that the clip has not been enabled for looping and will not extend.

You will be adding one more music track to this song. Audition is capable of using an unlimited number of audio tracks.

5 To view additional tracks, click the Zoom Out Vertically button (). You should see at least 2 remaining tracks in this multitrack session. Drag the clip WahClav08-DE.cel into Track 5. Use the Move/Copy Clip tool to place the start of the clip at Bar 13 beat 1 (13:1.00). Click on the handle on the bottom right and drag to the right to extend the clip to Bar 17 beat 1 (17:1.00).

6 Click and drag the WahClav13-AED.cel clip into Track 5. Place the beginning of the clip at Bar 17 beat 1 (17:1.00), then click on the bottom right of the clip and drag to the right, extending the clip to Bar 21 beat 1 (21:1.00).

7 Add the Suitcase04.cel clip to Track 5, by clicking and dragging it from the Files panel into this track. Place the beginning of the clip at Bar 21 beat 1 (21:1.00), click on the bottom right, and drag to the right, extending the clip to Bar 28 beat 1 (28:1.00). If you are having difficulty locating the exact spot on the timeline, use your start-time indicator to find the 28:1.00 mark and extend the end of the clip to the start-time indicator.

You can also use the left and right arrow keys on your keyboard to move the start-time indicator. In addition, you can use the Begin Selection field in the Selection/View panel to quickly set the start-time indicator to a specific location.

8 To add the final clip to your session, move the start-time indicator to Bar 28 beat 3 (28:3.00). Drag the KickCymbalRoll01.cel from the Files panel into Track 5 and align the beginning of the clip with the start-time indicator. Adding the Cymbal Roll extends the length of the song.

9 To view all the clips in the session, click the Zoom Out Full Both Axes. Press the Home key on your keyboard to return start-time indicator to the beginning of the session and then press the spacebar to hear your composition. You will be adding one more basic change to the structure of the song.

10 In the Files panel, click on the clip SmackFunkDrm24.cel. If necessary, click to select the Loop Play button in the Files panel and then click the Play button in the Files panel to hear the file. This is a drum fill, which you will add to your drum track. This breaks up the repetition of the main drum loop and propels the momentum of the song. Press the Stop button after listening to the clip. Move the start-time indicator to the Bar 7 beat 1 (7:1.00) mark, and then click the Zoom To Selection button ().

***Note:** The Zoom To Selection increases the magnification of a session and centers the start-time indicator. This is very useful when working on small sections of a clip.*

11 Select the Time Selection tool ( ) and click in the SmackFunkDrm18 clip in Track 1. Click and drag to create a selection that starts at Bar 7 beat 1 (7:1.00) and ends at Bar 8 beat 1 (8:1.00). Use the Selection/View controls to confirm your selection.

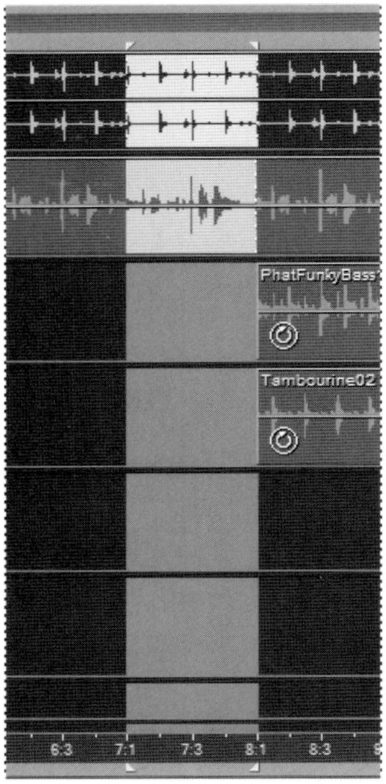

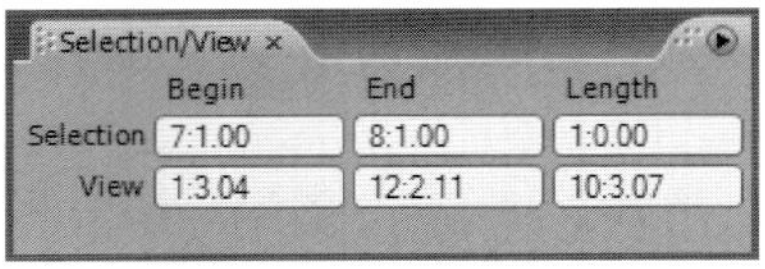

12 Choose Edit > Cut from the menu or press the Delete key on your keyboard to cut 1 bar from the main drum track. A 1 bar-long gap is created in the drum track.

13 Locate the clip SmackFunkDrm24.cel in the Files panel and using the Move/Copy Clip tool, drag it into the empty gap created in Track 1 where you cut 1 bar in the previous step. This 1 bar long drum fill perfectly fits the 1 bar gap in the drum track.

14 Press the Home key then move the start-time indicator to the 6 bar (6:1.00) mark, and press the spacebar to hear your composition play from this point. After the drum fill, press the spacebar to stop the session.

Note: *When you deleted a 1 bar section of the drum clip, a gap was created between 07:01.00 and 08.01.00. The actual length of the session remained unchanged. If you want to change the length of the session by adding or deleting a few bars, you can use the Edit > Insert/Delete Time command.*

Scrubbing

By dragging the start-time indicator, you can scrub the multitrack session to find important locations in your session. Audition also offers a dedicated Scrub tool for this purpose.

The term scrubbing comes from the pre-digital recording era when engineers had to manually move the reels of their tape machine while editing, causing the tape to scrub across the playback head. The speed of the moving reels determined how fast the tape would be scrubbed against the head. The direction of the movement determined whether the tape would play forwards or backwards. Scrubbing allowed them to hear and find exact locations on the tape for the purpose of editing and punching. The Scrub tool offers the same style of editing and movement within your tracks.

The Scrub tool is available in the Edit View as well as the Multitrack View, and can be activated by the keyboard shortcut A.

1 In the Multitrack View, choose the Scrub tool () and click once on the first clip in Track 2, called SmackFunkWah01-E, at Bar 8 beat 1 (08:01.00). The start-time indicator gets placed at this location.

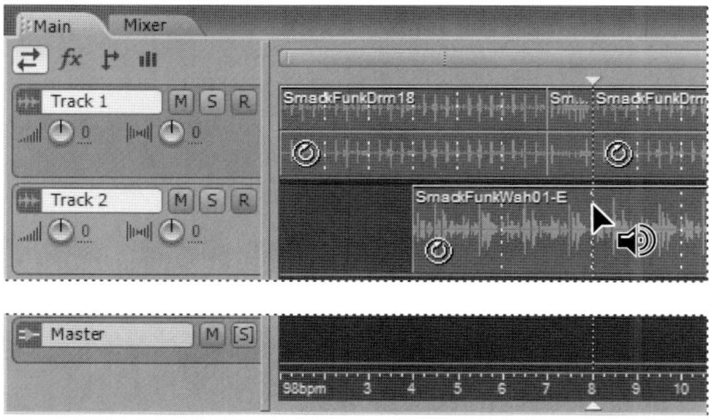

Scrubbing the guitar track using the Scrub tool.

2 Click at this location again, and without releasing your mouse button, drag toward the right of the start-time indicator. The Solo button (S) for Track 2 turns on and you can hear only the guitar clip being scrubbed. Move your cursor to different locations to the right of the start-time indicator and experiment with moving the cursor at different speeds.

The faster you drag toward the right of the start-time indicator, the faster the scrubbing will be in the forward direction. If you drag toward the left of the start-time indicator, scrubbing takes place in a backwards direction.

3 Release your mouse button to stop scrubbing. The Solo button for Track 2 turns off. Press the spacebar to confirm that you can now hear all the tracks in the session. Press the spacebar again to stop the playback.

The maximum speed of scrubbing you can achieve in this manner is the normal speed of playback of the session. Sometimes, you might want to scrub through a track at a much higher speed—just like pressing the Fast Forward button on a CD player—to quickly locate a section within a song. The Scrub tool works in combination with the Alt key to scrub at a higher speed.

4 Hold down the Alt key on your keyboard and scrub the guitar clip in Track 2. Drag the cursor toward the right while holding the Alt key. The faster you drag to the right, the faster the playback speed in the forward direction. This speed can be much higher than the playback speed. Similarly, if you drag toward the left, you can scrub through the track backwards at higher speeds.

You can hold down the Ctrl key while scrubbing to scan for audio sections in the waveform or session. Holding down the Shift key while scrubbing lets you make selections.

Mixing and effect basics

Creating your own composition in Audition is a matter of arranging music clips in time. Although Audition makes it simple to create multi-layered compositions using sound loops, you can modify the different tracks and instruments to create your own unique sounds and tracks.

1 Press the Home key to position the start-time indicator at the beginning of the timeline, then press the spacebar to play the session. As the song begins to play, click the Solo button (S) on Track 1 to play only the drums in this track. The other tracks are turned off and visually grayed out. Listen to the drums for a few moments and click the Solo button again, and the other tracks return to play in real time. By using the Mute and Solo buttons you control which tracks are played and which tracks are silent. Allow the song to continue playing.

2 While the song is still playing, press the Solo button on Track 1 again. Press the Solo button on Track 2, which is the guitar track. Now just these two tracks can be heard, the others are silent. Click the Solo buttons on both the drum track and the guitar track again to enable all your tracks, and then press the spacebar to stop playing the session.

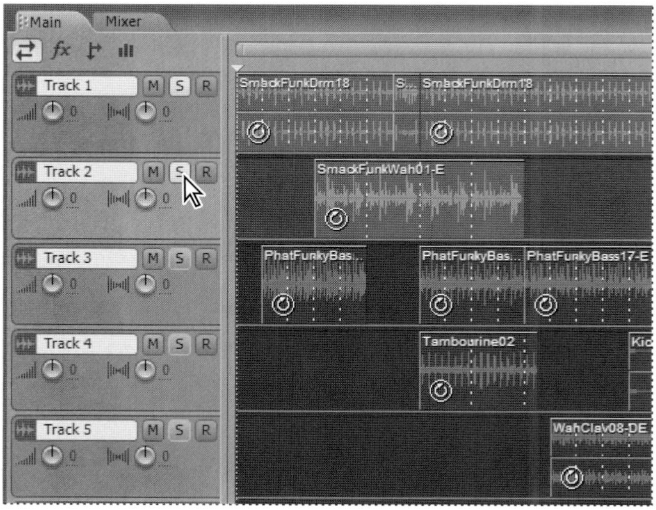

3 Press the Home key to return the start-time indicator to the beginning of the session and then press the Play button. Press the Mute button (M) in Track 1, which is the drum track, to mute this track. The other tracks continue to play while this track is muted. Press the Mute button for Track 2, which is the guitar track. This turns off that track as well. Click the Mute button again in Track 1 and Track 2 to make them audible again.

4 Choose Window > Workspace > Multitrack View (Default).

5 Click on the Mixer tab which is found next to the Main tab above your tracks. The Mixer panel comes to the forefront and overlaps the view of your tracks.

6 Click on the Mixer tab and drag it to the right edge of your screen display. Once the right edge of the screen has a pale green highlight, release your mouse to dock the Mixer.

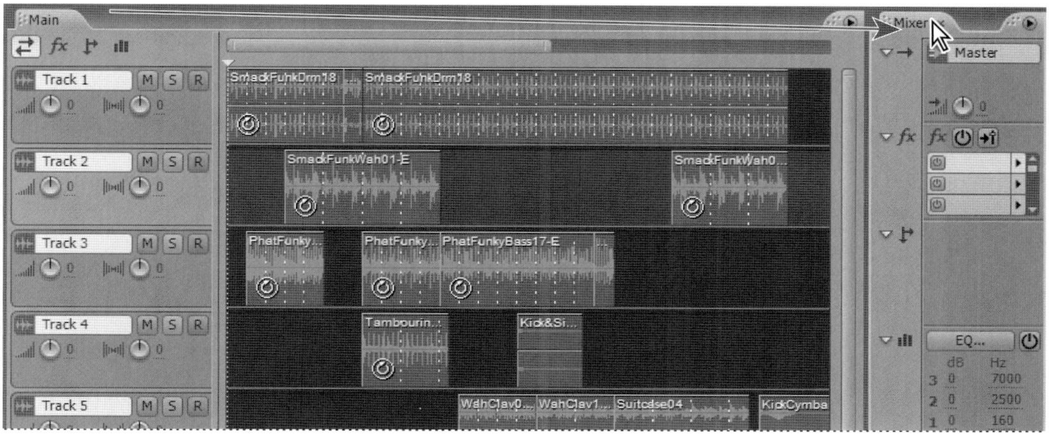

The Mixer panel can be docked to the right of the Main panel by dragging its tab.

Note: *If you are not familiar with moving tabs and panels, see "Working with panels and workspaces" in Lesson 2, "Audition Basics."*

7 Move the cursor over the left edge of the docked Mixer panel. When the cursor's shape changes to (+||+), click and drag to resize the Mixer panel toward the right until you can see nothing but the Master track, as shown in the image above.

8 Click on the volume fader of the Master track. Drag it down to approximately -2 dB.

Reducing the overall volume prevents your session from sounding distorted. When you add more instruments to a song, it becomes louder. You can control the overall session volume using the Master track, as well as the volume of individual tracks.

Note: *You'll have to resize the Mixer panel again to be able to see the individual tracks.*

You can control the volume of individual tracks either in the Mixer panel or directly in the track controls.

9 Press the Home key to return your start-time indicator to the beginning of the session and press the spacebar to play the session. Bring your cursor over the Volume knob for Track 1, which is the first knob on the left below the track's name. The Volume knob is currently set at 0. This is the default value for the Volume knob in this track. Click on the Volume knob and drag to the right to raise the volume to 2 dB. This increases the volume of the drums.

10 In addition to changing the volume of a track, you can also change the pan or balance. As your session is playing, bring your cursor over the Pan knob for Track 2. The pan of this track is in the center, which is 0. This is the default setting. Click on the Pan knob and drag all the way to the right, which is designated as 100.

Now the guitar plays exclusively in the right channel of your speakers or headphones. Drag the knob all the way to the left, which is the -100 designation, to hear the guitar in the left channel of your speakers or headphones. Panning to either extreme has a tendency to sound artificial, so place the guitar track at approximately -30 on the left channel.

11 Resize the Mixer panel by dragging its left edge to the left. Keep increasing the size of the panel until you can see the mixer strips for at least the first three tracks.

The Mixer panel emulates a mixing board. Notice that the volume and pan changes you made to the drum and guitar tracks are both visible in the Mixer panel as well.

Although controlling the pan and volume of individual tracks is fairly easy with a small session, the more tracks you add to a session, the more difficult it becomes to keep track of the individual settings. The Mixer makes it easier to manage a larger number of tracks.

12 Press the spacebar to play the session. In the Mixer, click and drag the volume slider for Track 1 toward the top. Notice that the volume of the drum track increases as you increase the volume. Move the slider to 2 dB. As the session plays back, move the volume faders for Track 1 and Track 2. Experiment a bit with the levels of other tracks and then return them all to 0 dB. Press the spacebar to stop the session.

13 Grab the Mixer by its tab and drag it back to its original location beside the Main tab as it was in step 5, or simply choose Window > Workspace > Reset Current Workspace. When Audition asks you if you really want to discard all the changes to the current workspace (Multitrack View (Default)), click on Discard Changes. Your workspace and windows are restored to their initial state.

Using volume and pan envelopes

Audition provides clip envelopes to dynamically change the volume and pan settings for individual clips.

About envelopes

With clip envelopes, you can automate volume and pan settings over time. For example, you can automatically increase clip volume during a critical musical passage and later reduce the volume in a gradual fade out. For tracks with real-time effects, you can also automatically change the ratio of dry to wet sound.

Envelopes operate non-destructively, so they don't change the original audio file in any way. If you open an original file in Edit View, for example, you won't hear the effect of any clip envelopes. Envelopes also operate in real time, so you can edit them as a mix plays.

You can identify envelopes by color and initial position. For example, volume envelopes are green lines initially placed across the top of clips. Pan envelopes are blue lines placed in the center of clips. You edit envelopes by dragging control points on these lines. With volume envelopes, for example, the top of a clip represents 100% of track volume, while the bottom of a clip represents full attenuation (silence). With pan envelopes, the top of a clip represents full left, while the bottom represents full right. If an envelope is too high or low, preventing you from raising or lowering control points, you can rescale it.

—From Adobe Audition Help

1 In the Multitrack View, start by editing the volume envelope of the first clip in Track 5, which is WahClav08-DE. Drag your start-time indicator to Bar 12 beat 1 (12:1.00), or use your keyboard's left and right arrows to reach this location. Press the spacebar to play the session. The clavinet clip currently begins at full volume. To create a smoother transition, you will create a fade into the clip. Press the spacebar to stop playing the session.

2 Using the Move/Copy Clip tool (), click on the WahClav08-DE.cel in Track 5. If not already checked, choose View > Show Clip Volume Envelopes, and choose View > Enable Clip Envelope Editing to select these options. Uncheck Show Clip Pan Envelopes from the View menu. A thin green line with control points on either side appears at the top of the clip. This is the volume envelope for this clip.

Clip volume envelopes off.

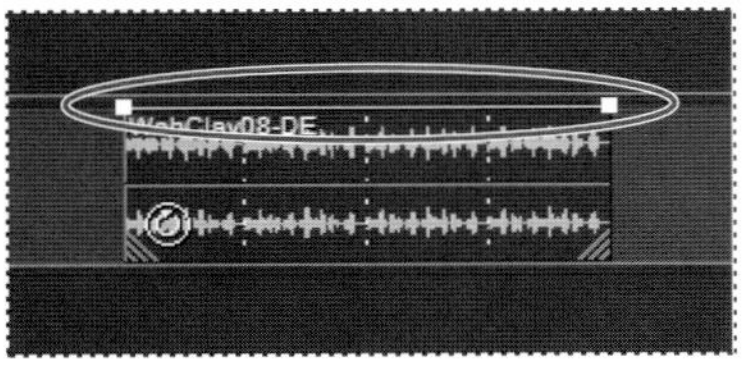
Clip volume envelopes on.

Place your cursor over the control point on the top left side and a small tooltip appears, indicating that the volume is at +0 dB (100%). Click the control point and drag it down to the very bottom of the clip. As you drag, the tooltip changes to reflect the volume level. Drag the point down to the bottom of the clip, reducing the initial volume of the clip to $-\infty$ dB (0%), which is silent. Press the spacebar to hear the effect of the envelope. When the first clavinet clip finishes playing, press the spacebar to stop playback.

3 To provide additional control over the level of the clip, you will add another control point to the volume envelope. Place your cursor on the volume envelope line at approximately the 14 bar mark. Before clicking, confirm that you see the small plus sign, which indicates that your cursor is positioned on the line, then click to add a control point. Drag the new control point up toward the top of the clip, using the tooltip to guide you in changing the volume to approximately -1.5 dB (85%) at the 14 bar mark. Press the spacebar to play the section again. Now, instead of a gradual fade in, the volume of the clip quickly fades in, and then becomes louder.

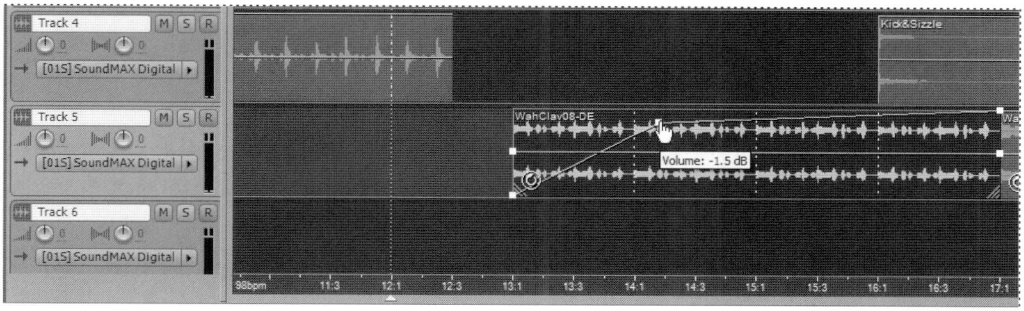

4 Right-click on the WahClav08-DE clip in Track 5. From the context menu that appears, choose Clip Envelopes > Volume > Use Splines.

The volume envelope changes to a slightly curved line. The control point is no longer on the line itself. Splines cause the volume envelope to change to a logarithmic curve. Press the spacebar to play. Select the second control point and drag it upwards to the top of the clip. The fade now sounds smoother, as the transition is more gradual. After listening to the clip, press the spacebar to stop playback.

5 Select the second control point in the WahClav08DE clip and drag it up and off the clip, as if you were dragging the control point into the track positioned above the clip. This removes the control point and resets the volume envelope to its previous state.

6 Select the control point on the left side and drag it back up to the top of the clip, restoring the volume to +0 dB (100%). Click in an empty area of Track 5 to deselect the clip.

7 You will now create a selection and allow Audition to create an automatic fade in. Using the Time Selection tool (), place your cursor at the beginning of the WahClav08-DE clip, and then click and drag to the right to make a selection of two bars starting at the beginning of the clip, 13:1.00, and ending at 15:1.00. Right-click on the clip and choose Crossfade > Logarithmic In from the context menu. This adds a series of control points within the selection to create a fade in. Press the spacebar to play just the selection and to hear the fade in. Press the spacebar to stop playing the selection.

8 You can also use Audition to create fade outs. Select the Suitcase04.cel clip in Track 5 by clicking on it. Place your cursor on Bar 25 and click and drag to the right to make a selection of three bars from 25:1.00 to 28:1.00. Right-click on the clip and choose Crossfade > Logarithmic Out from the context menu. This automatically creates a smooth fade out. Press the spacebar to play the selection and hear the fade out. Press the Home key to place the start-time indicator at the beginning of the session.

9 Envelopes can also be used to control the pan values, which is the positioning of a sound in stereo. Click and drag the start-time indicator to Bar 7 beat 1 (7:1.00). Click on the first tambourine clip in Track 4, then choose View > Show Clip Pan Envelopes, so that it is checked. A line with control points at each end appears in the middle of the clip. Drag the control point on the left side to the top, starting the pan at stereo left. Drag the second control point to the bottom of the clip, causing the clip to end the pan at stereo right. Press the spacebar to play the session, and note the tambourine moves in stereo space from left to right.

Using the Effects Rack

When working in Audition's Multitrack View, you can apply various effects to a track and never have to worry about altering the original clips in that track. Here you will add a non-destructive echo to the guitar track used in this session.

1 Press the Solo button (S) for Track 2, and place the start-time indicator at Bar 24 beat 1 (24:01.00). This is the beginning of the second guitar clip, SmackFunkWah01-E. Press the spacebar to listen to the soloed guitar clip for about 2 bars and then press the spacebar again to stop playback.

2 Bring your cursor just below the Volume and Pan knobs along the bottom edge for Track 2. When the shape of the cursor changes to two parallel lines with arrows (÷), click and drag downwards to increase the height of the track in order to reveal more controls and properties for Track 2.

3 Click the FX button (fx) from the row of four buttons above Track 1 to view the Effects controls for the tracks.

You should now be able to see the Effects Rack below the Volume and Pan knobs for Track 2.

4 Press the FX Power button (⏻) to switch on the Effects Rack for Track 2. Click on the black triangle on the first slot and choose Delay Effects > Echo.

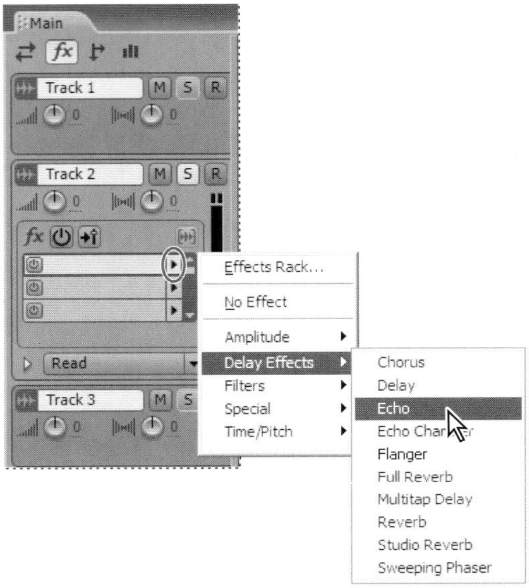

A new window, called Effects Rack: Track 2, opens. You can see on the left that Echo is the first effect in this Effects Rack. Its Power button has been turned on and the various settings of the Echo effect are visible on the right.

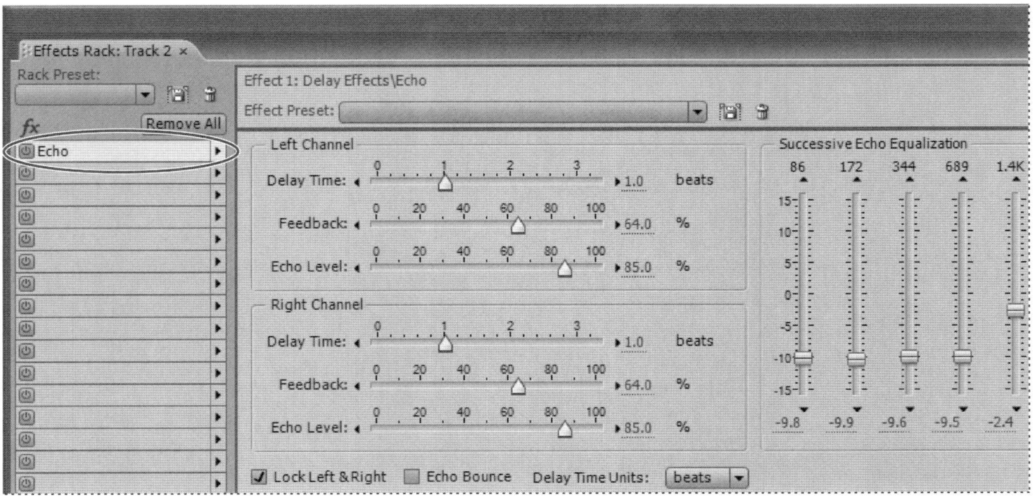

5 At the bottom of the settings for Echo, if the Delay Time Units menu is not already set to beats, select beats now. Click the Lock Left & Right option if it is not already checked.

6 In the Left Channel controls on the top, if necessary, click and drag the Delay Time slider to set it at 1 beat, and set the Echo Level to 85%. The Right Channel sliders move in sync because you chose to lock the left and right channel settings for the Echo effect.

7 Press the spacebar to hear the guitar track with a 1 beat echo applied to it. After listening for 2 bars, press the Power button ( ) for Echo within the Effects Rack to hear the dry guitar without any echo. Switch on the Power button again to hear the echo applied to the guitar track. Reduce the amount of effect applied to the original sound by using the mix slider on the bottom left of the Effects Rack. Reduce this from 100% to 85%. Press the spacebar to stop playback.

The different slots of the Effects Rack are used to chain different effects together. For example, you can add a Flanger and a Studio Reverb in the next slots and, when playing, you hear the combined result of the three effects applied to the track. Audition ships with a wide variety of effects that can be used for the Effects Rack within each track.

8 Close the Effects Rack window. Press the Home key to place your start-time indicator at the beginning of the timeline and then press the spacebar to listen to the soloed guitar track. The Echo effect is applied to the entire guitar track. Press the Solo button (S) for Track 2 again to hear all the tracks together. Stop playback by pressing the spacebar.

Effects used in the Multitrack View are non-destructive and don't change your original files. If you don't like the effects used on a certain track, you can open the Effects Rack for that track and make changes to the effect or remove the effect altogether. Additionally, effect settings in the Multitrack View can be controlled using automation lanes. These techniques are discussed in Lesson 8, "Mixing and Real-Time Effects" and Lesson 10, "Using Audition's Automation Tools."

9 Choose File > Save Session, and then choose File > Close All.

Congratulations! You have finished this lesson.

Exploring on your own

1 Change the mix of your saved song by opening the Mixer and using the track sliders to raise or lower the individual tracks as the session is playing. Adjust the pan of the clips to place the sound of a track in stereo left or right. Pay careful attention to the level meters and make sure that the overall volume of the session is not clipping.

2 Using the volume and pan envelopes, return to the session from the previous exercise and change the envelopes on alternate clips to create a different mix. Place different instruments in the foreground and note how the song changes. Be sure to use the spline curves by right-clicking on a clip and choosing Clip Envelopes.

3 Switch on the power to the Effects Rack for another track and follow the steps in the Using the Effects Rack section to experiment with the different effects installed with Audition. Try adding a Chorus effect to the guitar track or the Studio Reverb effect to the drum track.

4 Scrubbing also works in the Edit View. Experiment with different scrubbing speeds and the Alt+drag and Ctrl+drag combinations. Open Suitcase04.cel in the Edit View and try scrubbing the left and the right channels separately.

Review

Review questions

1 What is the difference between an audio file, sometimes called a one-shot, and an audio loop?

2 How do you make a copy of a file in the Multitrack View? What is the difference between a unique copy and a reference copy?

3 What is the difference between controlling the volume of an individual track versus controlling the volume using envelopes?

4 How do you apply a non-destructive effect to an audio track in the Multitrack View? How is the level of the effect modified?

Review answers

1 Audio loops have been configured to loop seamlessly when you bring them into the multitrack. You can visually identify music loops in the multitrack if there is a loop icon on the clip itself. Standard one-shot audio files are identified in the Files panel and have no icon when dropped into the multitrack.

2 There are several ways to make a copy of a clip in the Multitrack View. Selecting a clip and choosing Clip > Convert to Unique Copy creates a new copy of the clip. Alternatively, the Move tools can also make a copy of the clip, but the behavior is different based on which tool you choose. Using the Move/Copy Clip tool, right-click on a clip, drag to the desired location, and choose either Copy Reference Here or Copy Unique Here. Copy Reference makes an alias of the clip; any changes made to the original clip also change the copy. Copy Unique creates an independent copy; any changes to the original file do not affect the unique copy. Using the Hybrid tool, right-clicking on a clip while holding the Shift key and dragging to a desired location also creates a unique copy.

3 Raising or lowering the volume of a track using the track properties raises or lowers the volume of all the clips in the track by an equal amount. Volume envelopes, on the other hand, allow volume to be selectively raised or lowered on a clip-by-clip basis. In addition, clip volume envelopes allow you to dynamically raise or lower the volume to create fade ins and fade outs.

4 To add a non-destructive effect to a track, press the FX button to view the effects controls for a track. Use the Effects Rack for a track to add the effect or effects you desire from the list of installed real-time effects. The amount of the effect can be changed using the Mixer located in the Effects Rack. Additionally, you can use automation lanes to adjust the amount of the effect over time. This is covered in later lessons.

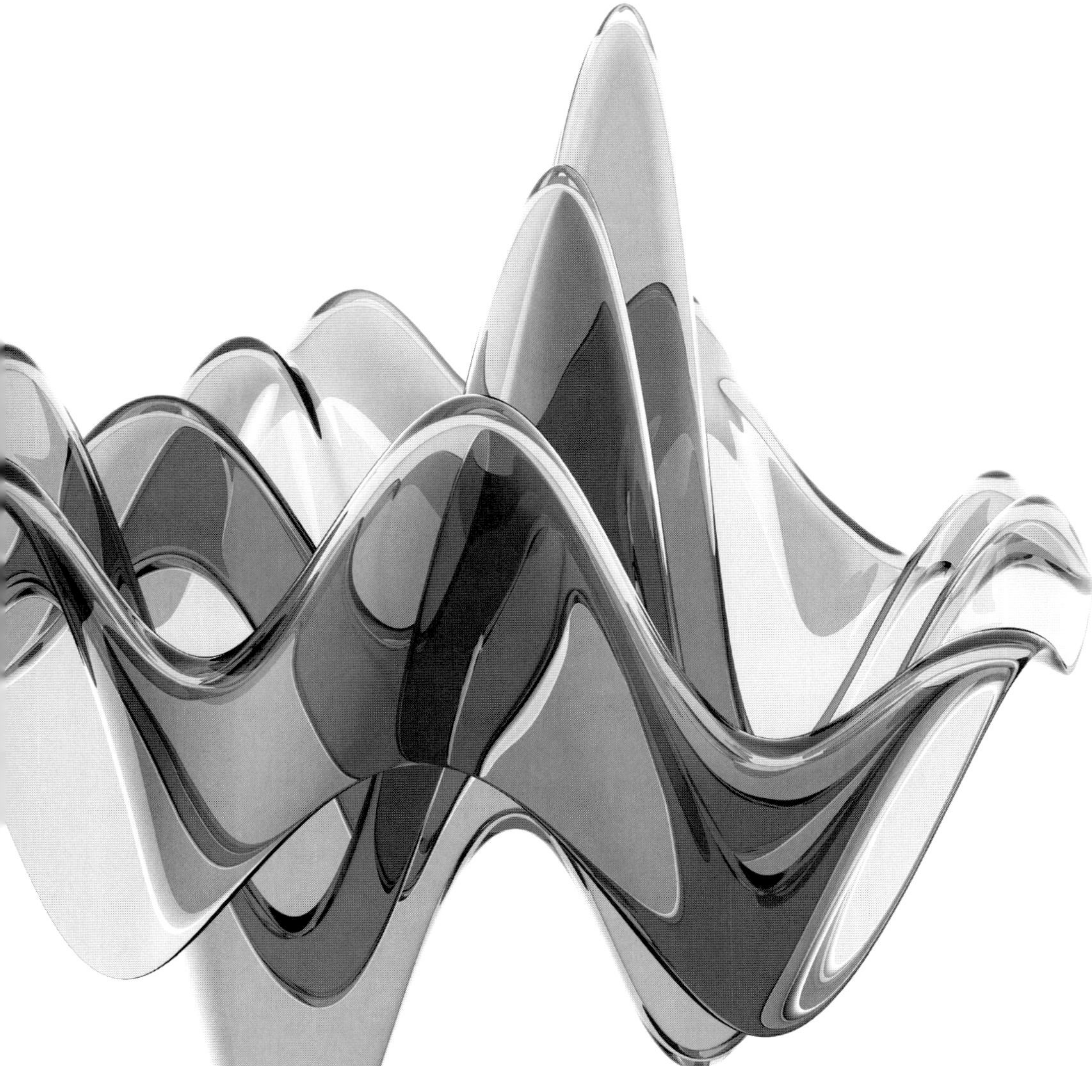

5 Working with Loops and Waves

You can use Adobe Audition to view and edit waveforms using multiple views. Using specific tools, you can isolate frequencies and varying lengths of a waveform. Adobe Audition also provides powerful tools for creating, viewing, and editing loops.

In this lesson, you'll learn how to do the following:

- Add loops to the multitrack.
- Create repetitions of a loop within the multitrack.
- Create a loop from a larger waveform.
- Manipulate the source waveform of a clip.
- Use markers to define locations and sections.
- Change the length of a clip by time stretching or shrinking.
- Change the pitch of a clip.
- Change the tempo of the entire session.

Getting started

In this lesson, you'll create a multitrack session from a library of loops and audio files. You will then modify their properties using different methods such as the Stretch effect, and tempo, to create your composition.

1 Start Adobe Audition. Click the Multitrack View button (▦) if it is not already selected.

2 If you have not already copied the resource files for this lesson onto your hard disk from the *Adobe Audition 2.0 Classroom in a Book* CD, do so now. See "Copying the Classroom in a Book files" on page 2.

3 Choose File > Open Session. Open the 05_Start.ses file within the AA_05 folder on your hard disk.

4 Choose File > Save Session As. Enter the file name **05_FirstTune.ses**, and save it in the AA_05 folder on your hard disk.

This Audition file appears completely empty with just the names of the tracks. You will import several loops into these tracks later in the lesson.

5 To review the finished session file, choose File > Open Session, and open the 05_End.ses file in the AA_05 folder within the AA_CIB folder. Click the Play button (▶) in the Transport panel controls or press the spacebar on your keyboard to play the file.

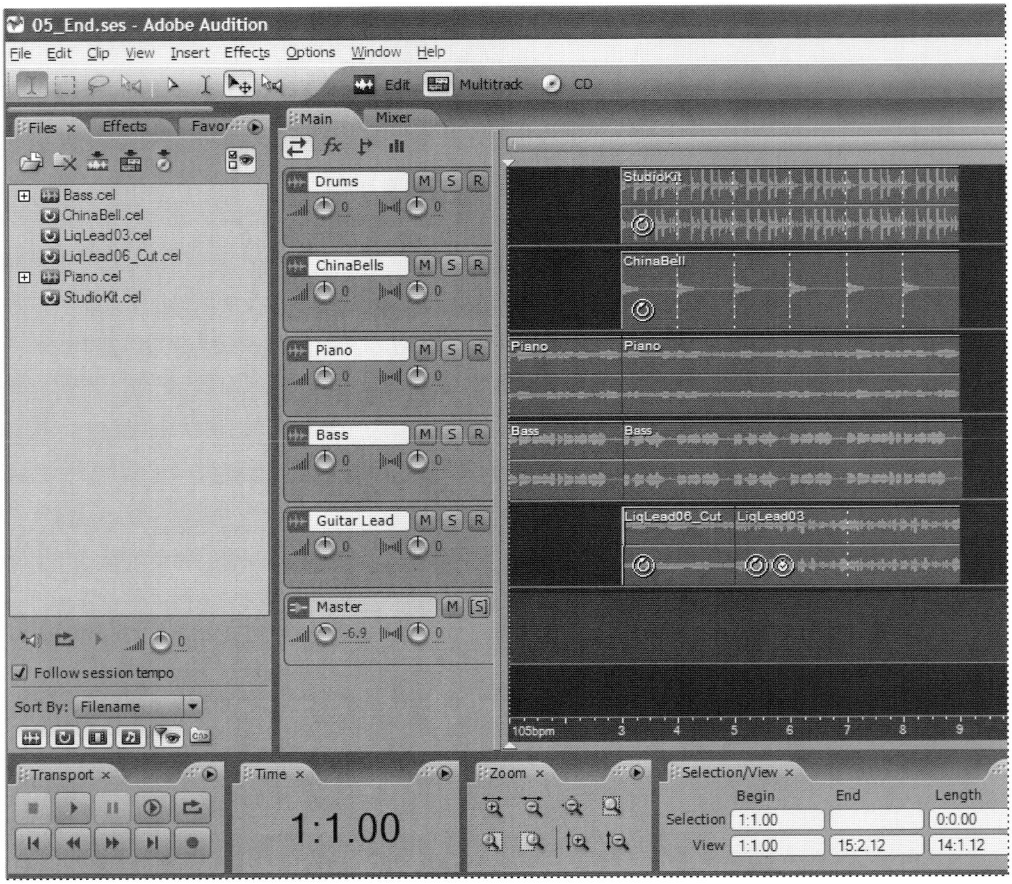

6 When you are ready to start the lesson, close the 05_end.ses and its contents by choosing File > Close All.

7 Open the 05_FirstTune.ses you just saved, by selecting File > Open Session, or choose it from the list of recent files listed under the File menu.

Adding loops to a multitrack

You will start building your session by importing loops from the AA_05 folder.

1 Choose File > Import. In the Import window that opens, check the Auto Play and Loop check boxes located in the bottom right of the window. Select the following loops located in the AA_05 folder by Ctrl+clicking them one at a time. You'll hear each loop play as you select it:

- Bass.cel
- ChinaBell.cel
- Piano.cel
- StudioKit.cel

2 Once you've selected the required files, click the Open button to import them into the session.

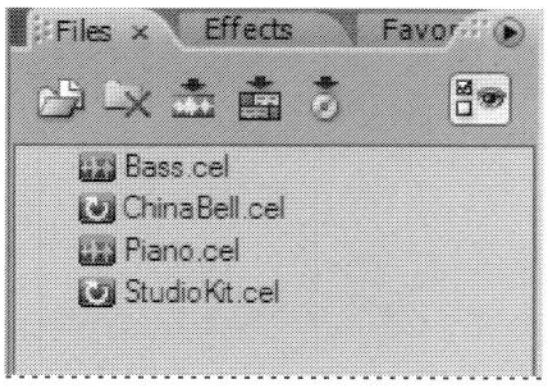

Each file is added to the Files panel located on the left side of the Audition interface. Two of these loops are single shot waveforms: Piano.cel and Bass.cel. These files have no looping information. This is indicated by the waveform icon ( ) next to their file names in the Files panel. The two remaining files are loops from the Adobe Audition Loopology DVD. In addition to their audio contents, these files contain special looping information that lets you use them at any tempo, and stretch for repetitions simply by clicking and dragging them. A loop is identified by the circular icon located to the left of the file name ( ). You'll learn how to create your own loops later in this lesson.

3 Select the StudioKit.cel loop from the Files panel by clicking on it. Drag the loop into the multitrack on the right and release the loop in the Drums track. Notice that the tracks have already been named based upon the instrument you will be placing in each track.

4 Repeat the previous step with the remaining loops in the Files panel, dragging each loop onto its appropriate track. Don't worry about placing the clips precisely within the multitrack at this time.

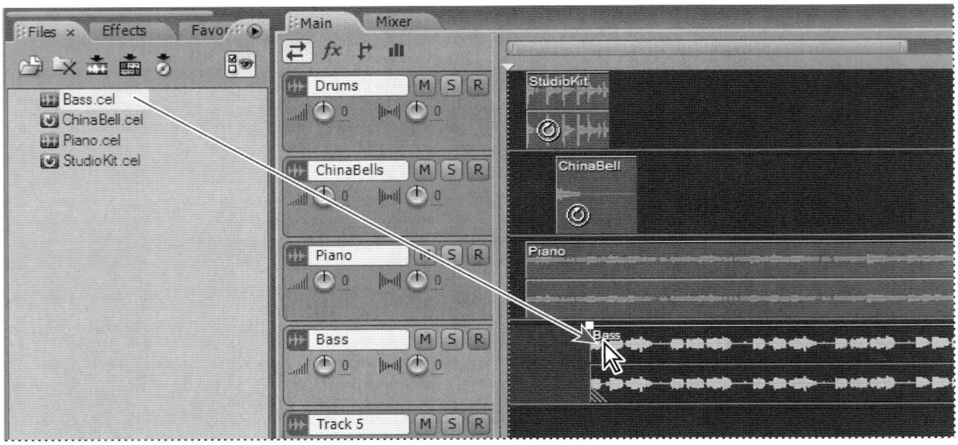

You will now align the starting position of each clip in the multitrack.

5 Position your mouse over the timeline across the bottom of the multitrack and right-click. From the context menu, select Display Time Format and confirm that the Bars and Beats option is selected.

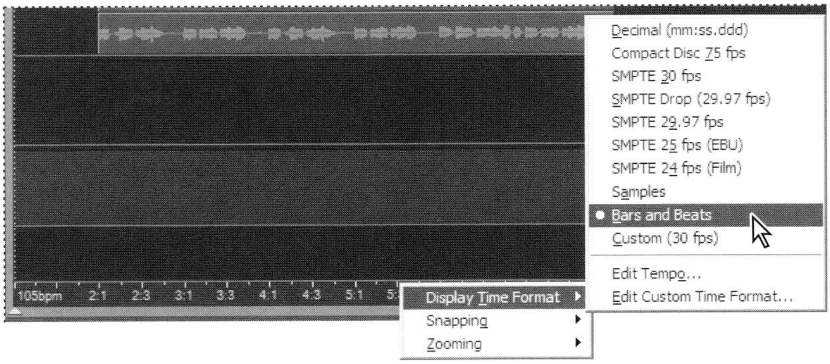

6 Right-click once again in the timeline and select Snapping. Confirm that the Snap to Ruler (Coarse) option is selected. If it is not selected, choose it now.

7 Choose the Move/Copy Clip tool ( ) from the Shortcut Bar at the top of the screen. Click on the StudioKit.cel clip in the first track and drag to move it to Bar 3 beat 1 (3:1.00) on the timeline. Placing the clip at this location on the timeline indicates that the clip will begin to play on beat 1 of the third measure. Notice that as you drag your clip, snap lines appear at points in the ruler.

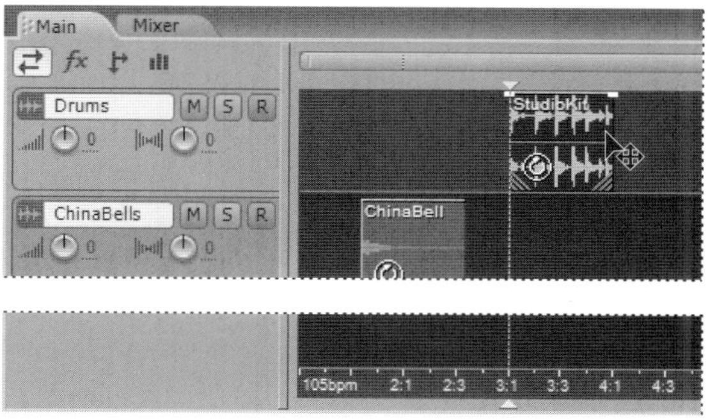

8 Repeat step 6, dragging each of the remaining clips so they start at the 3:1 position on the timeline.

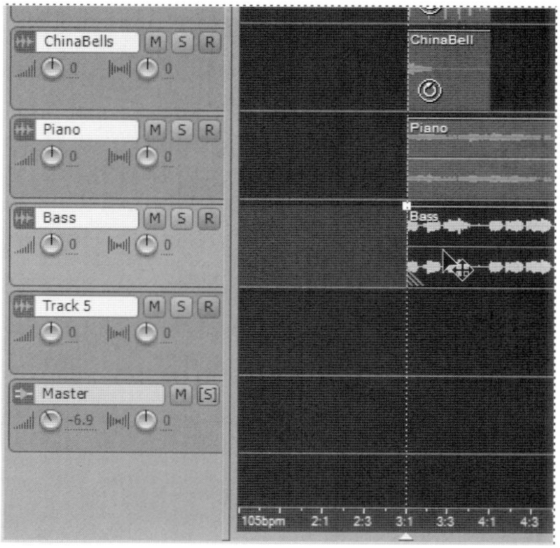

9 Save the session by selecting File > Save Session As, and click to select the 05_FirstTune.ses file in which you are currently working. In the Save Session As window that appears, check the Save copies of all associated files option in the lower left corner. Click the Save button, then click Yes to overwrite the file.

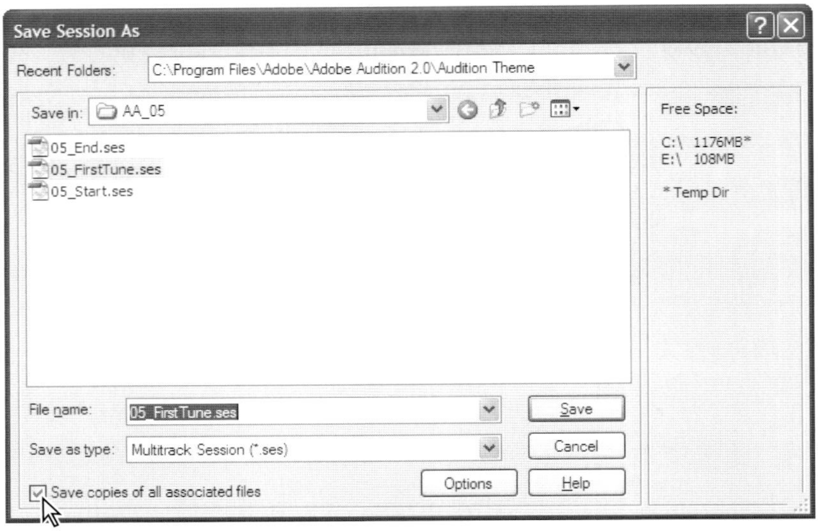

The Save copies of all associated files option packages all loops and waveforms into the same folder as the session file you are currently saving. This option makes it easy to transfer Adobe Audition session files from one computer to another by ensuring that all your component files are located in the same location as your .ses file.

10 Click the Play button ( ) in the Transport panel to listen to the session. You can also play the session by pressing the spacebar. Press the spacebar to stop playback once you have previewed your work.

Repeating a loop

You will now use loop editing to create repetitions of a loop without modifying the original file. Currently, the Piano and Bass track both play longer than the Drum track. You will extend the StudioKit.cel clip so the drums play through most of the session.

1 Click the Zoom Out Full Both Axes button ( ) in the Zoom panel, to view the entire timeline. Click the StudioKit.cel clip in the Drums track to select it. Position your cursor over the lower right corner of the clip. The cursor changes to the loop editing icon ( ). Click the bottom right corner of the clip and drag to the right, stopping when the end of the clip is at Bar 9 beat 1 (9:1.00) on the timeline.

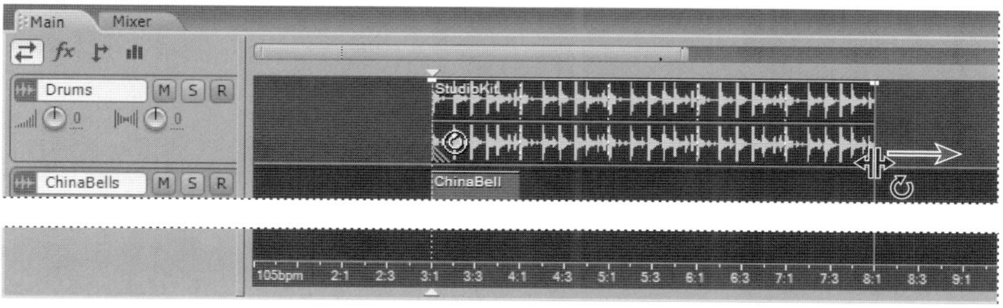

Click the Rewind button ( ) in the Transport panel to bring the start-time indicator to the beginning of the session, and then click the Play from Cursor to End of File button ( ) to hear your changes. If necessary, right-click the button to set its function. The Studio Kit loop now continues to play over the Piano and Bass track as it repeats itself.

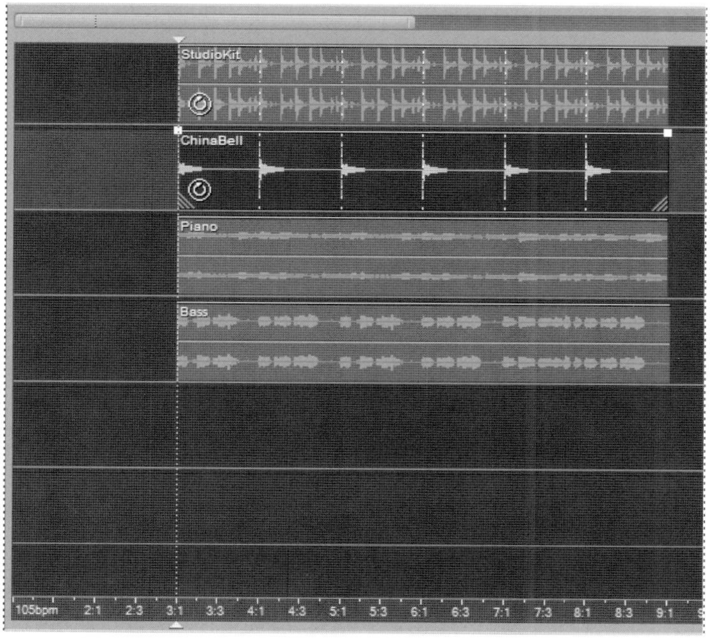

2 Repeat step 1, extending the ChinaBell.cel clip, causing it to continue to play at the same time as the Piano, Bass, and StudioKit clips are playing.

3 Press the Home key on your keyboard to move the start-time indicator to the start point of your session, then preview your new file by pressing the Play to End of File button ( ).

Making a loop from a larger waveform

Next you will create a new loop by isolating parts of a larger loop. You will then save the isolated portion as a unique file, which you will incorporate into the multitrack session.

1 Click the Edit View button ( ) to enter the Edit View. Click the Import File button ( ) in the Files panel. If necessary, navigate to the AA_05 folder on your hard disk. Select the LiqLead03.cel file, then hold down the Ctrl key on your keyboard and also select the LiqLead06.cel file. Click the Open button to import these two files into the Files panel.

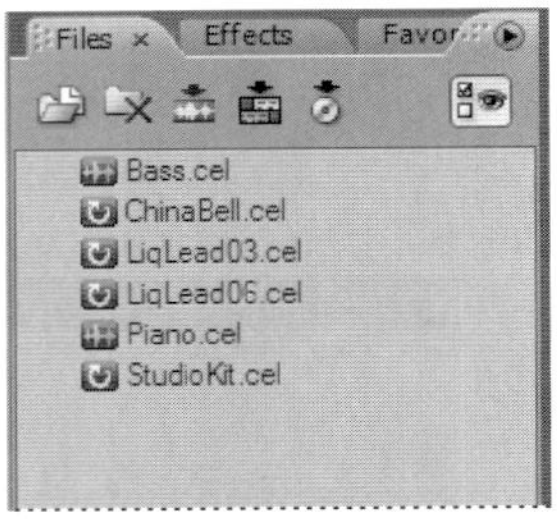

Preview each of these files by clicking on each file name and then clicking the Play button ( ) at the bottom of the Files panel. If the Loop Play button is selected, you may need to click the Stop button to stop playback.

2 Double-click the LiqLead06.cel file in the Files panel to view the waveform.

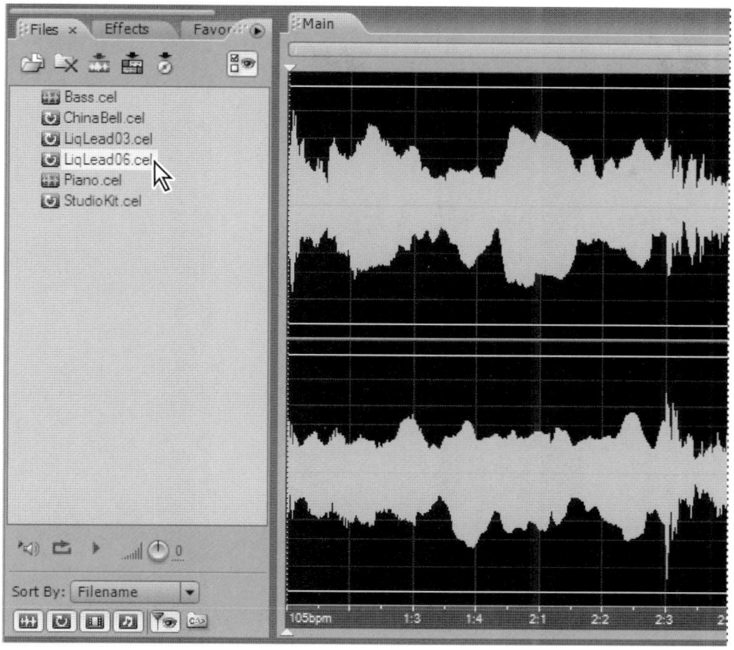

You will now isolate the beginning portion of this loop and use it within your multitrack session file.

3 Play the loop by pressing the spacebar. The play cursor moves from left to right as the file is played for you.

4 Play the loop again, noticing the location of the play cursor as the loop makes a musical run of notes. The musical phrase sustains on a long tone before rising again into another long run of notes. You should notice this point at approximately the Bar 3 beat 1 (3:1.00) point within the loop.

5 Click and drag the start-time indicator to Bar 3 beat 1 (3:1.00) on the timeline.

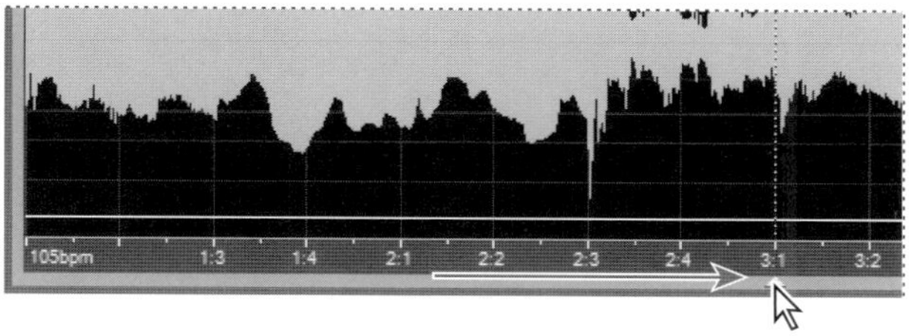

6 Choose the Time Selection tool (I) from the top left of the Edit View. Position your cursor over the center divider of the Edit View window at the 3:1 location. Click and drag to the right, to the end of the clip. This area becomes selected.

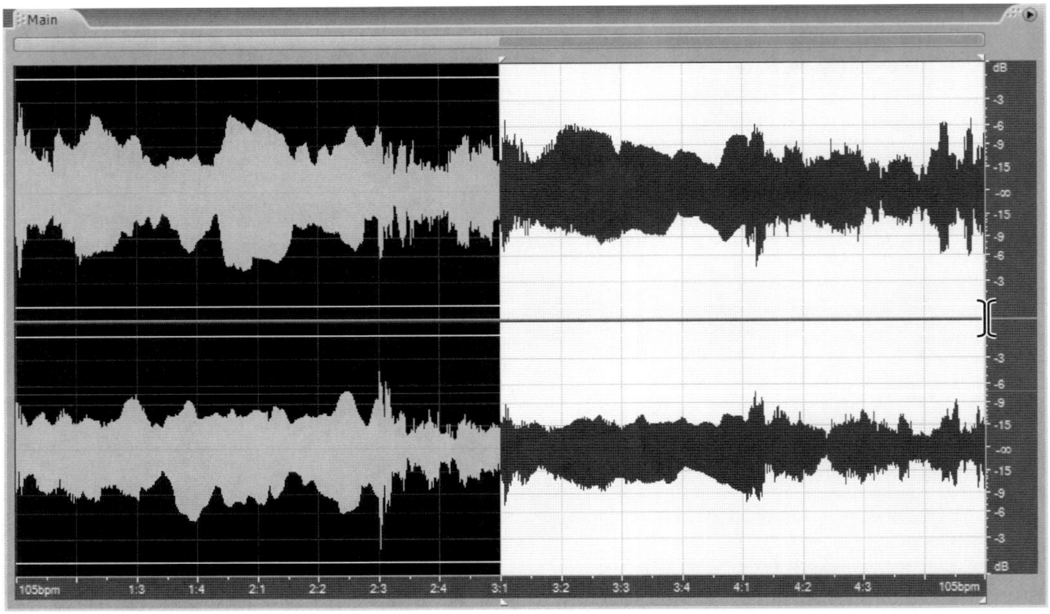

7 Press the Delete key, removing the selected portion of the clip. Press the Home key, and then review the remaining portion of the loop by pressing the spacebar on your keyboard to play the clip.

8 Select File > File Info to open the File Info window, and click on the Loop Info tab. Input **8** as the value for the Number of Beats, then click OK.

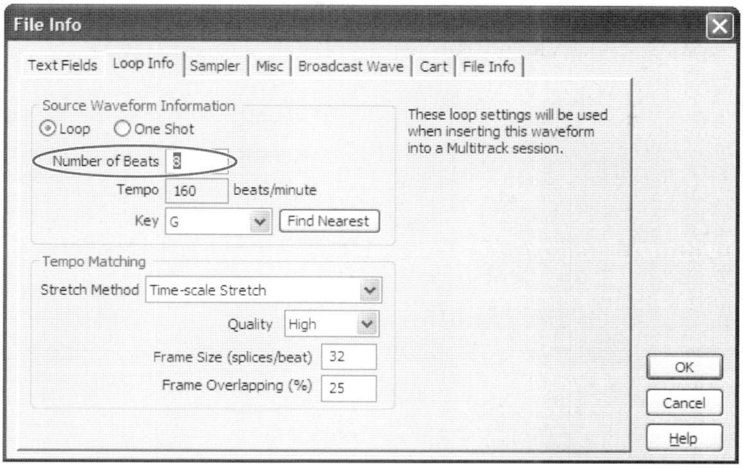

9 Save this new loop by choosing File > Save As. Name the file LiqLead06_Cut.cel, making certain to save this file within the AA_05 folder on your hard disk. A message appears asking if you want to overwrite this file, click Yes. If another window appears asking if you are sure you want to save this file in a compressed format, choose OK.

Note: *While working in the Edit View, Adobe Audition acts as a waveform editor. Actions and save commands in the Edit View affect only the loop in which you are working, and not the entire Adobe Audition session. Any changes made in Edit View are reflected in Multitrack View if the edited sound is part of a session.*

10 Click the Multitrack View button (▦) to view the complete session.

The LiqLead06.cel file is replaced by the LiqLead06_Cut.cel file in your Files panel. As an individual and unique loop, it is now ready to be used in a multitrack session.

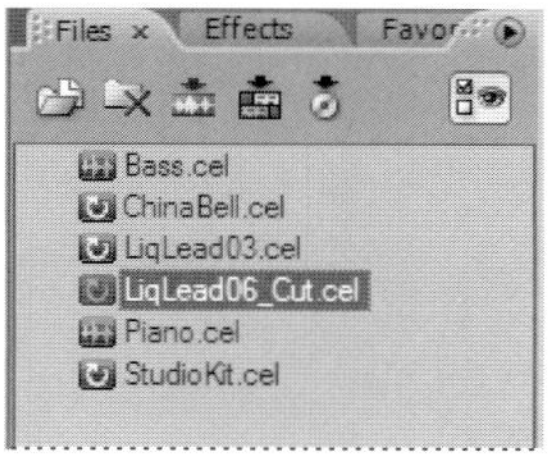

11 Click and drag the LiqLead06_Cut.cel file from the Files panel onto Track 5 in the multitrack session. If you cannot see Track 5 of the multitrack, click the Zoom Out Full Both Axes button (🔍).

12 Click the title area of the track controls for Track 5 to select this area. Rename the Track 5 title as **Guitar Lead**.

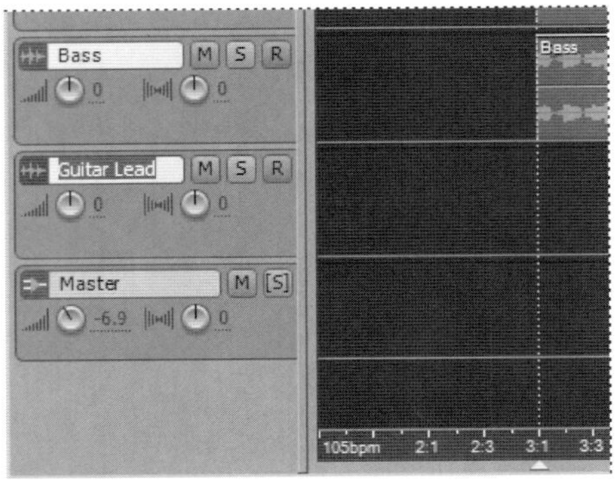

13 Choose the Move/Copy Clip tool (▸). Click and drag the LiqLead06_Cut.cel clip to position it at Bar 3 beat 1 (3:1.00) within the Guitar Lead track.

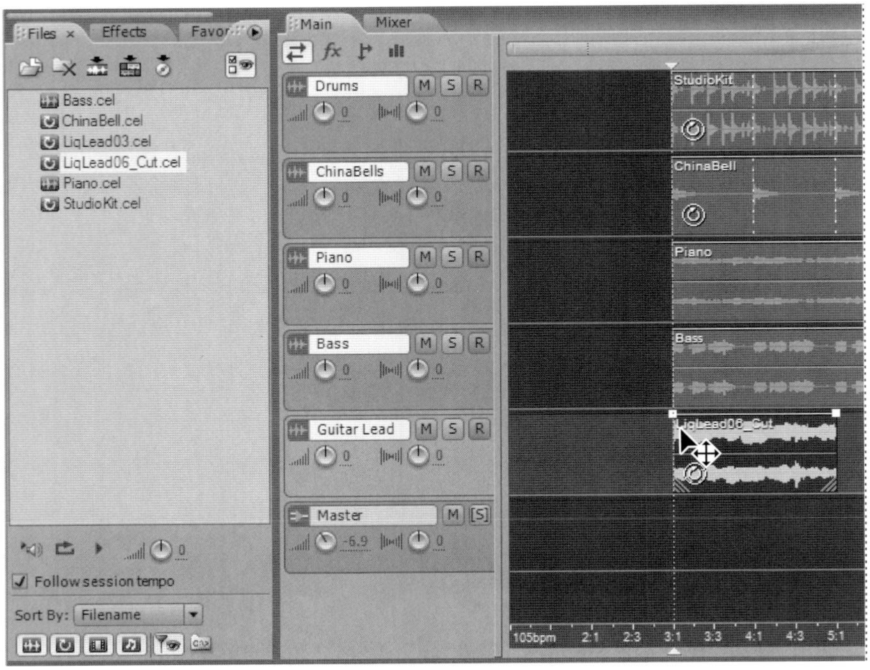

Note: *The Data Under Cursor position, located below the Master Level indicators, indicates your current cursor position as you move a loop within the multitrack session.*

14 Select File > Save Session.

Changing the source waveform

In the session file, the Guitar Lead track is substantially louder than the other tracks. As this track is playing, the level meters indicate that the session comes quite close to 0 dB, which might result in a clipped audio signal. You will use several of Audition's effects to normalize and alter the loops in this session, resulting in a more balanced session.

1 Right-click the LiqLead06_cut.cel loop in the Files panel and choose Edit File from the context menu. The loop opens in the Edit View. Right-click on the vertical measuring scale that appears at the right of the waveforms. In the context menu that appears, make sure that Decibels is selected as the unit of measurement.

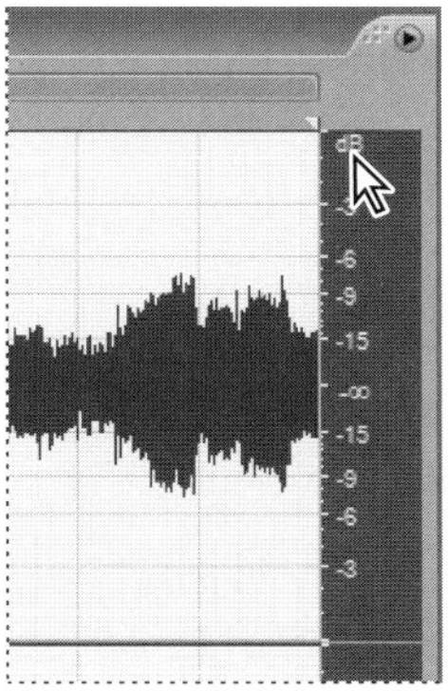

Notice that the waveform contains many peaks which reach just under the -4dB level in both channels. You will reduce the overall amplitude of this waveform to blend it more smoothly into the multitrack session with other loops.

2 Right-click between both the left and right channels, and choose the Select Entire Wave command. The entire waveform is highlighted from start to finish.

3 Select the Effects tab from the grouped panels to the left of the Main panel, and click on the plus sign (+) to the left of the Amplitude. This reveals all the available effects that relate to amplitude.

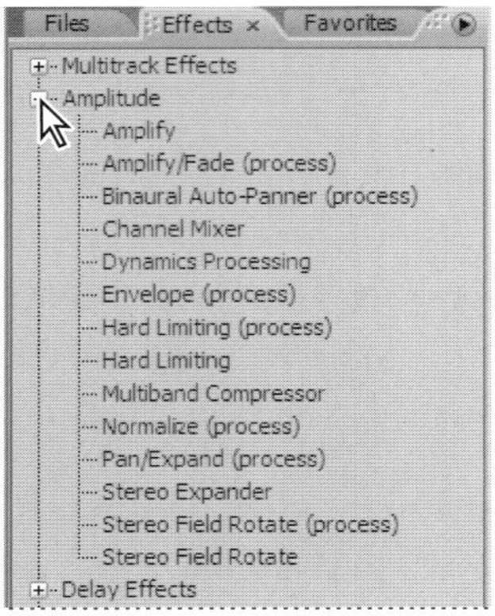

4 Double-click on the Normalize (process) effect.

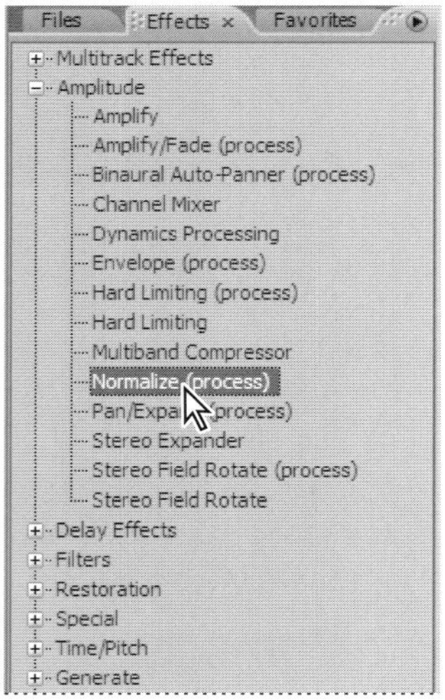

The Normalize window opens.

5 In the Normalize window, confirm that the option for Normalize L/R Equally is selected. Select the option Normalize to, and type **25** as the percentage and then click OK. This effectively reduces the amplitude of the selected waveform to 25%.

6 Preview the file by pressing the spacebar or clicking the Play button (▶). Notice that the peaks of the waveform now fall well below the -9dB level, resulting in the reduced volume (amplitude) of the file.

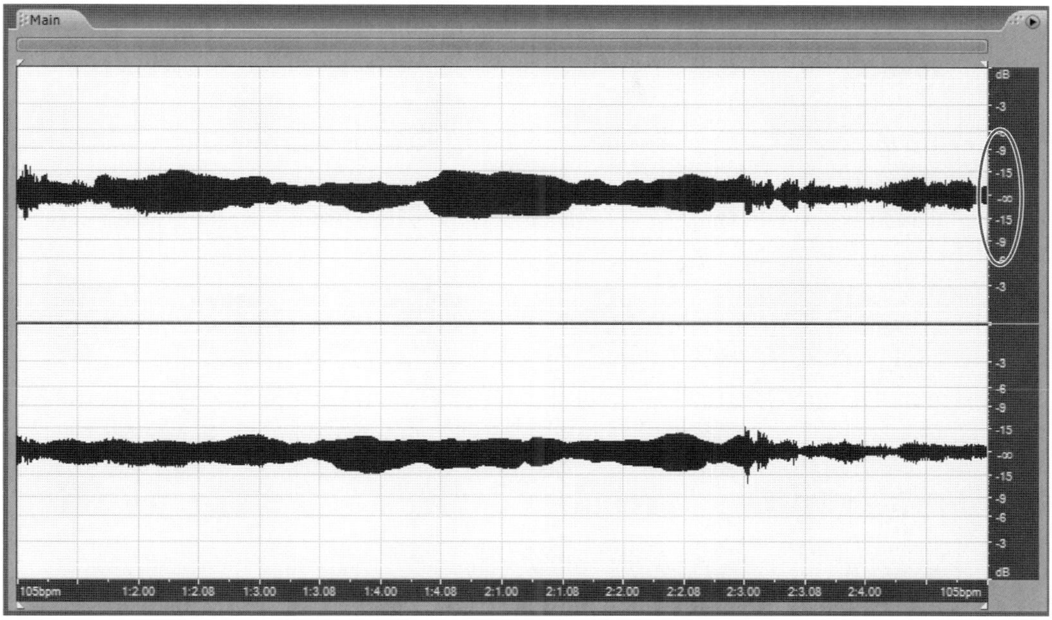

7 Select File > Save, overwriting the LiqLead06_Cut.cel loop. If Audition warns you about the file format, click OK.

8 Click the Multitrack View button (▦) or press the number 9 on your keyboard to switch to the Multitrack View.

9 Press the Home key and then play the session by pressing the spacebar on your keyboard. Note that your loop has been updated to reflect the changes you made to the LiqLead06_Cut.cel loop.

10 Select File > Save Session and leave the session file open.

Using markers

Markers are used to label important locations or sections in your waveforms or session. Audition offers different types of markers for different purposes. Cue and Beat markers are used when isolating particular points or sections of a waveform. Track and Index markers catalog multiple tracks and mark the start and end points for the creation of CDs.

You will start by isolating and marking subsections within the Piano track and within the Bass track so that you can easily use these subsections elsewhere in your multitrack session. You will learn how to place marked subsections into the session and use them just like any other clip.

1 In the Multitrack View, confirm that the Options > Synchronize Clips With Edit View option is not checked. If it is, deselect it.

2 Double-click the Piano.cel clip in the Piano track, opening it in the Edit View. If necessary, press Zoom Out Full Both Axes button to view the entire waveform.

3 Choose Window > Marker List to open the Markers panel.

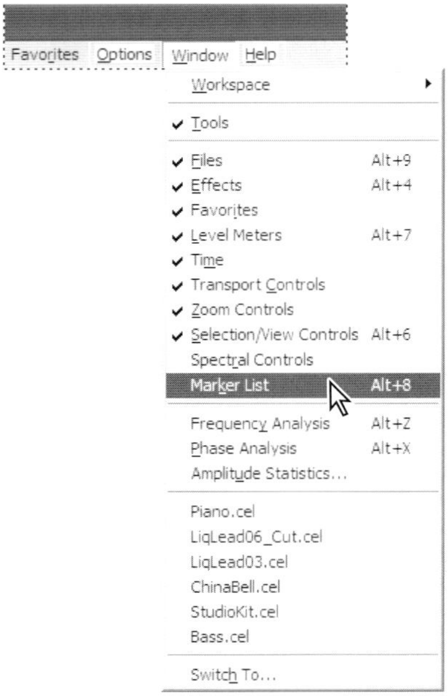

4 Click and drag on the title bar of the Markers panel to relocate it so that you can see the Edit window. Resize the Markers panel using its edges, if it covers up too much of the Edit View. In the Edit window, move the start-time indicator to the 5:1 position in this clip. Place your cursor over the waveform, then click and drag to the right, selecting from Bar 5 beat 1 (5:1.00) to the end of the clip.

5 Click the Add Marker button ( ) at the bottom of the Markers panel to mark your selection.

A new marker is added to the Marker List in the Markers panel. The marker includes its name, beginning and ending times, length, and type.

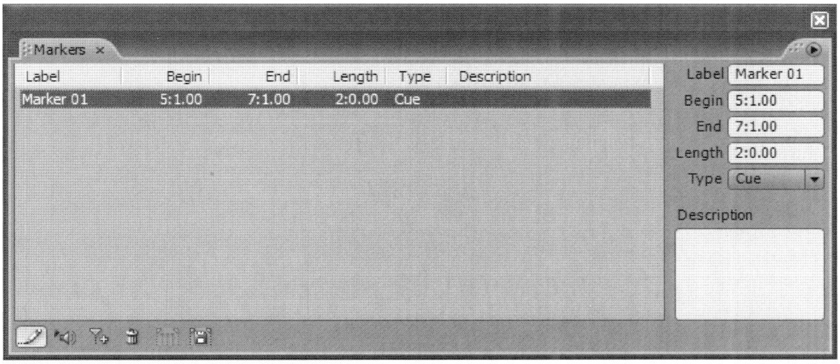

6 If it is not already selected, press the Edit Marker Info button ( ) toward the bottom left of the Markers panel. Then click once on the newly added marker to highlight it.

The fields on the right side of the Markers panel display the properties of the selected marker. You will now edit the properties of this marker using these fields.

7 On the right of the window, click into the Label field and enter **Intro** as the new label title.

8 Click into the Description field at the bottom right and enter **Two Bar Piano Introduction** as the description for this marker.

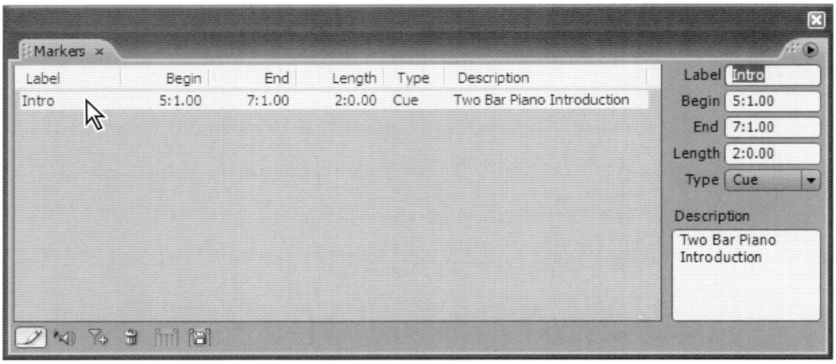

9 Similarly, create an Intro cue for the Bass.cel loop. Do this by repeating steps 1-8 after double-clicking in the Bass.cel clip in the Files panel. Enter **Intro** as the new label and **Two Bar Bass Introduction** as the description for this marker.

Note: *The Marker List for each audio file in the Edit View is different. You'll notice that the marker you created within the piano clip is not present in the Marker List for the bass clip, and vice versa. Audition allows you to mark an unlimited number of sections or locations within each file. When you save a file from the Edit View, remember to check the Save extra non-audio information option in the File > Save As window. This ensures that all the markers within that file will be saved too.*

10 Click the Multitrack View button (icon) to view the session. Select the Files panel.

Notice that the Piano.cel and Bass.cel files both now contain the markers you've created. This is indicated by the plus sign (+) to the left of each .cel file name in the Files panel. Clicking the plus sign reveals any markers which have been saved into the .cel files. These marked sections can be incorporated into your multitrack as independent clips.

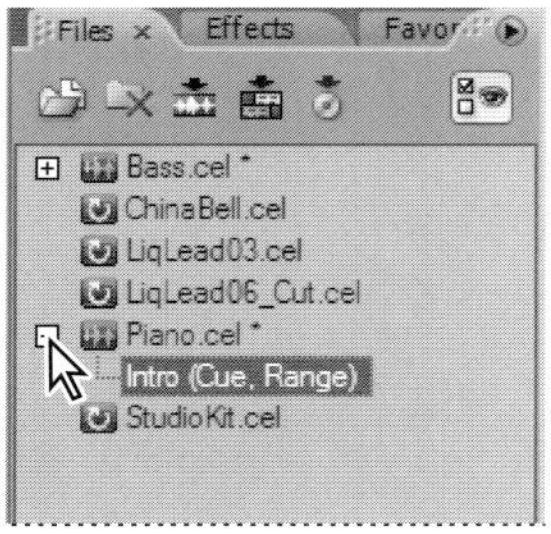

11 Select the Move/Copy Clip tool (). In the Files panel, click the plus sign in the Piano.cel loop, revealing its Intro marker. Click on this marker in the Files panel and drag it into the very beginning of the Piano track in the multitrack. When you release your mouse button, the section of the waveform represented by the marker is dropped into the multitrack as a separate waveform. Align this new clip to start at 1:1.00.

Ensure that there is no overlap between the first and second clip in the piano track. If there is a slight overlap, adjust the right edge of the first clip by clicking and dragging on this edge slightly toward your left.

12 Click the plus sign in the Bass.cel loop, revealing its Intro marker. Click on the marker and drag it into the very beginning of the Bass track. Align this new clip to begin at 1:1.00.

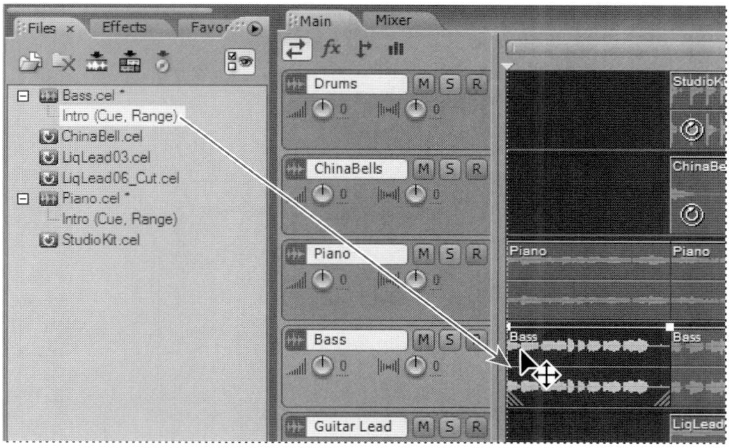

By creating markers, you can select and work with sections of files more effectively, rather than having to work with the entire file. You can also add markers in the Multitrack View to help you define important locations and regions. The Marker Lists for the Multitrack View are independent of the Marker Lists used in the Edit View.

13 Choose File > Save Session.

Changing the length of a clip

In the Multitrack View, you can change the length of a clip without altering its pitch. In this exercise you will use Adobe Audition's shrink/stretch method to shorten the length of a clip.

1 Using the Move/Copy Clip tool ( ), select the LiqLead03.cel file in the Files panel. Click and drag the file into the Guitar Lead track of your multitrack session. Release the clip immediately following the LiqLead06_Cut.cel file. Click and drag the file to begin at 5:01.00. Press the spacebar to listen to this addition to your composition.

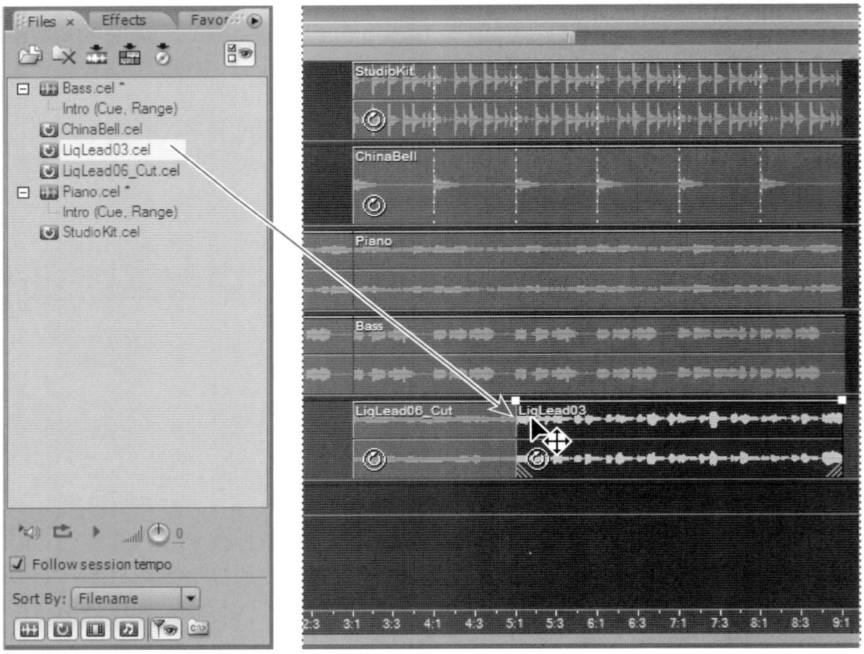

2 Confirm the LiqLead03.cel clip is selected in the session. Choose Clip > Clip Time Stretch Properties to open the Clip Time Stretch Properties window.

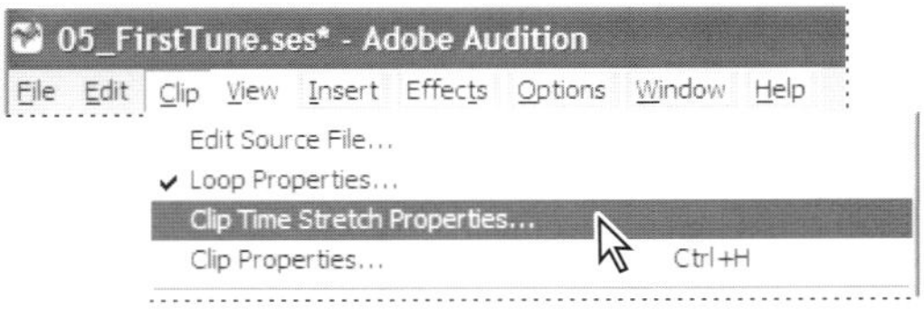

3 In the Clip Time Stretch Properties window, select the Enable Time Stretching option check box. In the drop-down menu within the Time Stretching Options section, confirm that the Time-scale Stretch option is selected. Enter **50** for the Time Stretch percentage and select OK.

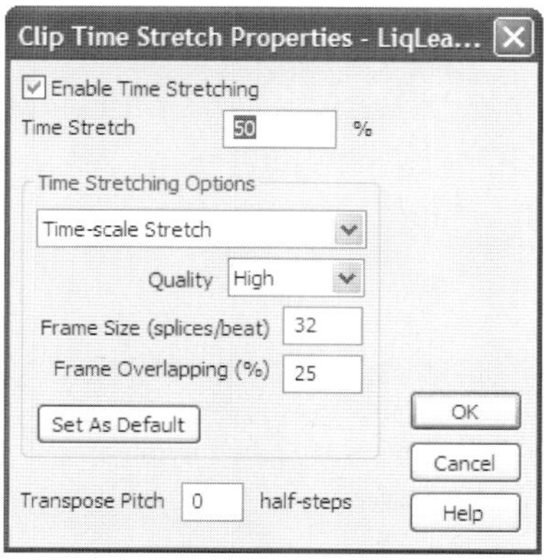

Note: *Adobe Audition's Time-scale Stretch option stretches or shrinks the clip to a percentage of its original length. This percentage is a fraction of its length in time, while maintaining all tonal properties of the original clip. Keep in mind that this effect is non-destructive too, which means that if you open up the clip in the Edit View, you will be able to hear the unaltered version of the clip.*

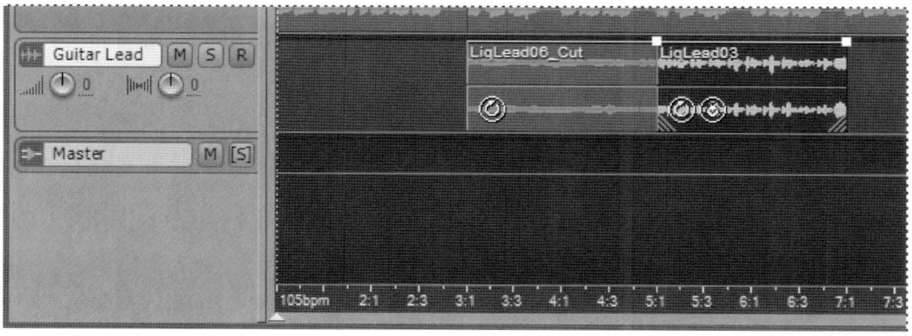

A special clock symbol ( ) appears on the LiqLead03.cel clip, telling you that this clip uses the time stretching/shrinking feature and has been altered from its original length.

4 Click onto the right edge of the LiqLead03.cel clip in the session and drag it to Bar 9 beat 1 (9:1.00). This causes the time-stretched loop to repeat itself once.

5 Listen to your session by selecting the Play button ( ) from the Transport panel or by pressing the spacebar.

6 Save the session by selecting File > Save Session.

Changing the pitch of a clip

Right now, the clips in the Guitar Lead track are in a different key and they clash with the rest of the song. You can also use the Clip > Clip Time Stretch Properties to change the pitch of a clip without affecting its length.

1 Right-click on the LiqLead06_Cut clip, which is the first clip in the Guitar Lead track. From the context menu that appears, choose Clip Time Stretch Properties. This is another way to access the Clip Time Stretch Properties window.

2 At the top of Clip Time Stretch Properties window, check the Enable Time Stretching option if it is not already selected. At the bottom of the window, click in the box for Transpose Pitch and enter **2**, then press OK. Press the spacebar to hear the changes in this clip.

The pitch of this clip is raised by 2 half-steps and it sounds more compatible with the rest of the song.

3 Similarly, right-click on the other clip in the Guitar Lead track to open its Clip Time Stretch Properties window and transpose its pitch by 2 half-steps as well.

Note: *There are 12 half-steps in the musical octave. For example, if you enter **12** half-steps in this dialog box, the pitch of the clip will be raised by an octave. You can also enter **-12** (negative twelve) half-steps to lower the pitch of the clip by an octave.*

4 Press the spacebar to hear the changes again. When you are done, save the session by pressing Ctrl+S.

Changing the tempo of the entire session

Tempo is measured in beats per minute (bpm). This can be calculated by counting the number of beats in a loop or waveform over a span of one minute. While the tempo of individual clips can be changed as described in the previous section, the tempo of all clips in a session can be changed together in a single step. You can do this by changing the session tempo in the Tempo field of the Multitrack View.

1 If the Session Properties panel is not visible at the bottom right of the display, choose Window > Session Properties.

*2 Click in the Tempo field in the Session properties panel and enter **120** as the new value for beats/minute or bpm. This becomes the new tempo for your multitrack session. Press Enter to initiate the tempo change in Audition. Wait until the progress windows show that the change has been completed.*

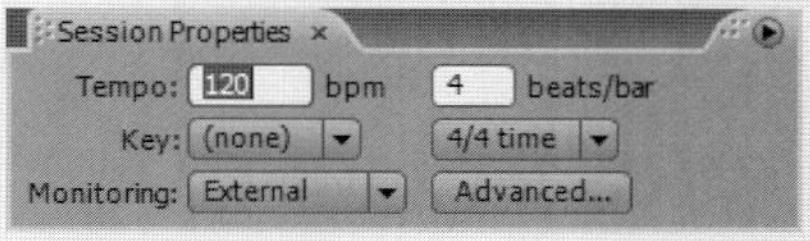

This process works primarily with loop files, as they contain tempo information that can be manipulated.

Exploring on your own

1 Extend the StudioKit.cell clip to several times its length and duplicate the clips in other tracks to create a longer multitrack session.

2 Modify the amplitude of the LiqLead03.cel clip to better balance the entire session, using Audition's Effects > Amplitude menu.

3 Create short fade ins and fade outs using clip envelopes to ensure that there are no abrupt transitions between any clips, their beginnings or endings. Select File > Save Session when you have finished editing the session.

Review

Review questions

1 What differences are there between simply pressing the spacebar, and using the Play controls from the Transport panel?

2 How is a loop-enabled file identified in Adobe Audition in the Multitrack View and in the Files panel?

3 What difference is there in using File > Save Session from Multitrack View or File > Save when working in Edit View?

4 How can you ensure that all your session files are saved in one central location on your hard disk?

Review answers

1 By default, the spacebar plays the entire session data from the start-time indicator to the end of your session. The default action of the Play button in the Transport panel also plays from the cursor location to the end of the file. The default action of the Play button with a circle surrounding it is to play only until the end of the area displayed on screen. Utilizing the circled Play button plays only to the end of the screen. The Play buttons can be customized by right-clicking them.

2 A loop-enabled file is identified both in the Files panel and in the Multitrack View by the loop icon.

3 The File > Save Session command while in Multitrack View will simply save the session file. Using the File > Save command while in the Edit View affects the file currently being edited in Edit View. Keep in mind that the shortcuts are the same while in both views (Ctrl+S), so be aware of the view you are using.

4 While in Multitrack View, and performing a File > Save Session As command, confirm that the Save copies of all associated files option is checked. This ensures that copies of all session files are saved in the same folder as the Adobe Audition Session (.ses) file. If you continue to work on a session file after performing a Save As, changes impact only the original file.

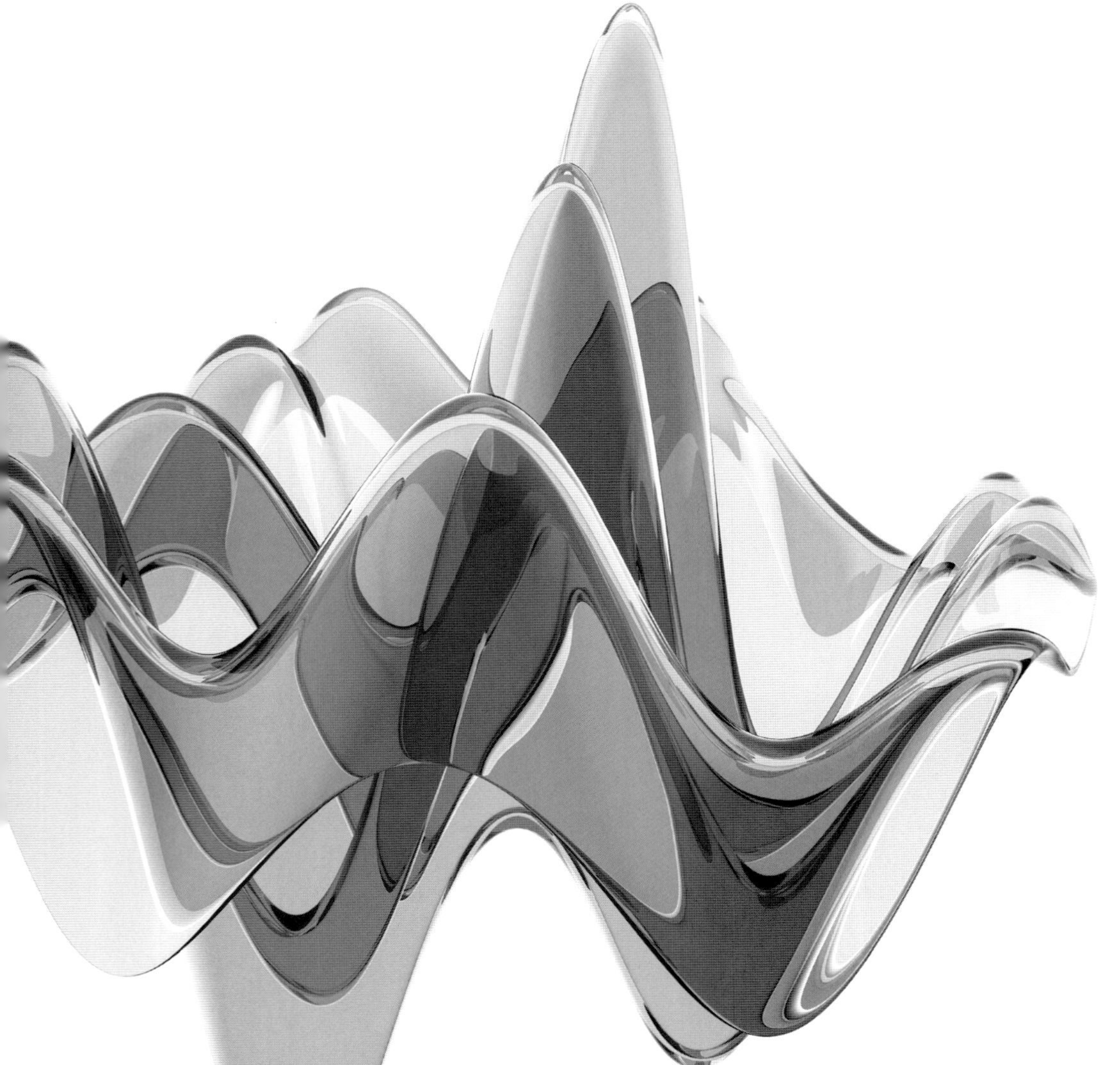

6 Noise Reduction

You can add new life to old or low-quality audio recordings using Adobe Audition's enhancement and restoration effects. Distracting hiss or background noise can easily be removed with the Noise Reduction effect. Pops, clicks, and crackles can be identified and removed using Audition's Spectral View.

In this lesson, you will learn how to do the following:

- Create and save a noise reduction profile.
- Remove pops, crackles, and hiss from a recording.
- Make selections in the frequency area to isolate specific frequencies.
- Use the Graphic Equalizer to improve the tonal balance of audio files.

Getting started

In this lesson, you will be utilizing Adobe Audition's built-in noise reduction effects to improve the quality of a waveform. Because many recordings do not take place in a sound booth or professional recording studio, noise is typically recorded along with the focus of your recording. Noise can be described as unrequired signals, usually at lower amplitudes, which are picked up by the microphone during the recording session. Street noise, crowd noise, and the buzz of nearby electronic devices—such as a fan, are all examples of noise which can get recorded unintentionally.

Noise and imperfections in a recording may also be related to the recording source itself. Creating a digital loop from an analog source, such as a record player, may result in crackles or pops throughout the recording, due to scratches or imperfections in the vinyl record itself.

In this lesson you will use some of the tools available in Adobe Audition for repairing or removing audio imperfections.

1 Start Adobe Audition and click on the Multitrack View button ( ), if not already selected.

2 If you have not already copied the resource files for this lesson onto your hard disk from the AA_06 folder on the *Adobe Audition 2.0 Classroom in a Book* CD, do so now. See “Copying the Classroom in a Book files” on page 2.

3 Choose File > Open Session, and open the 06_Start.ses file in the AA_06 folder, which is located in the AA_CIB folder on your hard disk.

4 Choose File > Save Session As, and name the file **06_Recording.ses**, and save it in the AA_06 folder.

5 To review the finished session file, choose File > Open Session, and open the 06_End.ses file in the AA_06 folder, which is also located within the AA_CIB folder on your hard disk. Play the session file by either clicking on the Play button ( ) in the Transport panel, or pressing the spacebar on your keyboard.

6 When you are ready to start working on the lesson, close the 06_End.ses file by choosing File > Close All.

7 Select File > Open Session to reopen the 06_Recording.ses file you created in the previous steps.

Tools to clean up sound

The lesson files in this chapter are modeled after an amateur radio commercial demo. The Voice Over track recording was created using a low–quality microphone in a non-studio environment. The Guitar track is a sampled loop recorded from an old, heavily used vinyl record. As you play this session file, note all the residual noise which is evident throughout the session. Listen to each track individually by clicking on the Solo button (S), then pressing the spacebar on the keyboard to play.

Notice that the Voice Over track has a substantial amount of noise in the background of the recording. The Guitar track contains hiss, pops, and clicks throughout the loop as a result of the wear in the vinyl record.

Audition offers several effects that can be utilized to repair such imperfections. These tools are available in the Edit View. As you know from the previous lessons, changes made to files in the Edit View are destructive in nature. This means that the changes will be saved into the file when you save. If you do not wish to alter the original file, you can choose to make a copy by choosing Edit > Copy to New, or by choosing the File > Save As command and entering a new name for the file.

Creating the Noise Reduction Profile

You will isolate the background noise from the Voice Over sample using Audition's Noise Reduction Profile feature. You will then use this profile to filter out the existing noise throughout the voice recording.

1 In the Multitrack View, double-click on the VoiceOver_Take1 clip in the Voice Over track. This opens the file in the Edit View.

2 Press the Home key and then click the Zoom to Selection button (🔍) three times to zoom in. When you previewed the file, you may have noticed a slight pause before the subject begins speaking. The file contains approximately 1 second of background noise during this pause. Isolate the first second of this waveform by clicking and dragging in the Edit View display window. Your selection should end prior to any significant change in the waveform.

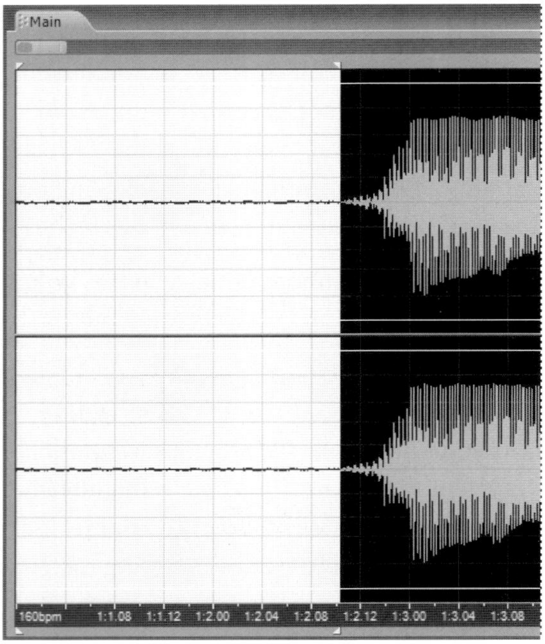

3 Click on the Effects tab in the group of panels to the left of the Main panel. Select the plus sign (+) positioned to the left of the Restoration category.

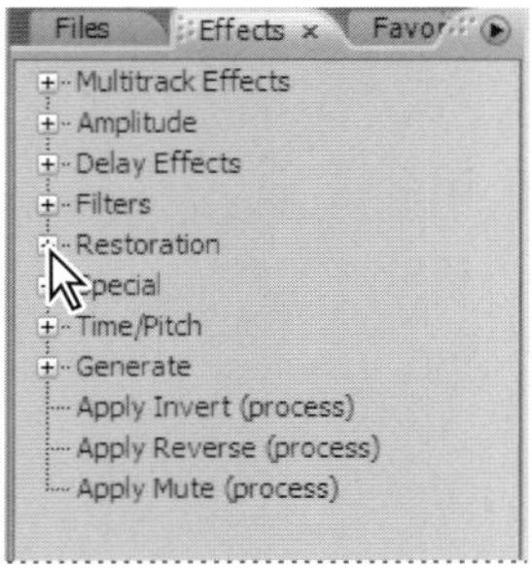

The category expands, revealing various effects that are available under this category.

4 Double-click on the Capture Noise Reduction Profile option from the Effects panel.

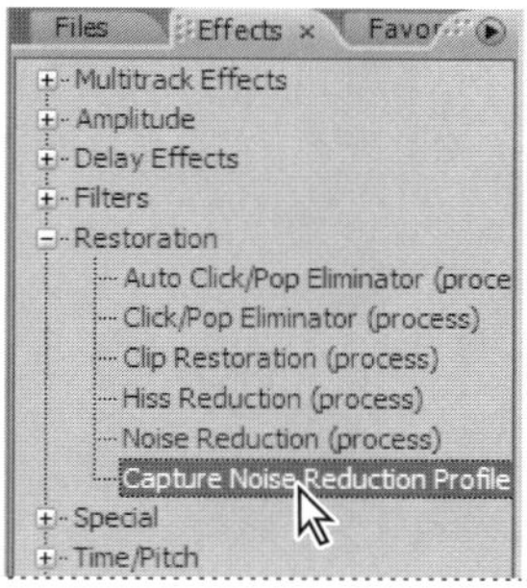

If an Alert window opens informing you that a profile is being created from the current selection, click OK. A window appears showing Audition's progress in creating the profile, and then the window closes after the profile is created. You will now use this captured Noise Reduction Profile to cancel out the noise present throughout the file.

5 Click anywhere in the waveform to clear the current selection and then press the Home key to place the start-time indicator at the beginning of the file. Double-click the Noise Reduction (process) effect in the Effects panel. The Noise Reduction effect window is displayed.

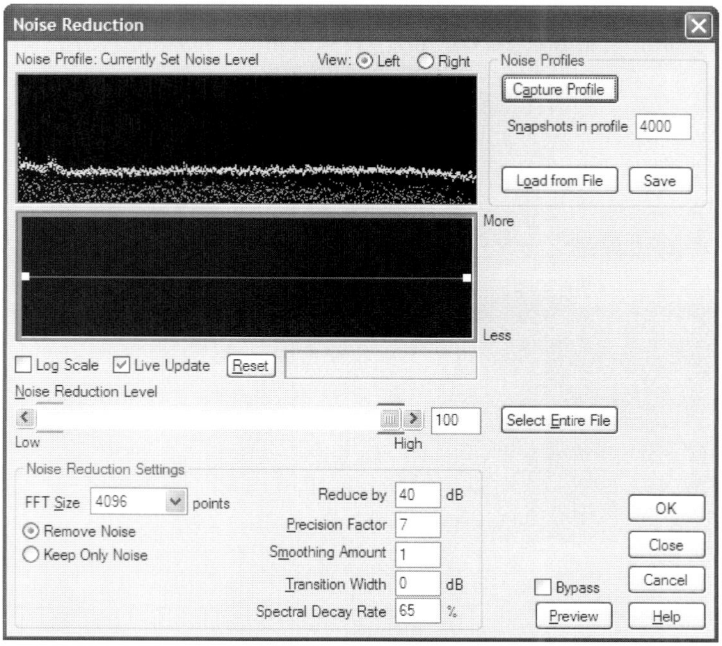

6 In the Noise Reduction effect window, press the Preview button to listen to the file as you make changes.

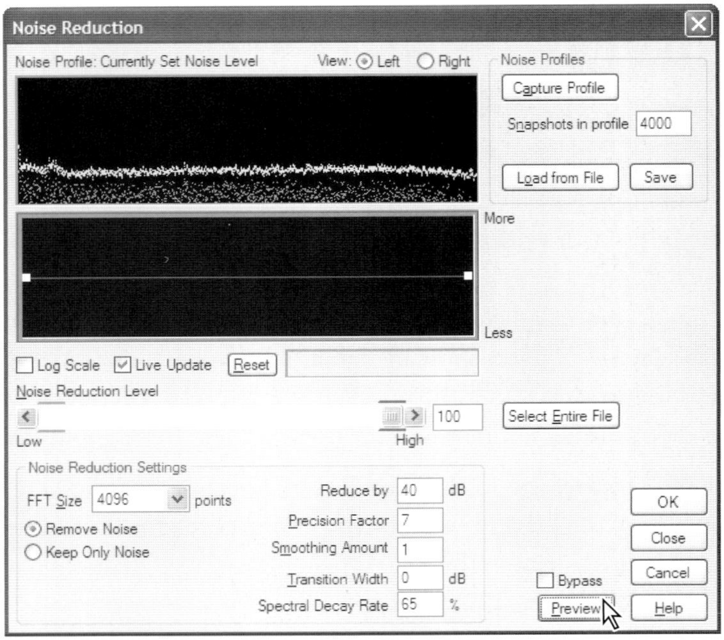

7 While the file is previewing, move the Noise Reduction Level Slider from left to right and back. As you do so, take note of its effect on the file. Move the slider to the 75% position, or click into the input area and enter **75** as the value. Allow the file to continue previewing.

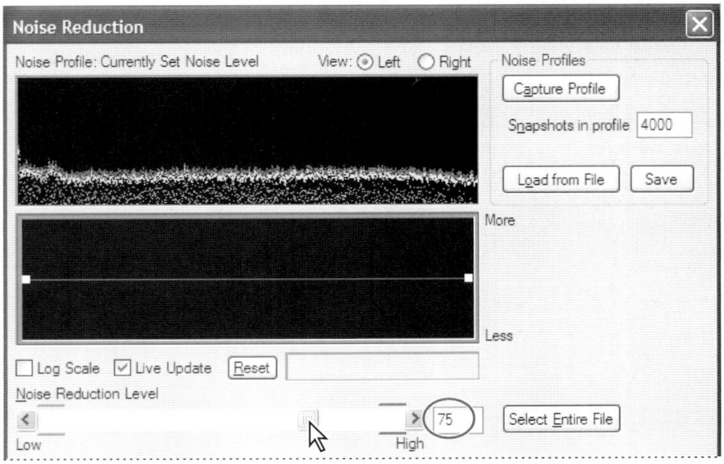

8 While the file is previewing, click the Spectral Decay Rate field at the bottom of the window and enter **25** as the value. Click the Bypass option to hear the original file. Click Bypass again to restore the effect. The background noise is much less prominent when the Noise Reduction effect is applied.

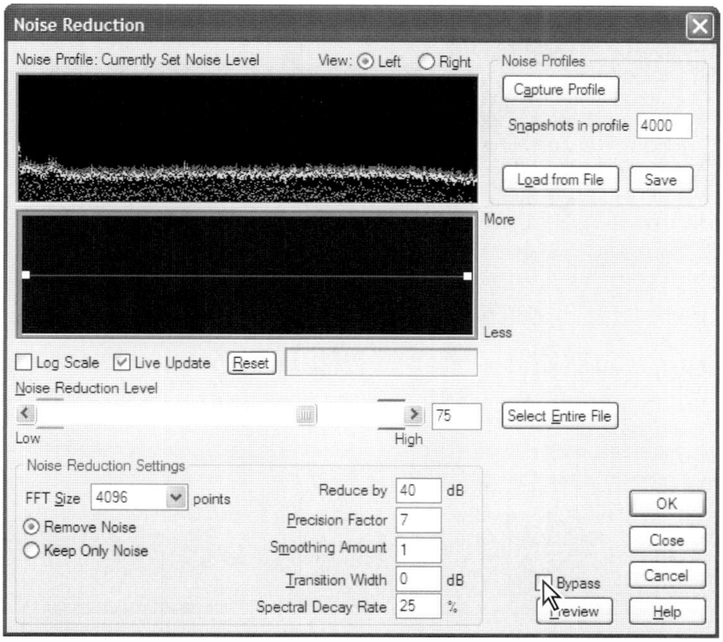

9 Return the Noise Reduction Level to 75, then click OK to close the Noise Reduction window and apply the changes to the entire waveform. Choose File > Save As to save this file under a different name. In the Save As window, enter the name **VoiceOver.cel** and then click the Save button. Click Yes to overwrite the existing file with the same name. If you get a warning saying that you might be saving to a lower-fidelity format, click OK.

To reduce noise added by a sound card during recording, start the recording with one second of silence. After recording is complete, use that silence as the Noise Reduction Profile. You can then remove the identifiable noise from the finished recording. In some cases, this process can increase dynamic range by a full 10 dB.

10 Press the F12 key to switch to the Multitrack View, and then play the session file using the spacebar on your keyboard or use the Play button in the Transport panel controls. Notice that the voiceover sounds much cleaner after applying Noise Reduction.

11 Save your session by selecting File > Save Session.

Removing pops, crackles, and hiss

Pops and clicks are artifacts which can be unintentionally recorded from an outside source. They may also be the result of an audio file having been cut and looped. The GuitarRiff_from_Vinyl loop, which is in the guitar track, contains several clicks which you will remove using Audition's Pop/Click Eliminator effects.

1 Near the top left of the Audition workspace, click the Files tab. Double-click on the GuitarRiff_from_Vinyl.cel file in the Files panel to open it in the Edit View.

2 Preview the file by pressing the spacebar, making note of the audible pops and clicks, and their connection to the large spikes in the waveform.

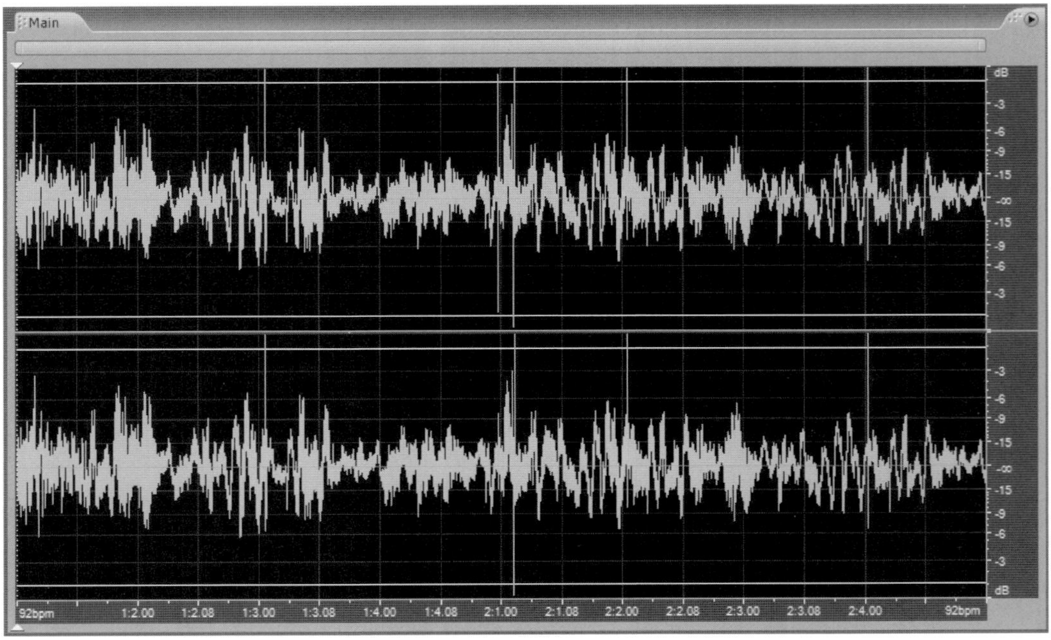

3 Click onto the Effects tab, next to the Files tab, to bring the Effects panel forward. Within the Effects panel, click the plus sign (+) for the Restoration category to reveal the Restoration effects. Double-click the Click/Pop Eliminator (process) effect, opening the Click/Pop Eliminator window.

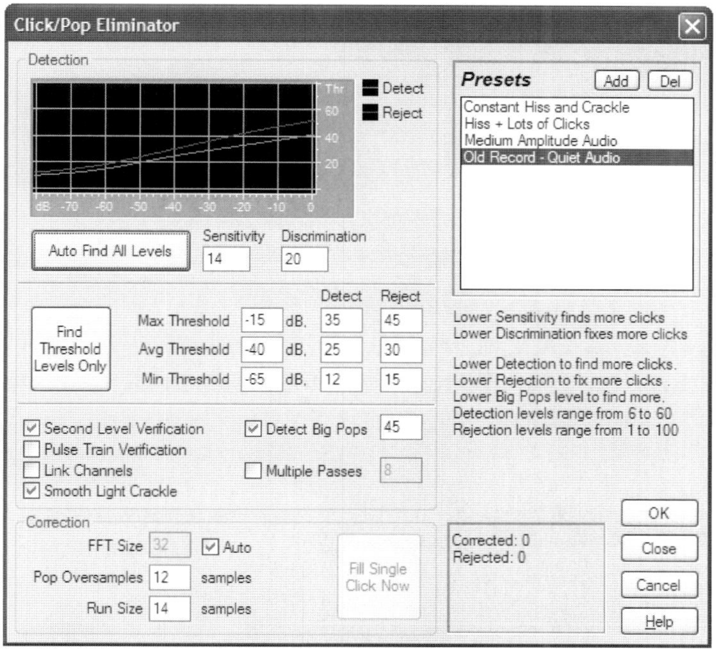

4 Select the Old Record - Quiet Audio option from the Presets portion in the top right corner of the window, then click the Find Threshold Levels Only button. This creates a threshold for minimum, average, and maximum decibels (dB).

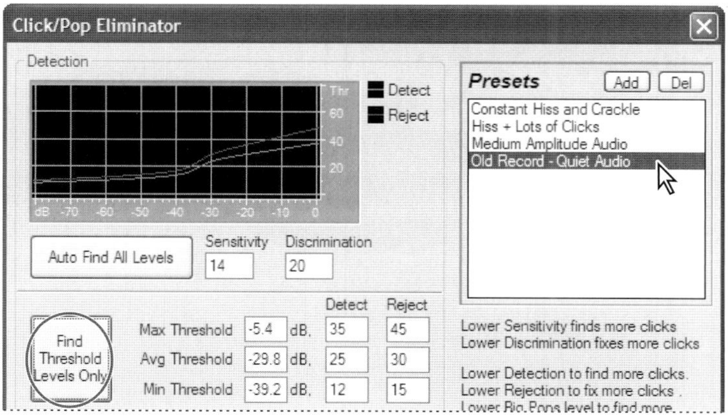

5 For each threshold value, input a new Reject value of **15**, causing Audition to isolate more clicks.

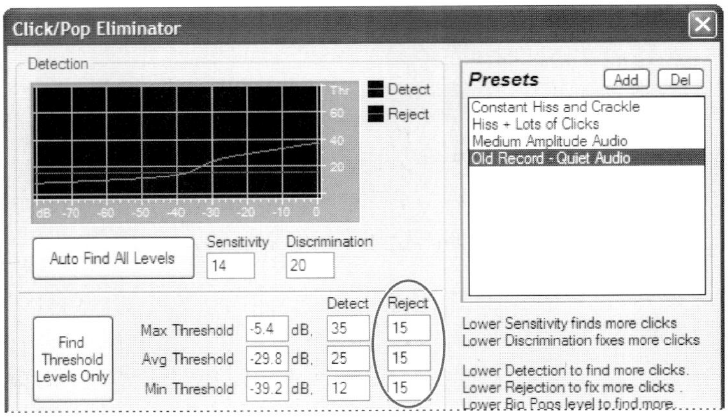

6 Save your options as a preset by clicking on the Add button in the upper right corner of the Click/Pop Eliminator window. Enter **Old_Vinyl** as the name for the preset and then click the OK button.

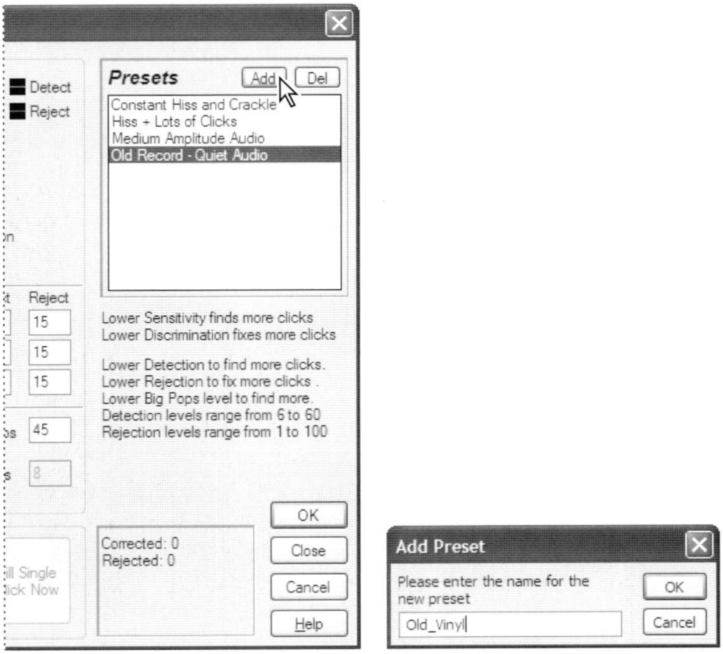

7 In the Click/Pop Eliminator window, click the OK button to apply the click/pop elimination process to the GuitarRiff_from_Vinyl file.

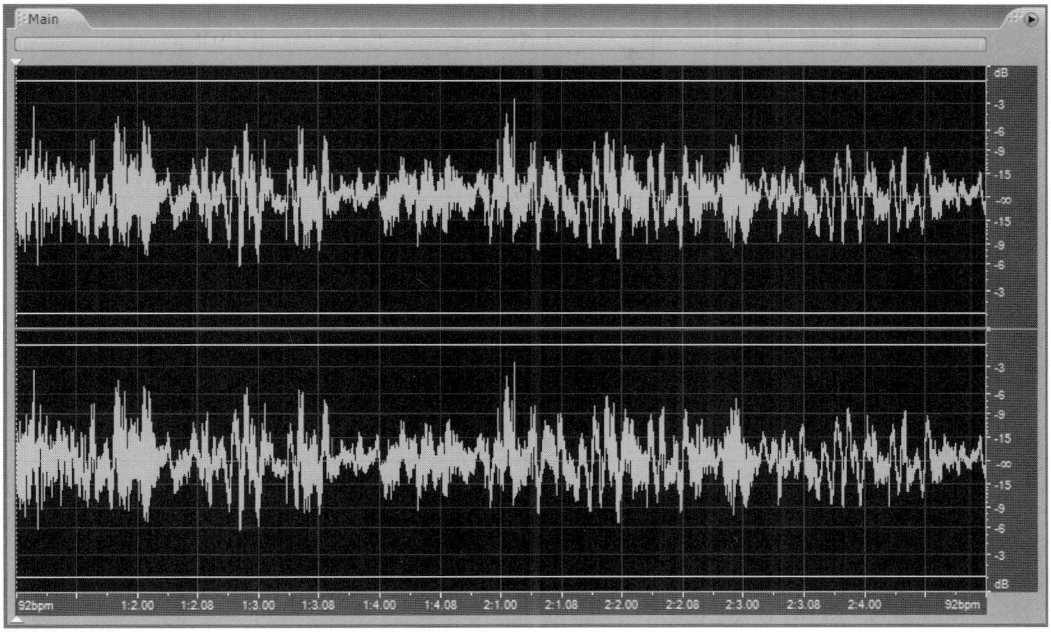

8 Play the modified file by pressing the Play button in Transport panel or use the spacebar on your keyboard. Most clicks are gone! You should notice a significant improvement in the overall quality of the recording.

9 Select File > Save As. If necessary, navigate to the AA_06 folder on your hard disk. Name the file **GuitarRiff.cel** and then click the Save button. Click Yes to overwrite the existing file with the same name. Click OK if you receive a notification that you might be saving to a lower-fidelity file format.

Using the Auto Click/Pop Eliminator effect

If you need to quickly remove crackle and static from vinyl recordings, first try the Auto Click/Pop Eliminator effect. You can easily select and correct a large area of audio, or a single click or pop. This effect provides the same processing quality as the Click/Pop Eliminator effect, but it offers simplified controls and a helpful preview.

By using some more specific effects, you will now isolate and eliminate the hiss which remains. Then you will also remove the remaining pop located midway through the loop.

10 Within the Restoration category in the Effects panel, double-click the Hiss Reduction (process) effect. The Hiss Reduction window opens.

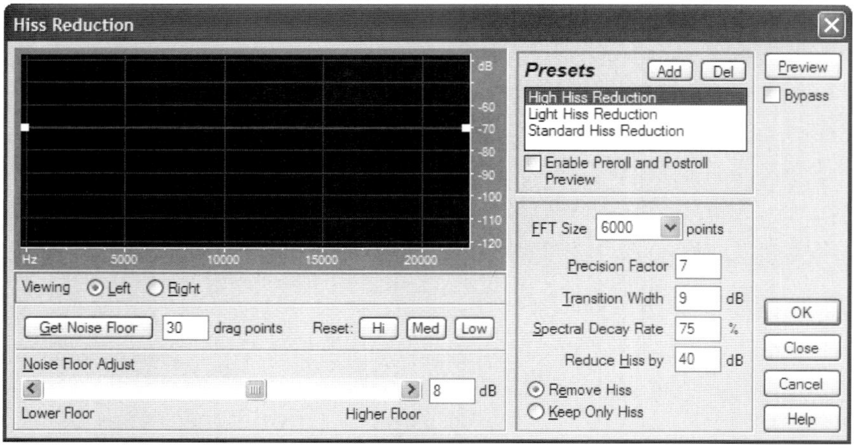

11 In the Presets portion of the window, select the High Hiss Reduction setting. Click on the Preview button to hear your changes. Allow the file to continue playing.

12 Drag the Noise Floor Adjust slider toward the right until a setting of approximately 10 dB is achieved. You can also manually enter values by clicking into the input box and entering the value from your keyboard.

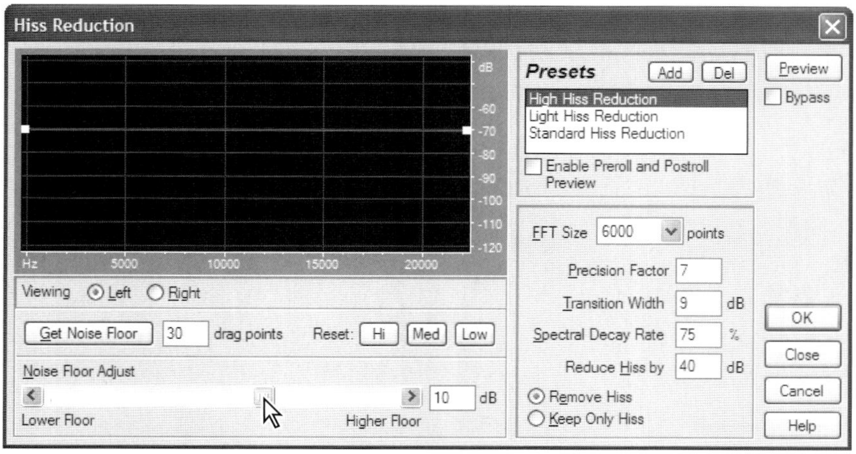

13 Click the OK button to confirm the settings and apply this Hiss Reduction effect to the guitar sample. Play the file to hear how the hiss that was present in the sample earlier has been drastically reduced. You can compare the result of hiss reduction by choosing Edit > Undo and Edit > Redo commands. Finally, choose File > Save to save the revisions to the GuitarRiff.cel file.

Isolating specific frequencies within your files

1 Select View > Spectral Frequency Display, to display the spectral analyzer. Spectral View displays the guitar waveform by its frequency components.

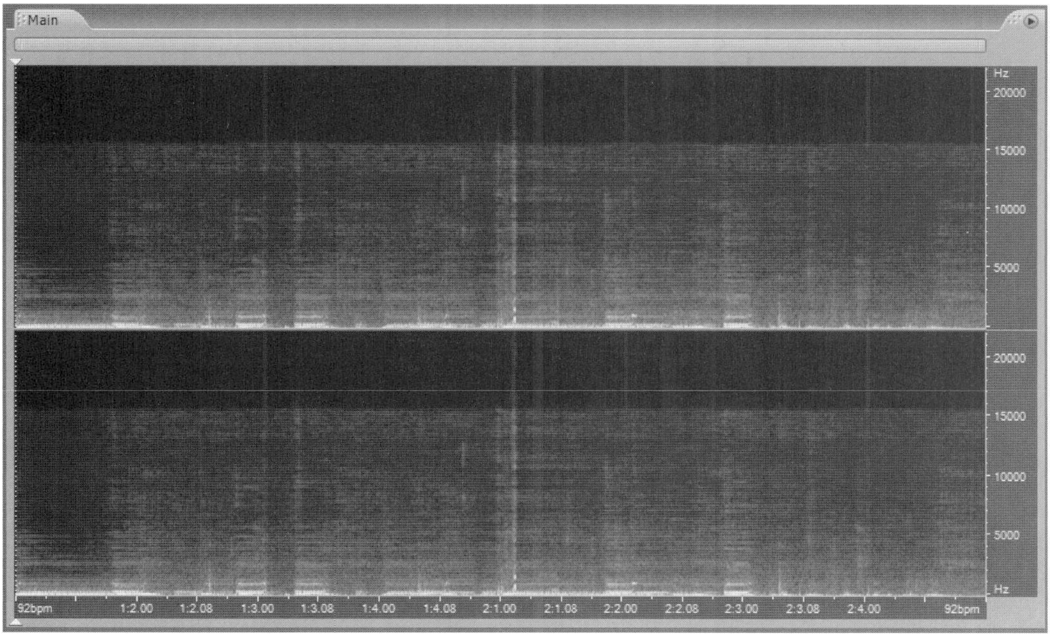

In the Spectral Frequency Display, the x-axis (horizontal) represents time and the y-axis (vertical) measures frequency. This view lets you analyze audio data to see which frequencies are most prevalent in your file. The greater a signal's amplitude component within a specific frequency range, the brighter the displayed color. Colors range from dark blue, indicating that the frequencies are very low in amplitude, to bright yellow, indicating that the frequencies are high in amplitude. This is a linear display. You can right-click along the vertical axis displaying the Hz levels and choose Logarithmic to show a logarithmic display.

2 Press the spacebar on your keyboard to play the file. Notice that the pop correlates to the large spike indicated in the spectral view at around Bar 2 beat 1 (2:1.00) of the waveform.

3 In the timeline, right-click and then drag to zoom into the area of the pop. Audition zooms into the highlighted area. Select the pop in the Spectral View window by left-clicking and dragging, to make the selection.

Note: *Toward the top left of the Spectral View display, you can find different tools that let you make precise selections within the frequency area. To make rectangular selections in a specific frequency range, you can choose the Marquee Selection tool ( ). If you want to make free-form selections, you can choose the Lasso Selection tool ( ).*

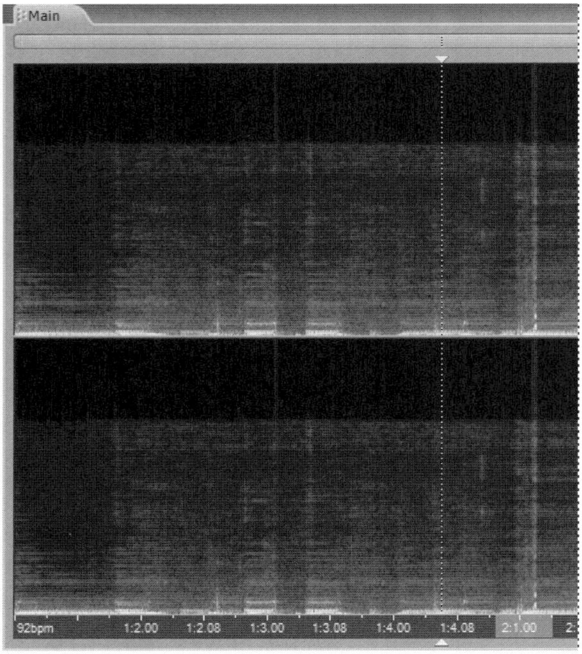

Before zooming.

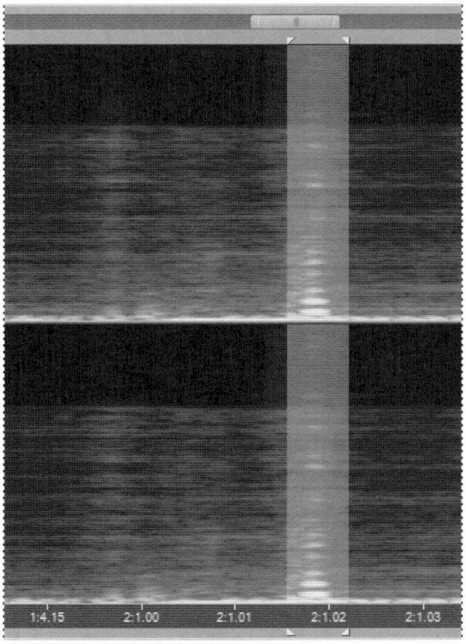

After zooming.

Note: *If you zoomed into an incorrect view by mistake, you can click the Zoom Out Full Both Axes button to expand the view. You can also right-click in the timeline and choose Zooming > Zoom Full.*

4 In the Effects panel, go to the Restoration category and double-click the Click/Pop Eliminator (process) effect. The Click/Pop Eliminator window opens.

5 In the Click/Pop Eliminator window, select the Old_Vinyl Preset you previously saved. This is located in the Presets portion of the window. Keep the Click/Pop Eliminator window open.

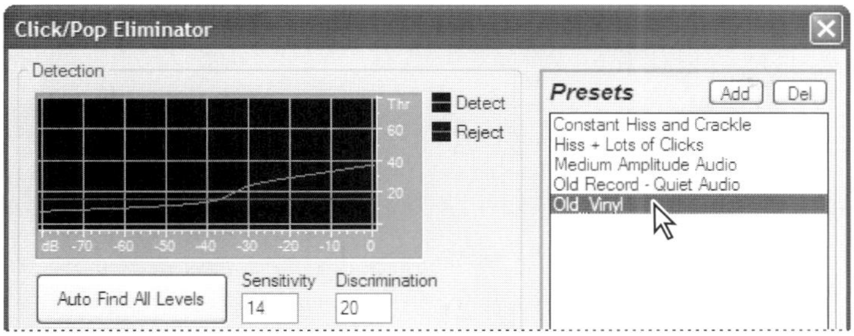

6 Select the Fill Single Click Now button. This action repairs an individual click contained within your selection.

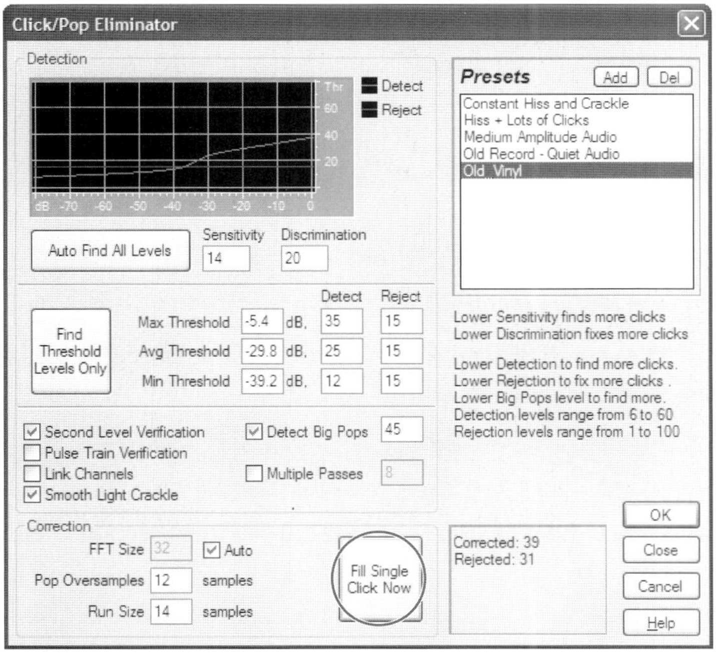

7 Choose View > Waveform Display, or use the Shift+W shortcut.

8 Choose File > Save to save your changes.

Repairing single clicks

The Favorites panel contains several effect presets. The Repair Transient preset is an effective tool for repairing single clicks or pops in an waveform. In the Edit View, make your selection, then double-click on the Repair Transient command in the Favorites panel, and Audition will repair the single instance in the waveform.

Being able to make accurate selections in the frequency area gives you a lot of power and flexibility to manipulate your samples. For example, you could select just the bass area (say, below 150 Hz) and apply compression to those frequencies only. The frequencies that were not selected will remain totally unaffected. To give another example, you could apply reverb to all the frequencies between 10,000 Hz and 15,000 Hz, without letting the reverb affect the lower frequencies, which might have otherwise caused muddiness or boominess in the sample. In order to make precise selections in the frequency area, you can zoom in and out for the y-axis (frequency) by using the same procedure as in step 3, or use the Zoom panel controls toward the bottom of the display.

Using Graphic Equalizer to change sound quality

The Graphic Equalizer provides you great control over the tonal balance in an audio file. It allows for modification of specific frequencies. By isolating typical frequencies produced by the human voice, the recorded VoiceOver.cel file can be improved.

1 Click to select the Files tab to bring the Files panel forward. Double-click the VoiceOver.cel file, opening the file in the Edit View.

2 Click on the Effects tab to bring the Effects panel forward. If the waveform is not selected, choose Edit > Select Entire Wave or alternatively, press Ctrl+A.

3 In the Effects panel, click the plus sign (+) to the left of Filters category, and double-click the Graphic Equalizer effect.

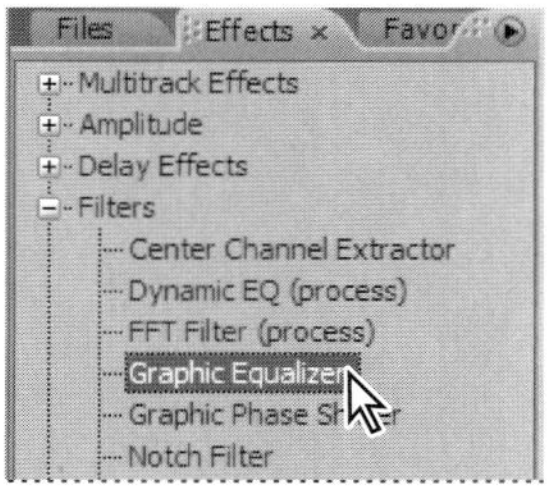

The Graphic Equalizer window opens.

4 In the Graphic Equalizer window, switch off the Power button ( ) at the bottom left by clicking on it once. Press the Preview button ( ) next to the Power button to hear your file without any EQ applied to it.

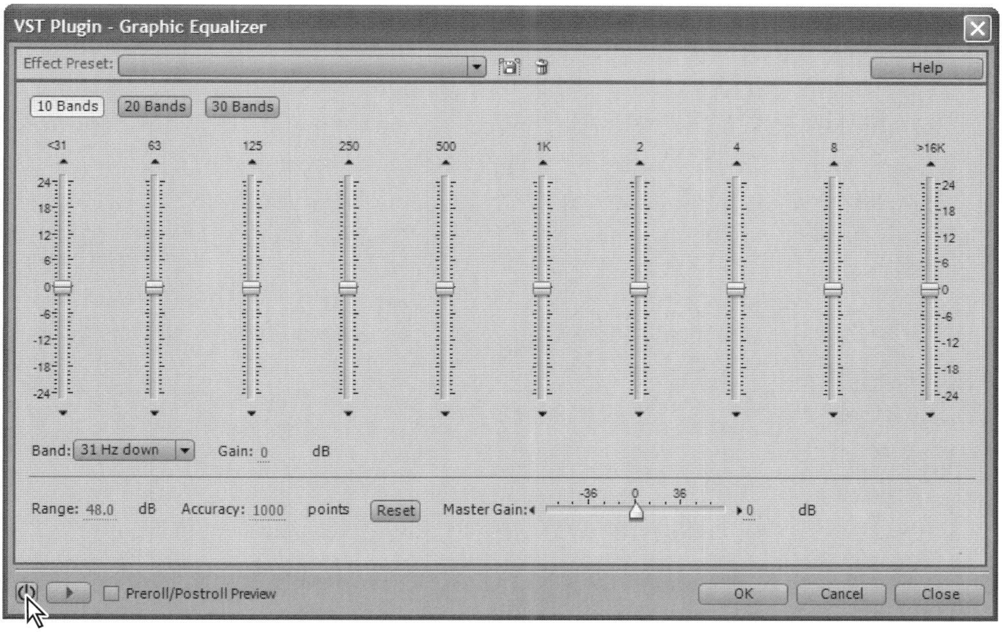

Preview buttons in effects windows change to Stop buttons ( ) when you are previewing the effect. You may also utilize the spacebar to toggle playback of files if the Preview button is active.

5 Press the Preview button again to stop the playback of the file. Switch on the Power button.

6 Confirm that the 10 Bands button has been selected above the sliders. Press the Reset button toward the bottom of the sliders to set all sliders at 0 dB. Now click on the 125 Hz slider and drag it up to +3 dB level. Release your mouse button. Click the Preview button ( ) to play the file with this Graphic Equalizer effect applied. At this point you should notice an increase in the lower frequencies of the voice, resulting in a broader, fuller sound. Click the Stop button. Click OK to apply this effect.

7 Select File > Save to save your changes to the VoiceOver.cel file.

8 Click on the Multitrack View button ( ) to view your session. Preview your file by clicking on the Play from Cursor to End of File button ( ) or pressing the spacebar. When you have finished listening to your file, select File > Save Session.

Exploring on your own

The graphic nature of the FFT (Fast Fourier Transform) Filter (process) effect makes it easy to draw curves or notches that reject or boost specific frequencies. This effect can produce filters such as high- and low-pass filters (to maintain high and low frequencies, respectively), narrow band-pass filters (to simulate the sound of a telephone call), or notch filters (to eliminate very narrow frequency bands).

In order to round out the session file in a final step, an FFT Filter allows for the limiting of higher frequencies over an entire wave file. Reducing these frequencies helps to push the guitar file farther into the background of our session file, leaving the Voice Over track as the main focus.

1 In the Files panel, double-click the GuitarRiff.cel file, opening it in Edit View.

2 Click to select the Effects panel.

3 Select the FFT Filter (process) option from the Filters category in the Effects panel by double-clicking.

4 In the Presets portion of the window, scroll down and select The Club Downstairs preset. Click OK.

5 Preview the file by pressing the spacebar or clicking the Play button.

6 Save the file by choosing File > Save.

Review

Review questions

1 What are some typical causes of noise and artifacts in sound files?

2 How can you set up a recording to later eliminate any existing background noise from the session?

3 What tools and options can be used to improve sound quality?

Review answers

1 Electronic equipment, poor recording source, or improper loop creation are some typical examples.

2 Allow for at least one second of silence at the very start of your recording. You can use this to build a Noise Reduction Profile which can be used later for the entire waveform.

3 Along with Noise Reduction, numerous tools exist for improving audio quality. These include the Repair Transient option found in the Favorites, the Click/Pop Eliminator, Hiss Reduction, and the Equalizer.

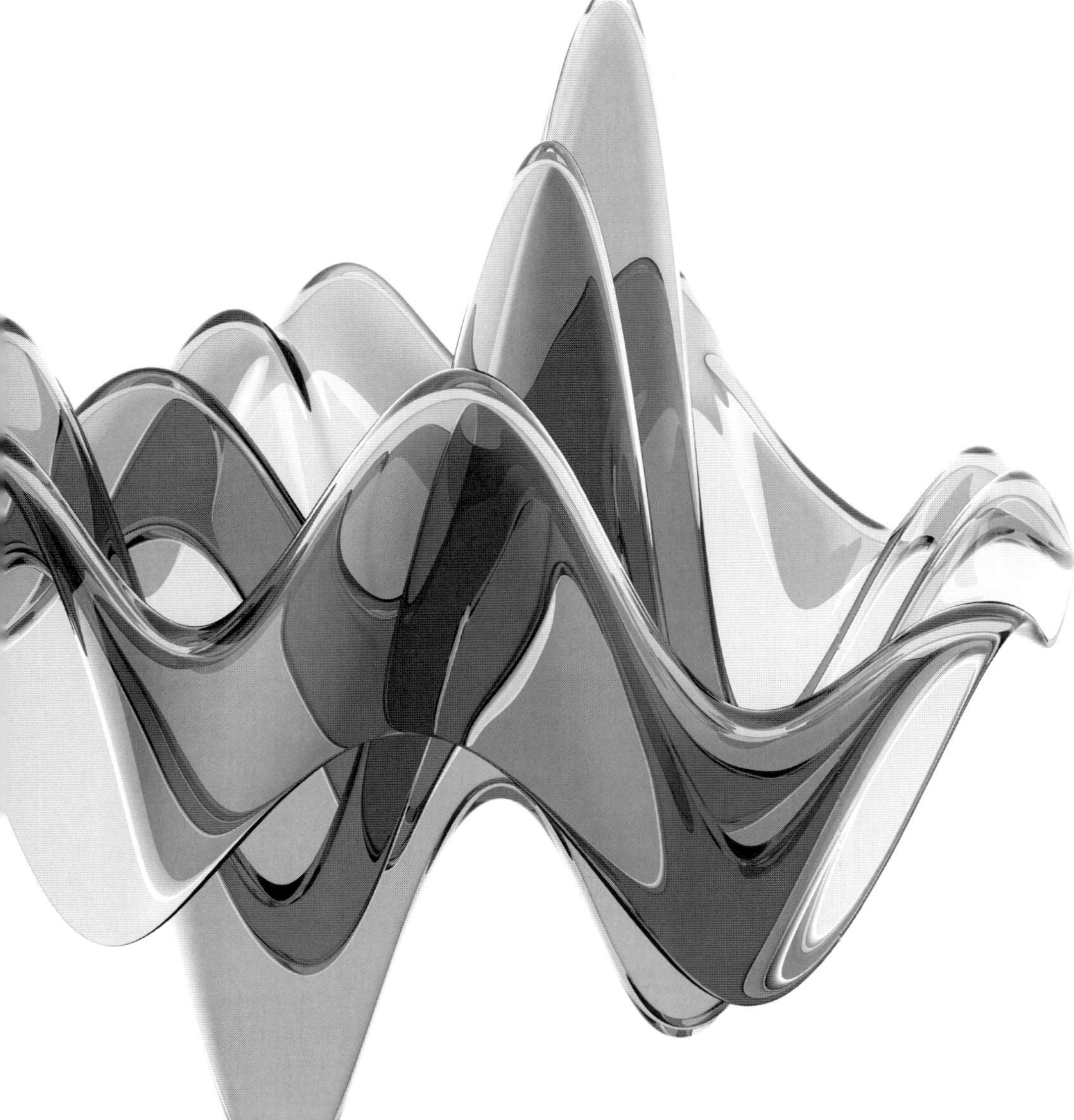

7 Editing Voices

Audition's editing tools make it possible to produce professional-quality audio recordings. In this lesson, you'll learn how to do the following:

- Split clips and save selections from larger clips.
- Work with and manipulate speech tracks.
- Use the Delete Silence feature to automatically remove gaps in an audio file.
- Use a bus to group the voice tracks together.
- Add an effect with the Quick Filter.
- Use the Mixer to pan the tracks in stereo space.
- Export the completed session as a stereo .wav file.

Getting started

In this lesson, you'll work with a series of files and place them in the Multitrack View to create a one-minute radio commercial.

1 Start Adobe Audition and click on the Multitrack View button ().

2 If you have not already copied the resource files for this lesson onto your hard disk from the AA_07 folder from the *Adobe Audition 2.0 Classroom in a Book* CD, do so now. See "Copying the Classroom in a Book files" on page 2.

3 To play the finished session file, choose File > Open Session. Open the 07_end.ses file in the AA_07 folder, which you just copied into the AA_CIB folder on your hard disk. Play the session file by either clicking on the Play button () in the Transport panel or pressing the spacebar.

4 When you are ready to start working, you can close the 07_end.ses file by choosing File > Close All.

5 Choose File > Open Session and open the 07_start.ses file in the AA_07 folder, which is located in the AA_CIB folder on your hard disk.

6 Choose File > Save Session As, and name the file **07_RadioAd.ses**, and save it in the AA_07 folder.

Splitting clips and saving selections

In this exercise you will arrange several clips in your multitrack to create a radio commercial. You will use Audition's editing and processing tools to create a session which is exactly one minute in length. Commercial scripts are rarely read live. Different actors may read their parts at different times and might not even be in the same room at the same time. It is often up to the studio engineer to shape the raw material to exact time requirements.

1 Click on the Import File button () in the Files panel and Ctrl+click the following files from the AA_07 folder:

- Announcer_1.wav
- Announcer_terms.wav
- Announcer_tincan.wav
- Announcer_welcome.wav
- SkyCellTell_theme.wav
- Woman1_cantbelieve.wav
- Woman1_thankyou.wav

If you have the Auto Play and Loop options checked on the right side in the Import window, each file will play as you select it. Once all the required files are selected, press the Open button to import all these files into the session. The files show up in the Files panel once they are loaded.

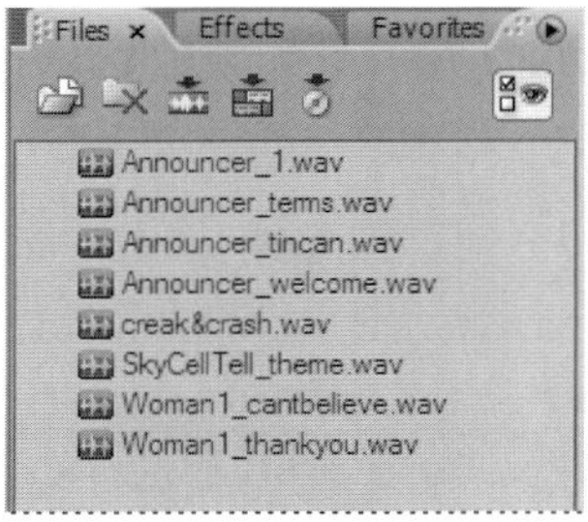

2 Double-click on the Announcer_1.wav clip to open it the Edit View. Press your spacebar to hear the clip, which is approximately 20 seconds long.

This clip was read in one take, you will be splitting it to create two separate clips.

3 To ensure you are working in the correct time format of minutes and seconds, choose View > Display Time Format and select Decimal (mm:ss.ddd) if it is not already chosen. Using the Time Selection tool (I), click and drag to select from the beginning of the clip to the 7.5 second mark.

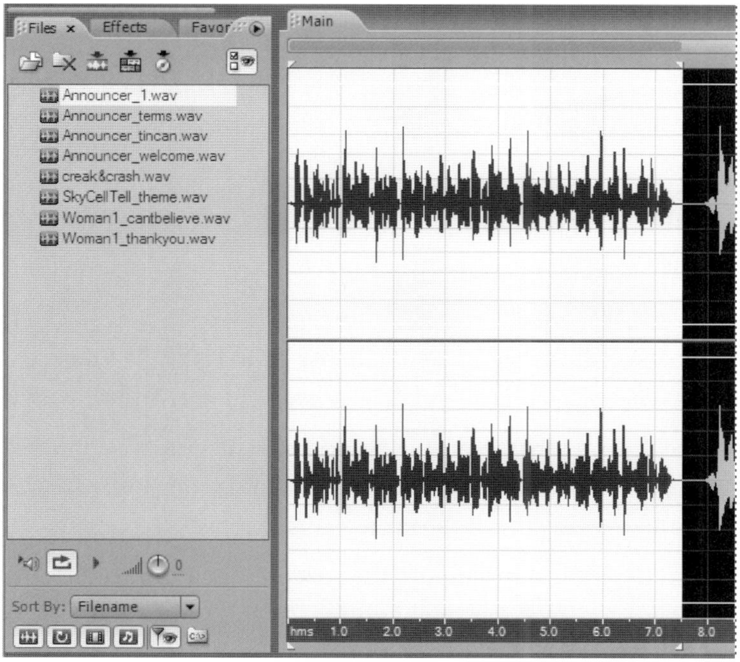

4 Choose Edit > Copy to New.

The selection becomes its own waveform and it appears in the Edit display. This is also reflected in the Files panel where a file called Announcer_1(2)* has been created. This indicates that the source of this new file was the Announcer_1.wav file. You will now save it under a different filename.

5 Choose File > Save As and save the file as **Announcer_intro.wav** into your AA_07 folder, located in the AA_CIB folder on your hard disk. If prompted to overwrite the file, click Yes, then click OK, if presented with a dialog about the file format.

6 Double-click on the file Announcer_1.wav in the Files panel. Notice that your initial selection remains highlighted, which makes it easier to create a second selection.

7 Click on the waveform at the 8 second mark and drag to the right, selecting the second half of the waveform.

8 Press the Play button and note how the announcer repeats the first phrase "Well, it's true." To edit out the first instance of the phrase, Shift+click near the separator between the top and bottom waveforms at the 9.4 second mark. This moves the left boundary of the selection to the right and reduces the current selection by about 1.4 seconds.

Note: *In addition to Shift+clicking on the selection, you can also drag the range boundaries (represented as yellow triangles at the top and bottom of the timeline) to the left or to the right to expand or contract the selection.*

Trimming and placing a clip

In the next steps you will start placing and trimming various clips to create the final session.

1 After having performed the previous steps, choose Trim from the Edit menu. Trimming a clip retains the selected area and deletes everything else.

2 Choose File > Save As and rename the file **Announcer_itstrue.wav** and save it into your AA_07 folder, which is located in the AA_CIB folder on your hard disk. If prompted to overwrite an existing file of the same name, choose Yes.

3 You will now begin to place your files into the session. Click the Multitrack View button () and rename Track 1 by highlighting the track name and entering **Announcer**. Repeat this process to rename Track 2 to **Woman**, Track 3 to **Sound Effects**, and Track 4 to **Music**.

4 Target the Announcer track by clicking on it. The fact that this track is now targeted is shown by a lighter shade of the track. Press the Home key to send the start-time indicator to the beginning of the session. Click on the Announcer_intro.wav file in the Files panel to select it and then press the Insert key on your keyboard (Ins on some keyboards) to insert the clip into your multitrack in the targeted track.

This clip gets inserted at the beginning of the session (0:00.00) because the start-time indicator was located there.

5 Click and drag the woman1_cantbelieve clip into the Woman track. Using the Move/Copy Clip tool (), move the clip so the beginning aligns with the end of the Announcer_intro.wav.

The edges of the two clips aligned because of a feature called Snapping. While this is helpful with music-based sessions, it is not always helpful with vocal projects where you may wish vocals to overlap slightly.

6 Choose Edit > Snapping and uncheck both the Snap to Clips and the Snap to Loop Endpoints options to deselect them. Additionally, deselect the Snap to Ruler (Coarse) option so that it is not checked. Select the Snap to Ruler (Fine) option so that there's a check mark next to it. Position the woman1_cantbelieve.wav so the clip begins at 0:07.00. Look at the time readout in the status bar as you drag the clip to the required position.

Note: *Audition measures time in the decimal format down to a thousandth of a second. We have rounded off all measurements in the text to tenths of a second; the actual numbers in your session may differ slightly.*

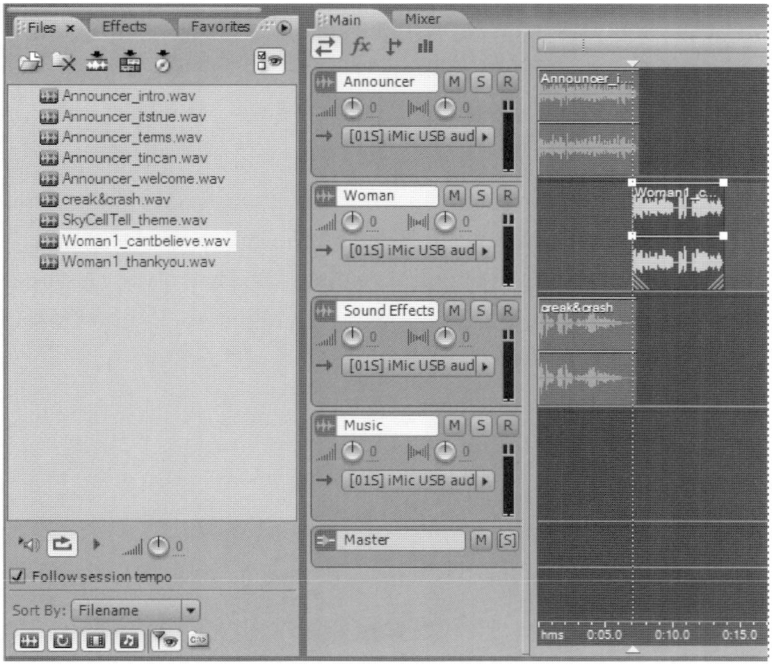

7 The start-time indicator is the vertical yellow dotted line with the yellow triangles at the top and bottom of the multitrack. Click and drag the start-time indicator to 0:14.00 on the timeline. Drag the file Announcer_itstrue.wav into the Announcer track and align the beginning of the clip to the start-time indicator.

Note: *Sometimes it is helpful to zoom into the session using the Zoom In Horizontally button ( ) to move the start-time indicator by very small amounts.*

You can also use the left and right arrow keys on your keyboard to move the start-time indicator to its left or right by small increments. If you are still having trouble placing the start-time indicator exactly at the 14 second mark, you can use the Selection/View panel below the multitrack. Type in **0:14.00** in the Selection Begin and Selection End fields and press Enter. The start-time indicator should jump to the 14 second mark.

8 Bring the start-time indicator to 0:23.90. Drag the file Announcer_tincan.wav into the announcer track and align the beginning of the clip to the start-time indicator.

9 Move the start-time indicator to 0:35.70. Place the clip Woman_thankyou.wav into the Woman track and align the beginning of the clip on the start-time indicator.

Note: *If you run out of room to place the additional clips, you will need to click the Zoom Out Horizontally button ( ) in order to view more of the timeline.*

10 Move the start-time indicator to 0:50.20. Place the clip Announcer_welcome.wav into the Announcer track and align the beginning of the clip to the start-time indicator.

11 Place the Announcer_terms.wav into the Announcer track next to the Announcer_welcome.wav approximately at (1:01.36). Press the Home key to send the start-time indicator to the beginning of the session and press the spacebar on your keyboard to play. If you hear obvious gaps or overlaps between clips, adjust them now by selecting the Move/Copy Clip tool ( ) and dragging the clips to the left or the right.

12 Press the Home key to place the start-time indicator at the beginning of the timeline and then press the spacebar to begin playing the session.

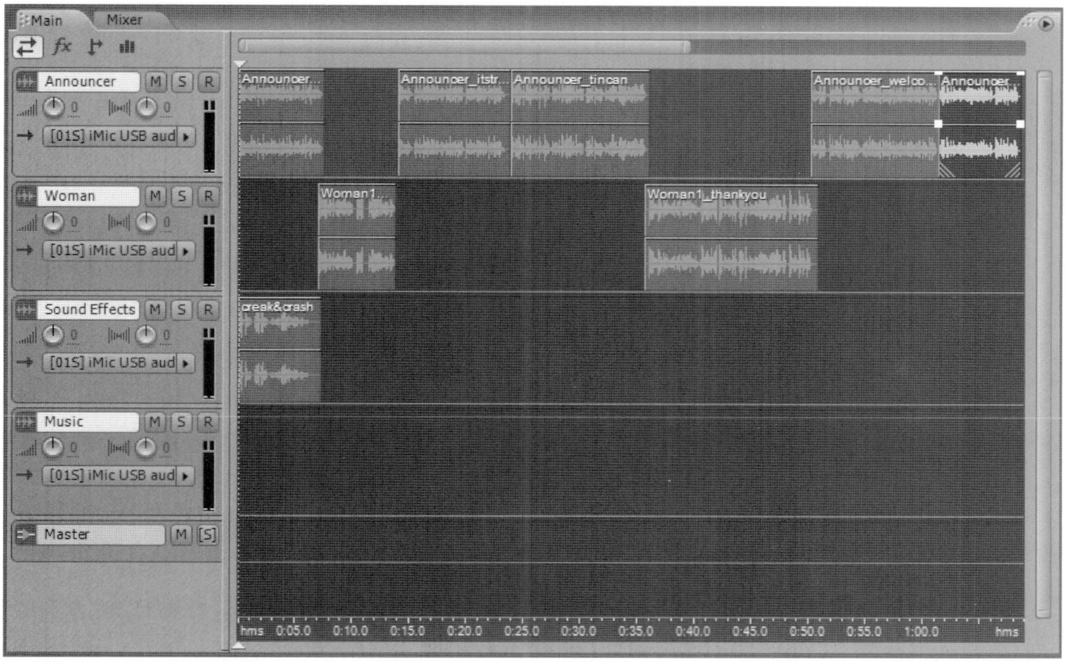

When the creaking chair sound effect stops at the 7 second mark, press the spacebar to stop playing the session. Playing the creaking chair sound effect over the voice-over may have seemed like a good idea, but in practice the two tracks are competing with each other. You will move the other files to the right of the creaking chair effect.

13 In the Multitrack View, with the Move/Copy tool still selected, place your cursor in the lower right corner of track 2. Click and drag up and to the left to create a marquee which selects all the clips within tracks 1 and 2. When all the clips within these two tracks are selected, release your mouse button.

You will now move all these selected clips to the right, such that the Announcer_intro clip begins playing when the creaking chair sound effect is about to finish.

14 Bring the start-time indicator to the 0:4.100 second mark. Click and drag all the selected clips to the right, making sure the beginning of the Announcer_intro clip is aligned with the start-time indicator.

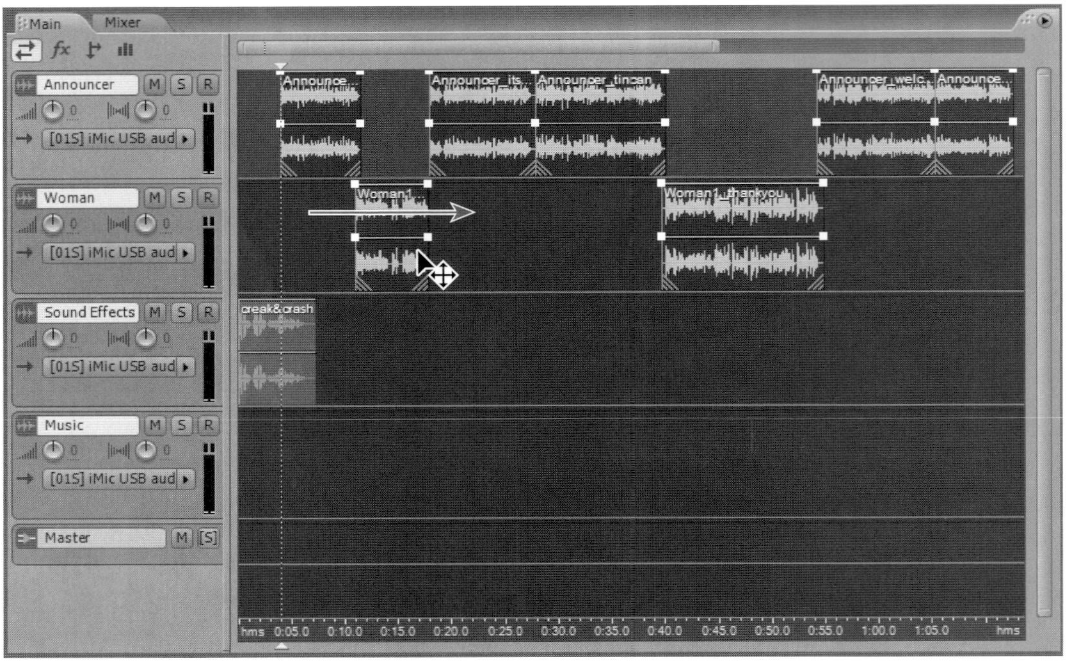

15 Press the Home key to place the start-time indicator at the beginning of the session. Press the spacebar to hear the effect of the changes you just made and press it again to stop playback. Click on the Zoom Out Full Both Axes button (). In your Selection/View panel toward the bottom of the display, note the overall length of the commercial is around 12 seconds longer than one minute. Our session length is 1:12, your numbers may differ slightly.

You will need to do some more editing in order to shorten the overall session length and make it fit into one minute.

16 Click once on an empty area in the multitrack to lose your current selection. Click and drag the start-time indicator to the beginning of the Announcer_tincan clip. If you need help in identifying a clip name, place your cursor over the various clips in the timeline and the full name of the clip appears in the status bar at the bottom of the display window. Press the spacebar and listen to the clip. When the clip is done, press the spacebar to stop playback.

17 Move the start-time indicator to 0:34.500 second mark and press the spacebar to play from this point. You will be near the announcer's phrase "But don't take my word for it, listen to what Jennifer Smith of Fargo, North Dakota has to say." If you hear this phrase cut off, or if you hear a part of the previous phrase, adjust the start-time indicator and press the spacebar again. Once you have located the beginning of this phrase, click the Time Selection tool ( ) and click and drag from the start-time indicator to the end of this clip to include this phrase into your selection.

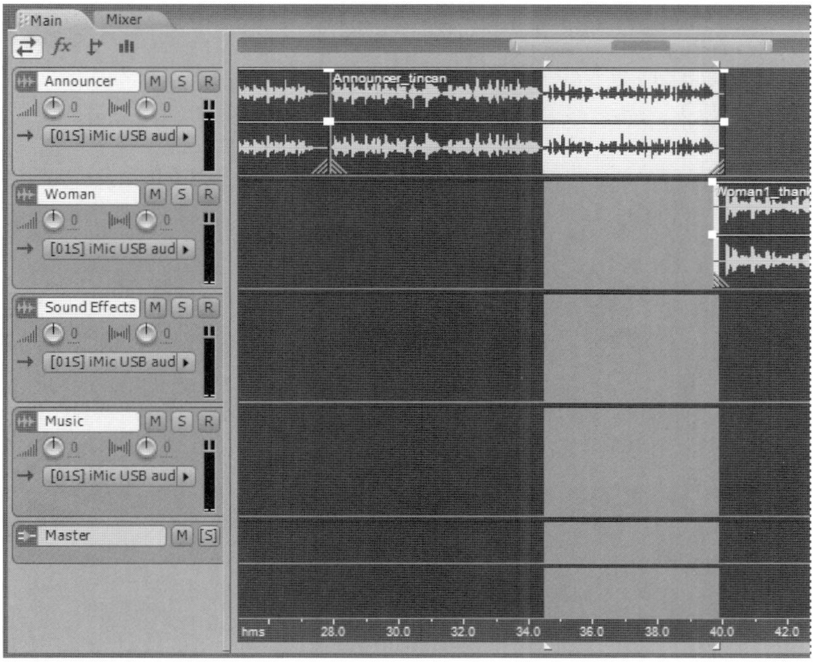

18 Choose Edit > Cut to remove this section from the multitrack. This removes the phrase contained in the selection but also creates a gap in your session. While this feature might be useful for some occasions, right now you want to cut down the total time of the session as well.

19 Press Ctrl+Z or choose Edit > Undo to undo the last action. Your previous selection becomes visible again. Choose Edit > Insert/Delete Time > Delete Selected Time and press OK.

The selection is cut and in addition, the rest of the session automatically moves to the left to fill up the resulting gap. This helps you to cut down the total time of the session without having to manually relocate each clip to the right of the gap in order to fill up the gap that results from Edit > Cut.

20 Place your cursor at the beginning of the next clip, Woman1_thankyou.wav. Highlight the entire clip from beginning to end by clicking and dragging across the clip. Click the Zoom to Selection button ( ) to view the entire waveform in the display window.

21 Press the spacebar to listen to the clip. You will be deleting the phrase "I've gone though several cell phone companies and none of them lived up to my expectations." Place your start-time indicator at approximately the 39 second mark and press the spacebar. The phrase you want to keep is "SkyCellTell has the best reception, best price, best customer service of any company I've ever known. Thank you SkyCellTell!" You may need to move your start-time indicator and press the spacebar a few times until you find the correct location.

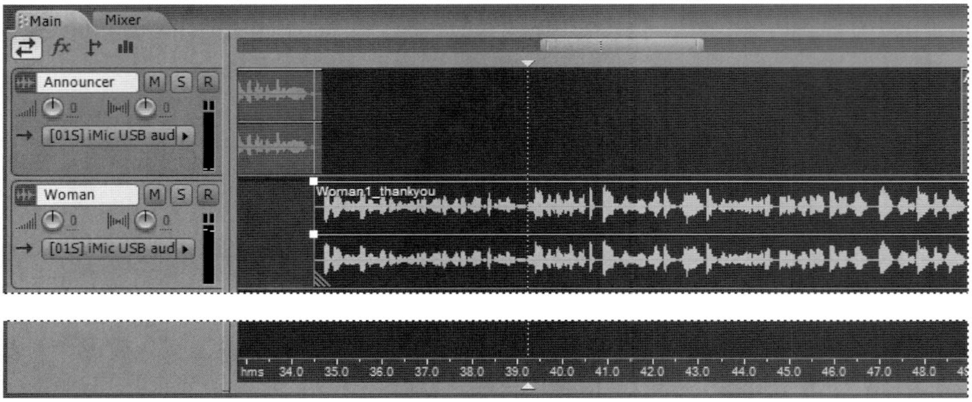

22 Once you have located the phrase, click the handle at the bottom left corner of the Woman1_thank you clip and drag it to the right until it aligns with the start-time indicator. This cuts the first phrase and shortens the clip.

When used with looped files, the handles on the bottom left and right of the clips repeat and extend music loops. On standard audio clips, the handles are still useful. If you cut too much off the beginning or end of a clip you can drag the handles to restore portions of the original audio.

23 Click the Zoom Out Full Both Axes button ( ). Your session should now fit in approximately 1 minute and 7 seconds. Using the Move/Copy Clip tool ( ), manually shift each clip so that there is the least amount of gap between them and the resulting session sounds as natural as possible.

In order to move several clips at once, Shift+click on the clips and drag them to the left or right. Align the beginning of the clip Woman1_thankyou.wav with the end of clip Announcer_tincan.wav.

24 Press the Home key to return the start-time indicator to the beginning of the session. Press the Play button to listen to the entire commercial. If there still are any obvious gaps between clips, use the Move/Copy Clip tool to adjust the position of clips as necessary.

Using the Delete Silence command

Removing some content from your commercial got you closer to the 1 minute mark, but the length of the session is still a few seconds too long. You will now use Audition's capability of automatically deleting the silence between words and phrases.

1 Double-click on the clip Woman1_cantbelieve.wav in your Files panel. This opens the file and displays the waveform in the Edit View. Press the spacebar to hear the clip. The actor's delivery includes a pause between words, visible as valleys in the waveform. The Delete Silence command automatically removes multiple areas of silence within a clip.

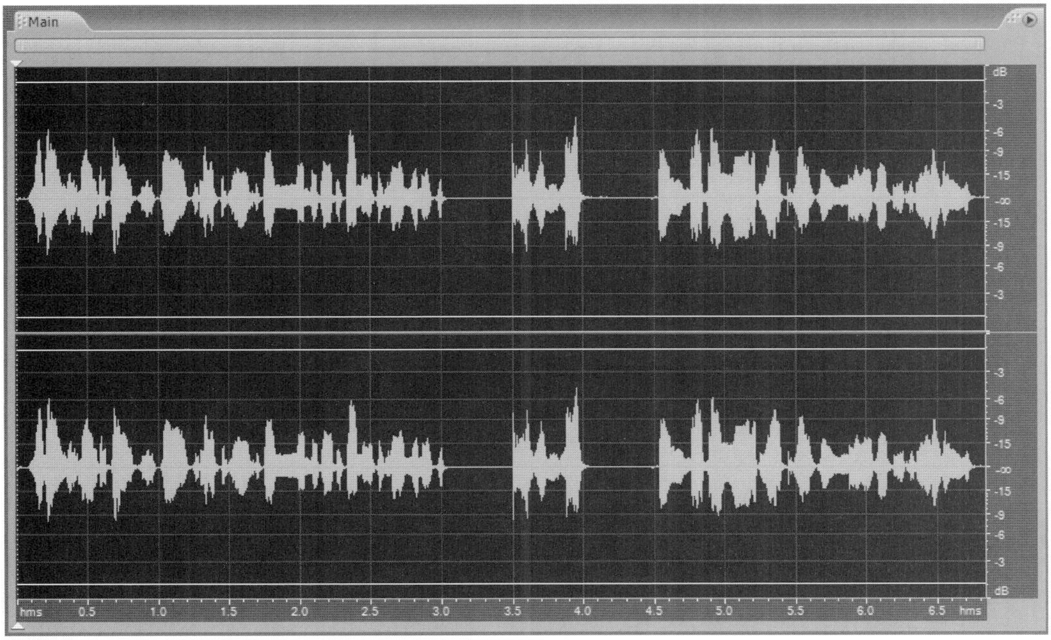

2 Choose Edit > Delete Silence and the Delete Silence window opens. In the Delete Silence window, click the Find Levels button. Audition scans the waveform for areas which it considers silence.

Applying the Delete Silence command analyzes and deletes silence across the entire waveform by default. You can also make a selection before choosing the command to impact only a specified portion of the waveform.

3 Click the Scan for Silence Now button. Audition previews the scanned area and gives you an approximation of how much silence will be deleted. For this waveform, the results should be slightly more than one-quarter of one second (0.28). Click the OK button.

4 Press the Play button or use the spacebar on your keyboard to hear the edited clip. You should notice the phrase is shorter, but there are still gaps between the words. Press Ctrl+Z to undo the Delete Silence. Click once in waveform to clear any selection and press the Home key. You will modify the default settings to remove more of the gaps between the words.

5 Choose Edit > Delete Silence. Click the Find Levels button. In the Silence field, change -64 dB to **-54 dB**. In the Audio field, change –59.4 dB to **-49.4 dB**.

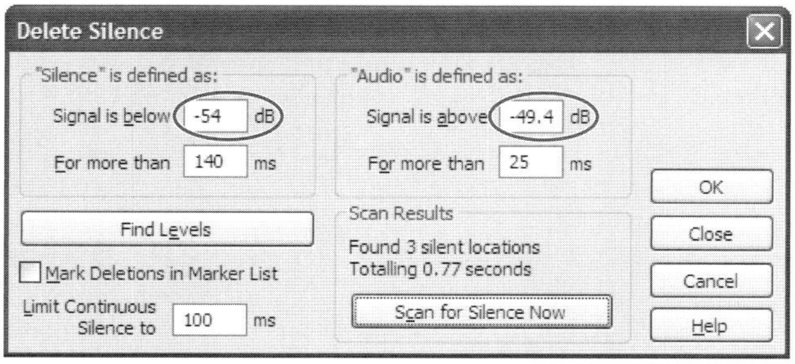

6 Click the Scan for Silence Now button. Audition will locate more silence as you broaden the definition it used when locating silent portions of the waveform. Using the values you entered in step 5, Audition should locate additional silent locations and remove approximately three-quarters of one second. We removed .77 seconds in 3 locations. Click OK and then click the Play button to hear the new waveform. There should be a very minimal pause between the words.

To better hear the difference between the two clips, press Ctrl+Z to undo the Delete Silence command and play the clip. Redo the Delete Silence by pressing Shift+Ctrl+Z. Listen carefully to the clip and make sure that none of the vocals have been cut. If you find that words or parts of words are being cut, you should undo the command and adjust the parameters for the audio and the silence levels. In general, if words or phrases are chopped off, you should lower the signal level values. If not enough silence is removed, increase the signal level values.

7 Choose File > Save As. Enter the name **Woman1_cantbelieve(edited).wav**.

Because the Delete Silence command is performed in the Edit View, the changes are destructive. By choosing Save As and renaming the file, you maintained a copy of your original audio in case you need it later. If you are prompted about overwriting an existing file of the same name, choose Yes to confirm your decision.

8 Click the Multitrack View button ( ) and note that within the Woman track, the previous clip has been replaced with the new Woman1_cantbelieve(edited).wav. Deleting silence from a clip has the desired effect of making the clip shorter; however you will now need to adjust the subsequent clips to avoid gaps between the voices.

9 Choose the Move/Copy Clip tool ( ). Shift+click to select the five clips to the right of the Woman1_cantbelieve(edited) clip. Drag the clips to the left, aligning the start of the Announcer_itstrue.wav clip with the end of the Woman1_cantbelieve(edited) clip. You can use the Snap to Clips snapping option to help align the clips.

10 Click on the Zoom Out Full Both Axes button ( ). Note the overall length of the session in your Selection/View controls, the length should read approximately 1:01.

You will now be using the Time Stretching feature of Audition to reduce the length of the last clip in the Announcer track, (Announcer_terms.wav), from 5 seconds to around 4 seconds.

11 Click on a gray area in the multitrack to lose your current selection, and then click on the last clip in the Announcer track, (Announcer_terms.wav) to select it. Choose View > Enable Clip Time Stretching.

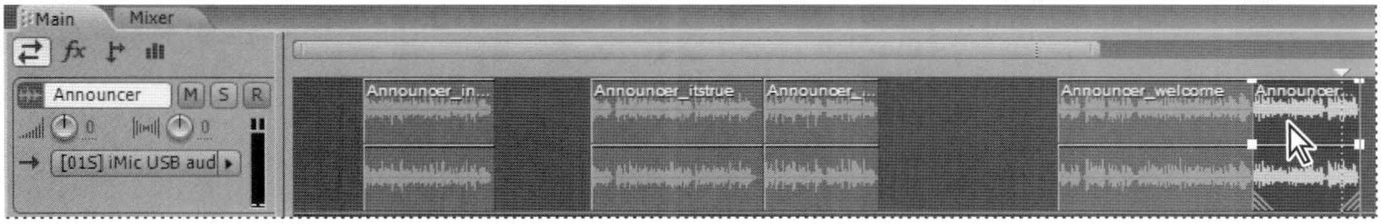

12 Move the start-time indicator to the 1 minute mark in the timeline. On the right side of the Announcer_terms clip, select the handle and drag until the end of the clip snaps to the start-time indicator. A clock icon appears on the clip to show you that it has been time-stretched.

When you took your cursor near the bottom right handle of clip, the cursor changed to the time stretch icon ( ). Normally, when time stretching is not enabled, moving this handle to the left would have determined how much of the contents of the clip are played. In case of loops, you could have dragged this handle to the right to create more repetitions. But now, since you enabled the time stretching option for this clip, when you move the handle of a clip using the time stretch tool, you will actually stretch or shrink the time that this clip takes to play. When you do so, a pop-up readout appears telling you the percentage of time stretching that will take place and the new duration of the clip. Like other features in Multitrack View, time stretching is nondestructive, so you can remove this feature from a clip by dragging the handle back to stretch it to 100% time. For most occasions, it's best to keep the Time Stretching feature disabled so that it doesn't interfere with your routine editing work. As a shortcut, you can hold down the Ctrl key while dragging a clip's handle to force time stretching for a clip.

What is Time Stretching?

Time stretching lets you change the length of an audio clip without changing its pitch. This technique is particularly helpful for fitting audio clips to video scenes or layering clips for sound design. You can time stretch a clip either by dragging or by setting time stretch properties. When you time stretch by dragging, Adobe Audition analyzes a clip's contents and attempts to select the most natural-sounding time stretch method. When you set properties for time stretching using Clip > Clip Time Stretch Properties, you also specify the method of time stretching to use.

Time stretching changes the tempo of a clip. If you time stretch a loop-enabled clip, it won't match the session tempo.

13 With the Announcer_terms clip still selected from the previous step, select View > Enable Clip Time Stretching again to disable this option. Press the Home key on your keyboard to return the Play cursor to the beginning of the session and then press the spacebar to review your edits to the commercial.

Using bus effects

You can route the outputs of several tracks into a special type of a track called a "bus." A bus helps you to process several tracks together, and manage them more easily. For example, in the following exercise, you are going to route the output of the Announcer track and the Woman track into a bus. You will also insert a Reverb effect into that bus. As a result, the reverb will be applied to the Announcer track as well as the Woman track because they use the same bus as their output.

Although you could insert the Reverb effect individually into the two tracks, sending them through the same bus track will save you time, especially if you decide to modify the effect. Additionally, this conserves your computer's processing power because you end up using just one instance of the Reverb effect instead of two. There are various ways in which a bus can be used, as you will be learning in the next lessons. In this lesson, you'll learn how it can be used to group tracks.

1 Click on the Mixer tab next to the Main tab to bring up the Mixer panel.

Note: ***By default, the Mixer tab is docked at this location. However, it is possible that you might have closed the Mixer in one of the previous lessons. If you don't see this tab for some reason, choose Window > Mixer. If the Mixer has been undocked and is currently an independent window, then you can grab it by its tab and drop it over the multitrack to dock it back to its default position. See Lesson 2, "Audition Basics" for details about docking and undocking windows.***

In the Mixer, you see the Announcer, Woman, Sound Effect, and the Music tracks corresponding to the four tracks used in the multitrack. You can also see a Master track on the right. Looking at each track from the top to bottom, you'll find the controls for the track's input, effects (fx), sends, EQ, automation, panning, track status, volume, and output. You can choose to show or hide some of these settings by clicking the Show/Hide Controls buttons (▷) near the left edge of the Mixer panel.

2 Click in an empty area within the strip for the Music track to make it the current track. The current track is distinguishable from the others by its lighter color. Select Insert > Bus Track to add a bus to your session.

A new bus track titled Bus A gets added to the right of the existing four tracks. Take a moment to note the physical differences of a bus track as compared to the other tracks. You'll find that a bus track does not have an input at the top. Secondly, it cannot be armed because the Arm for Record button (R) is absent. Its Solo button and fader are also different in appearance because they behave differently as compared to the other tracks.

3 Click the Title of Bus A and enter **Reverb Bus** as the new text.

4 Click on the Show/Hide Controls button (▷) for fx section, if it is not already showing fx inserts, to view the effects settings for your tracks.

You can see that currently none of the tracks have any effects inserted into them because all the slots in each Effects Rack are empty. You will now add a reverb to the Reverb Bus track.

5 Click in the FX Power button (⏻) in the Reverb Bus to switch it on. Just below it, click the black triangle for the first effect slot. Choose Delay Effects > Studio Reverb from the drop-down menu.

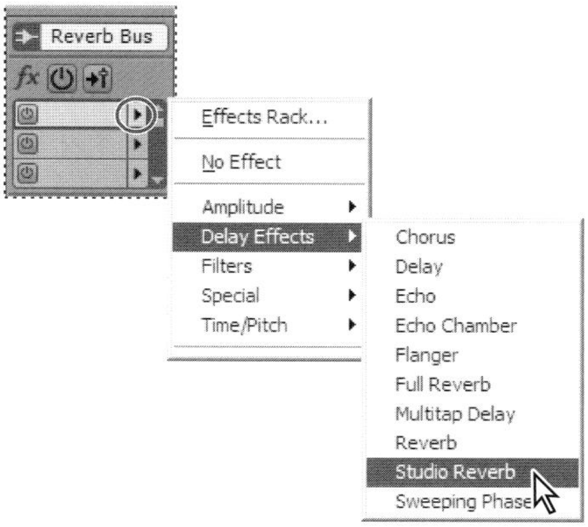

The Effects Rack window Reverb Bus opens up. On the left, you can still see the Effects Rack for the Reverb Bus. The Studio Reverb effect has been added to the first slot and its Power button has been turned on. On the right is the window for various settings pertaining to the Studio Reverb effect.

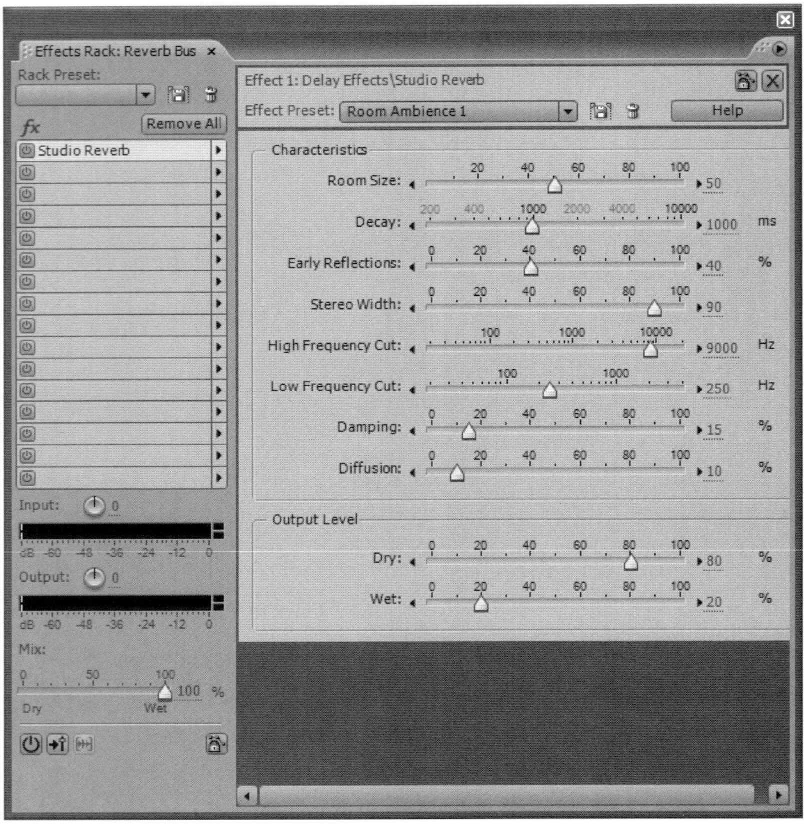

6 Click on the Effects Preset menu near the top of this window and choose Room Ambience 1 from the list of presets. Close the Effects Rack window by clicking the Close button (☒) on the top right of the window.

The Reverb effect has now been added to the Reverb Bus but you cannot hear it yet because none of the tracks is using this bus. You will now route the Announcer track to pass through the Reverb Bus.

7 All tracks are currently routed to the Master Bus. At the bottom of the Announcer track in the Mixer, click the black triangle to see the various possible output destinations for the Announcer track. From the context menu that opens, choose Reverb Bus.

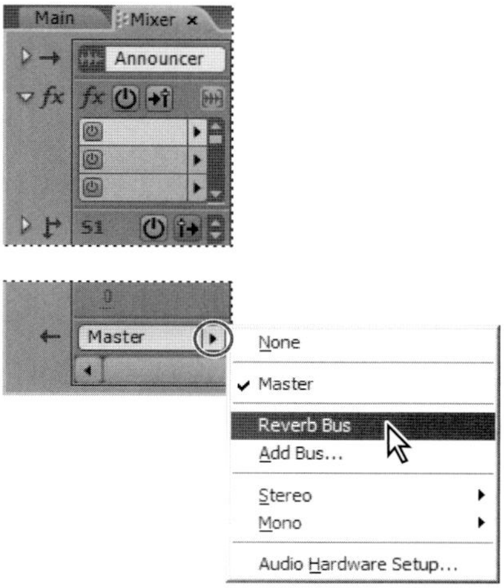

The Announcer track will now pass through the Reverb Bus that you created in the previous steps. Because you have already inserted the Studio Reverb effect to the Reverb Bus, this reverb will also be applied to all contents of the Announcer track.

8 Press the Home key to return the start-time indicator to the beginning of the session, click on the Main tab to view the multitrack, and press the spacebar to begin playing.

Note the difference between the Announcer's voice and the woman's voice. While the woman's voice seems dry, it seems that the Announcer is speaking from a spacious room. The Studio Reverb effect is responsible for this simulation. The Room Ambience 1 preset that you chose for this effect places the Announcer's voice inside a small room. Keep in mind that because the effects applied in the Multitrack View are non-destructive in nature, the original clips in the Announcer track are not altered.

You will now route the Woman track to the Reverb bus in order to apply the reverb to its contents as well. But this time, you will make the routing changes in the multitrack itself, without using the Mixer.

9 If the session is still playing, press the spacebar to stop playback. Just below the Main tab, press the Input/Output button (⇄) to view the input and output settings of your tracks.

10 In the track properties for the Woman track, click on the menu next to the Output icon (←) and choose Reverb Bus as the output destination for this track. If you don't see this menu, you might have to resize the track vertically by clicking and dragging its border. Press the spacebar to play the session and hear the results.

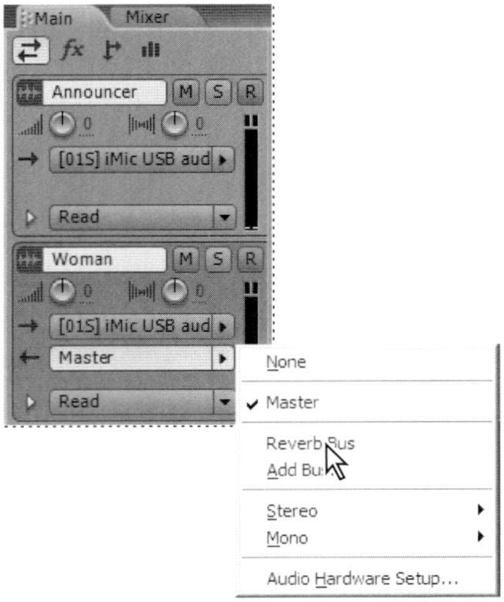

This menu is similar to the output menu you used in the Mixer in step 7 and it has exactly the same function.

Now that you have routed the Woman track to the Reverb Bus, the reverb will be applied to both the Announcer and the Woman tracks. A benefit of routing multiple tracks to a single bus is that changes made to the bus properties automatically affect all the tracks using the bus. You will hear this when you use the volume slider on the bus.

11 Click the Mixer tab again to view the Mixer. Press the spacebar to begin playing the session. Click on the golden volume slider for the Reverb Bus and drag it down to -6 dB. Both the Announcer and Woman tracks are affected because both of them use this bus as their output. Reducing the level of the bus by lowering the golden fader simultaneously reduces the levels of the Announcer and Woman tracks. Bring the golden volume slider back to 0 dB and press the spacebar to stop playing the session.

12 Make sure that the effects slots are visible in the Mixer. If not, use the Show/Hide Controls button (▷) for the fx section near the left edge of the Mixer panel to make them visible.

13 In the Effects Rack for Reverb Bus, the first slot has the Studio Reverb inserted into it. Click on the black triangle for this slot and choose Effects Rack from the menu. This action opens up the same Effects Rack window for Reverb Bus that you saw earlier.

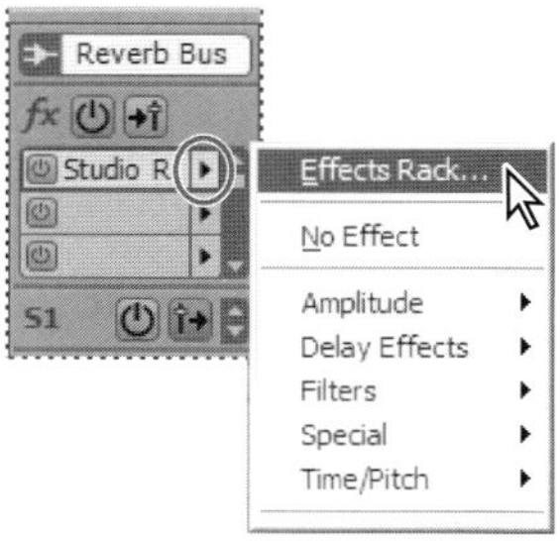

You can also double-click on the one of the slots to quickly open up the Effects Rack window for a track.

14 Press the spacebar to start playing the session. Right now there is more reverb being applied than is necessary. Near the bottom left of the Effects Rack window, click on the Mix slider and drag it to the 25% value. This reduces how much effect is applied.

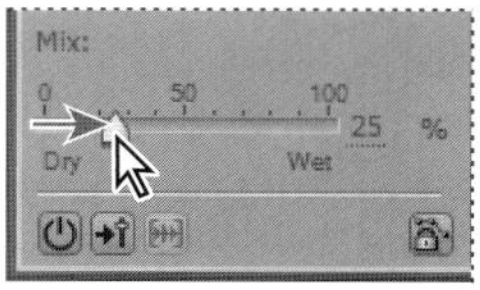

The Mix slider controls the balance between the original signal (dry) and the signal with effects applied to it (wet). Since you are just using one effect in this Effects Rack, the Mix slider determines the amount of reverb applied to the bus. This in turn affects the sound of the Announcer and the Woman tracks.

15 Close the Reverb Bus window and click on the Main tab to bring up the multitrack.

Adding effects and equalization

To add the finishing touches to your commercial, you will add an effect to the announcer's voice, add a music track, and then mix down the file.

1 In the Files panel, double-click the clip Announcer_tincan.wav to open it in the Edit View.

2 Choose the Time Selection tool (I), then click the waveform and drag to the right to create a selection that is 3.4 seconds long, starting at the beginning of the clip. This selects the phrase "Most cell phones sound like you're talking through a tin can..." Be certain that you do not include the remaining part of the sentence: "...With SkyCellTell it sounds like you're in the same room." If necessary you can adjust the selection by grabbing the yellow range marker and dragging it to the left or to the right.

3 Choose Effects > Filters > Quick Filter (process). The Quick Filter window opens.

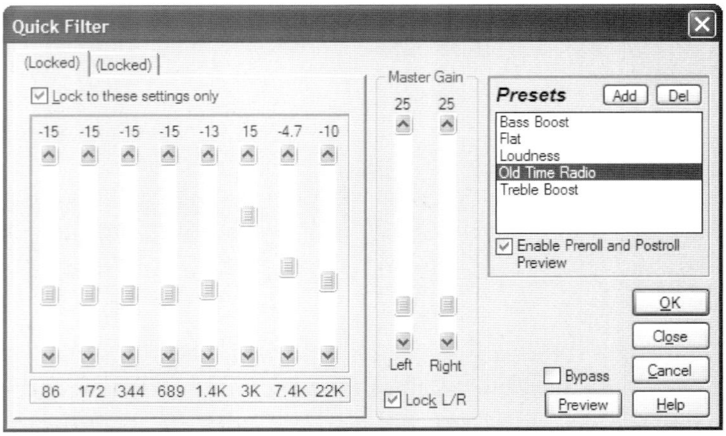

4 In the Quick Filter window, click to select the Old Time Radio preset. Check the Enable Preroll and Postroll Preview check box, if it is not already selected, and then click the Preview button. You will hear the phrase you selected take on a higher, tinnier tone. Because you have the Postroll Preview checked, you can also hear a second of unaltered audio after the end of the selection, allowing you to compare the effect of the Old Time Radio filter. Press the Stop button to stop playing the selection.

Quick Filter effect (Edit View only)

The Filters > Quick Filter effect is an 8-band graphic equalizer that you can easily customize to suit many filtering needs. Unlike a standard graphic equalizer, settings for the individual frequency bands interact with nearby frequencies. For example, significantly boosting the level of the highest 22 kHz frequency band moderately boosts the level of lower frequencies. This behavior helps you to quickly and easily enhance audio tone.

—From Adobe Audition Help

5 In the settings for Master Gain, check to select the box for Lock L/R. Increasing the EQ frequencies often increases the volume of the waveform as well. Locking the Left and Right Gain ensures that we are reducing the volume of the left and right channels equally.

6 Click the Preview button to hear the selection again. The clipping of the audio is noticeable as a crackling noise at the highest levels of the waveform. Grab the left slider and drag it down to a lower value, and listen until you no longer hear the crackling noise. We used a value of 25. Click the OK button to commit the effect. Note the changes to the selected part of the waveform.

7 Click on the Multitrack View button ( ). Press the Home key to return the start-time indicator to the beginning of the session and then move your start-time indicator 20 seconds into the session. Press the spacebar to play the session from the 20 second point forward.

Remember that effects made to a file in the Edit View are destructive, although the changes do not impact the file until it is saved. If you need to make a change to an effect, return to Edit View, undo the effect and apply it again using different settings.

8 Double-click the Announcer_tincan.wav clip to return to the Edit View. Select File > Save As to open the Save As window. Enter a name for this file **Announcer_tincan_edited.wav**. Click Yes if asked to overwrite a file of the same name.

9 Switch to the Multitrack View by pressing the Multitrack View button (). Move the start-time indicator to 2.2 seconds in the timeline. From the Files panel, drag the audio file SkyCellTell_theme.wav into the track named Music. Align the beginning of the clip with the start-time indicator. If necessary, use Snap to Clips to align this clip.

Note: *If you do not have the SkyCellTell_theme clip in your Files panel, you will need to import it from the AA_07 folder by choosing File > Import.*

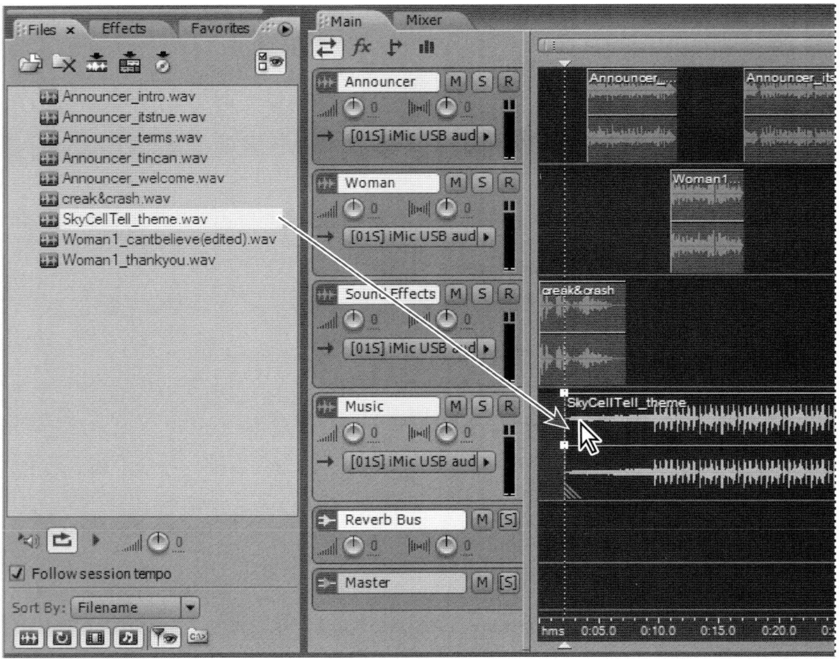

10 Press the Home key to return the play cursor to the beginning of the session. Press the spacebar to play the commercial. The music track was designed to be background music, but its sound levels are competing with the vocals. Press the spacebar to stop playing the session. Choose Window > Mixer to bring up the Mixer panel, or click the Mixer tab.

11 Press the spacebar to begin playing the session. In the Mixer panel, click on the golden slider for Reverb Bus and drag it up to 2.5 dB.

This step makes the Announcer and the Woman tracks slightly louder because you connected them to this bus earlier in the lesson. Note that the volume sliders for all other tracks are set at 0 dB. All the Pan knobs are set at their center positions too. You will now change the panning positions of the Announcer and Woman tracks.

12 Click on the Pan knob for Announcer track and drag to the left, setting a value of -32. This places the Announcer's voice slightly to the left of center in the stereo field.

13 Click on the Pan knob for the Woman track and drag to the right, setting a value of 32. This places the Woman's voice slightly to the right in the stereo field. Placing the two voices in opposite directions in the stereo field creates depth, and adds to the illusion of a conversation.

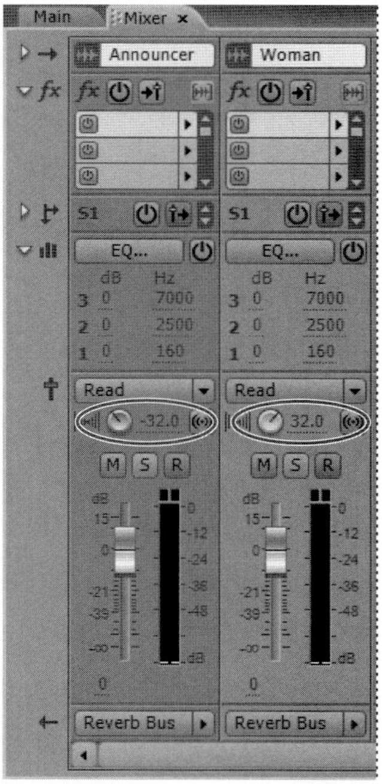

14 Click on the Main tab to bring up the multitrack.

15 Select File > Save Session.

16 Now you will mix down from 4 tracks to 1 track with 2 channels. Choose File > Export > Audio Mix Down. The Export Audio Mix Down window appears.

In the Mix Down options on the right, choose Master as the source, Entire Session as the range, 32 bit as Bit Depth. Choose Stereo in the box for Channels. Check the Embed Edit Original link data option. This will allow other Adobe programs, such as Premiere Pro, to link to this file. Check the Insert Mixdown Into option and choose Edit View in its menu.

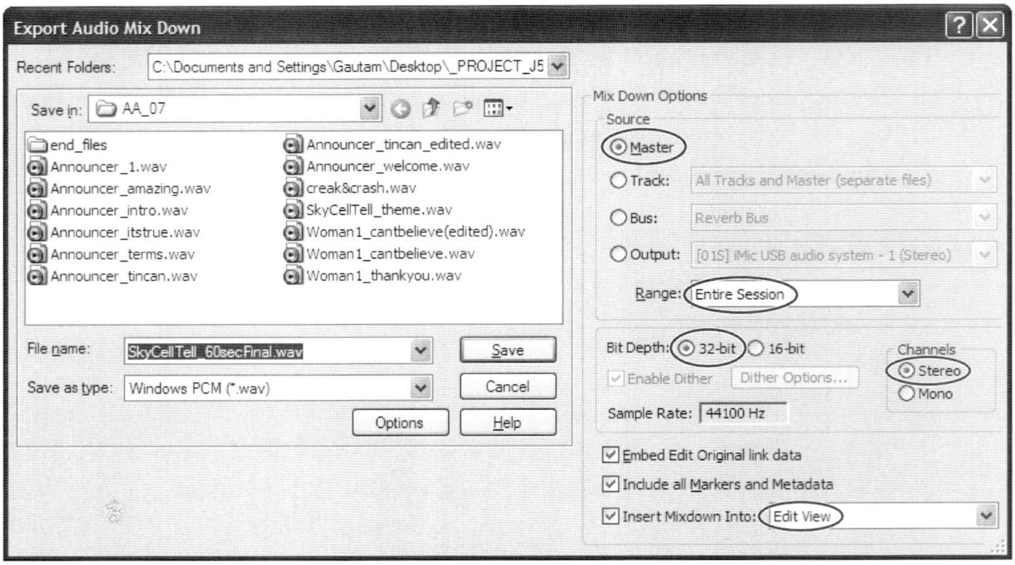

17 In the field for File name, enter **SkyCellTell_60secFinal.wav** and click the Save button. Audition takes a moment to export this session into a stereo file and, when done, it adds it to the Edit View.

18 You have now completed this lesson. Press the spacebar to preview the finished file.

Exploring on your own

1 Perform the Delete Silence on the remaining clips in the multitrack. The Announcer_itstrue.wav still has a silence between the first and second phrases.

2 Add a new bus and apply a different effect, such as Chorus or Echo, to it. Experiment with combining the two buses and layering the effects.

3 Using the Mixer, mix the session using different settings. Experiment with different levels for the two vocal tracks as well as the music track. Experiment with the pan levels.

Review

Review questions

1 What is the Delete Silence command and when is it used?

2 What is a bus and what are the advantages of using a bus?

3 When and how is the Mixer used?

Review answers

1 Delete Silence is found in the Edit menu of the Edit View. It is used to automatically delete areas of silence in an audio wave. It has the effect of speeding up your audio by reducing the pauses between words. Too much deletion of silence can result in audio which sounds artificial and can even delete words or phrases if not used properly.

2 There are various ways to use a bus. In this lesson, you learned to send the signals of two or more audio tracks into a bus. This allows you to add a single effect to the bus and have it applied to all the tracks that use the bus. A bus can also be used to control the panning, volume, and other track settings of multiple tracks.

3 The Mixer is accessed via Window > Mixer. It can also be docked into the Audition interface. Although volume, pan and effects can be controlled in the multitrack, controlling the tracks with the Mixer is useful when you have multiple tracks.

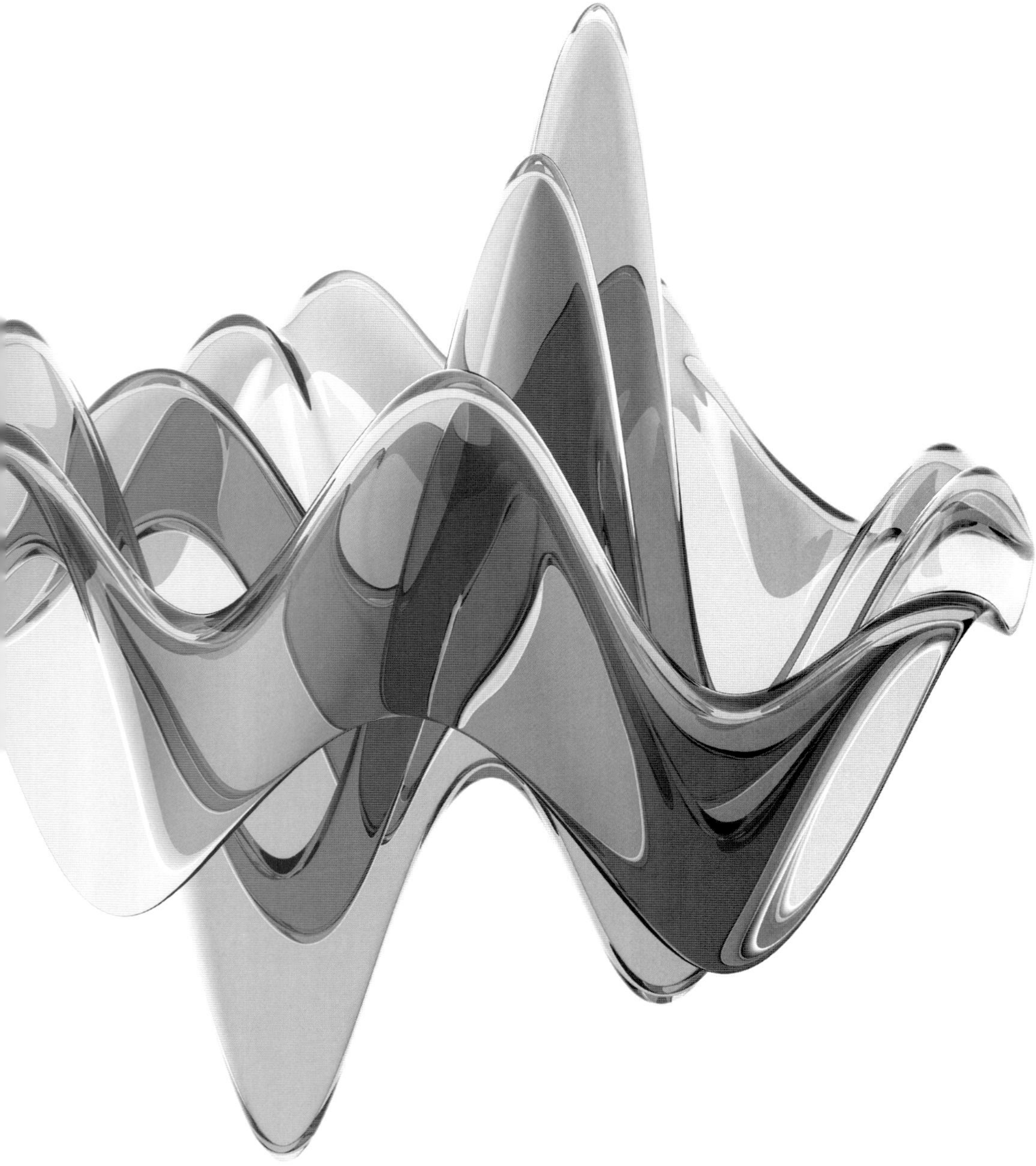

8 Mixing and Real-Time Effects

Audition provides a visual interface for mixing and applying effects for added control of your tracks. You can also conduct real-time effects processing using Audition's Multitrack View.

In this lesson, you will learn how to do the following:

- Use real-time effects as insert effects.
- Use the Effects Rack for a track to view and set effect parameters.
- Save your own effect presets and rack presets.
- Use the buses and sends for applying effects.

Getting started

In this lesson, you will learn how to use Adobe Audition's real-time effects from the Multitrack View. This method allows you to add effects to a track without altering the original clips contained within the track.

You saw in the earlier lessons that when you apply effects to a file in the Edit View, they physically alter the file. This is called destructive effects processing. On the other hand, the effects you apply in the Multitrack View do not alter the original waveforms. This type of effects processing is non-destructive.

1 Start Adobe Audition and switch to the Multitrack View, if it is not already selected, by pressing the Multitrack View button ( ).

2 If you have not already copied the resource files for this lesson onto your hard disk from the AA_08 folder from the *Adobe Audition 2.0 Classroom in a Book* CD, do so now. See "Copying the Classroom in a Book files" on page 2.

3 Choose File > Open Session, and open the 08_Start.ses file in the AA_08 folder, which is located in the AA_CIB folder on your hard disk. Press the spacebar to begin playback.

This is a short blues progression with lead guitar, piano, and drums. No effects have been applied to these tracks yet, so there's no sense of spaciousness in this session.

In this lesson, you will learn how to use various real-time effects on these tracks to make this session sound 'live,' as if the sounds were taking place in a hall.

4 Choose File > Save Session As. Name the file **08_Effects.ses**, and save it in the AA_08 folder on your hard disk.

5 To play the finished session file, choose File > Open Session, and open the 08_End.ses file in the AA_08 folder, which is located within the AA_CIB folder on your hard disk. Play the session file by either clicking on the Play button (▶) in the Transport panel or pressing the spacebar on your keyboard.

6 When you are ready to start working, close the 08_end.ses file by choosing File > Close All, and reopen the 08_Effects.ses file you just saved by selecting File > Open Session.

7 Press the Mute buttons (M) for the piano and drum tracks to mute them. You will be focusing on the guitar track for the following exercises.

Applying real-time effects in Multitrack View

You will now use two effects on the guitar track by accessing its Effects Rack. You will modify the settings of these effects and save your changes as presets that can be re-used later.

1 In the Multitrack View, press the FX button (fx) at the top to view the effects settings for the Blues Lead Guitar track.

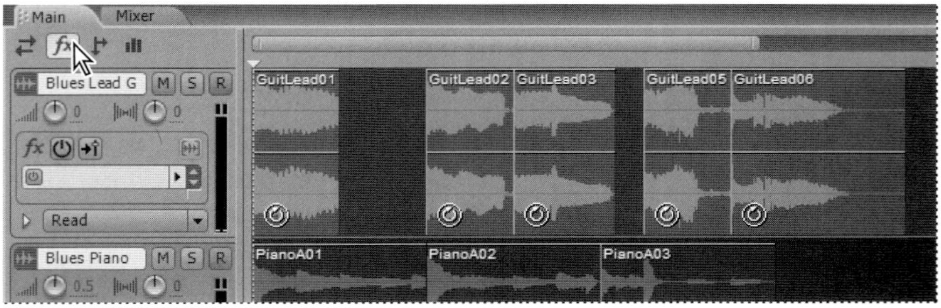

2 Bring your cursor over the separator between the Blues Lead Guitar track and the Blues Piano track until it changes to the (‡) shape. Click on the separator and drag downwards until you can see at least the first four slots for the Effects Rack for the Blues Lead Guitar track.

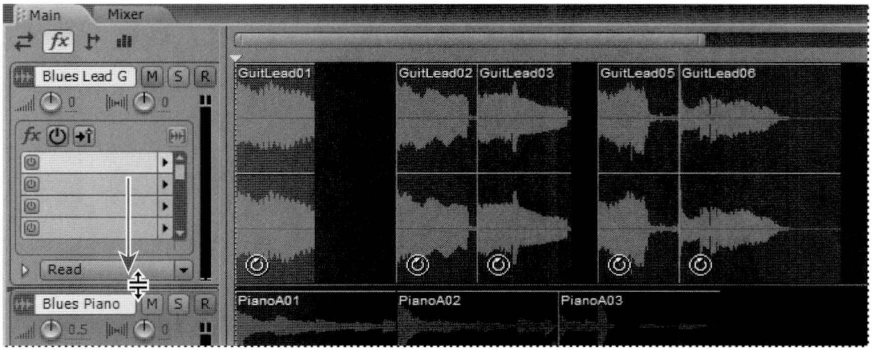

3 Click on the FX Power button (⏻) for the Lead Guitar track to turn it on.

4 In the first effect slot for the guitar track, click on the black triangle at the right to open up a categorized list of various effects that can be inserted into this slot. From this menu, choose Chorus from the Delay Effects category.

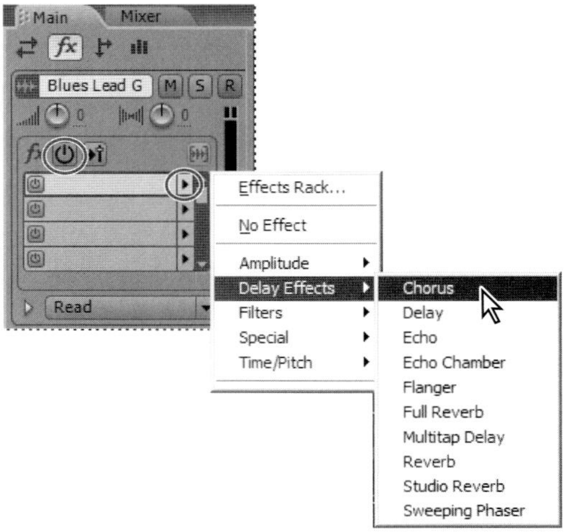

A new window called 'Effects Rack: Blues Lead Guitar' opens up and shows you that the Chorus effect has been inserted as the first effect in the Effects Rack for this track. On the right side, this window shows the various settings and controls that are available for this Chorus effect.

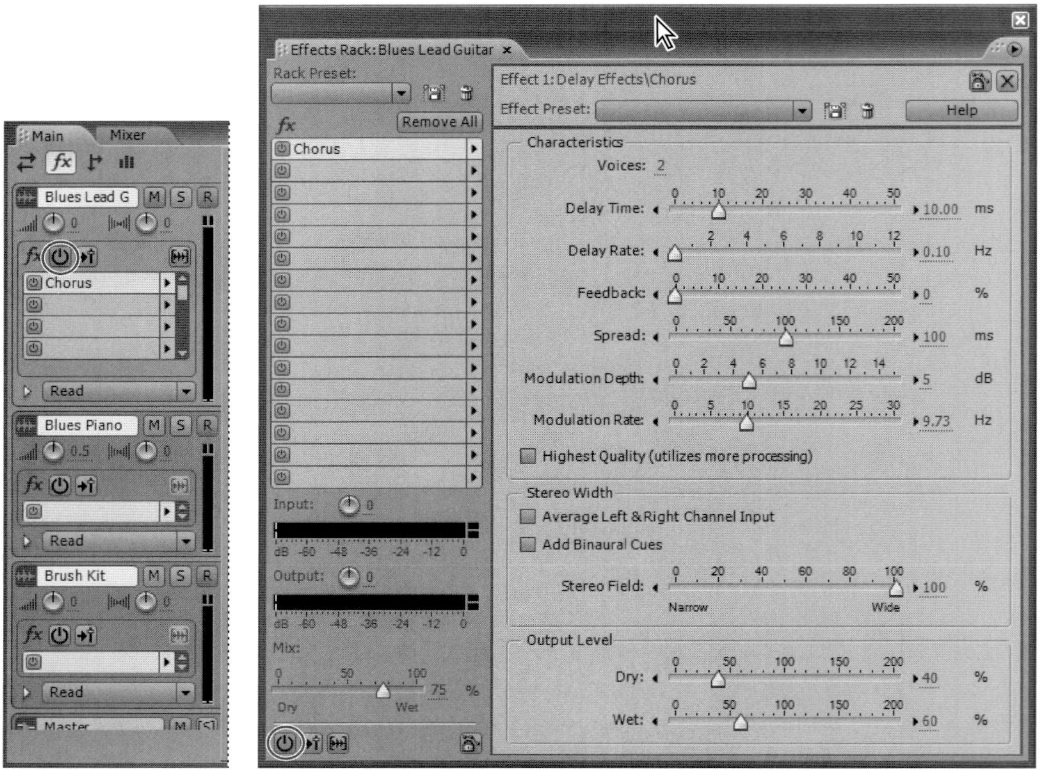

5 Click on the top of this window and drag it so that you can also see the track properties of the Blues Lead Guitar track in the underlying multitrack.

Note the similarities between the rack shown in the Effects Rack window and the one that appears in the Multitrack View. The small Power button ( ) for the Chorus effect has been turned on in both, and so is the bigger button ( ) for the power to the entire Effects Rack.

6 Click on the Effects Preset menu at the top of the settings for the Chorus effect and choose the Rich Chorus preset.

7 Press the spacebar to hear how the guitar track sounds with the Rich Chorus effect. Let the playback continue for a few seconds. While the session is still playing, click on the small Power button to the left of the Chorus effect in the rack to turn it off. The sound of the track becomes thinner and less rich in comparison to when the Chorus effect was on. Switch on the Chorus effect again and note the difference in the sound.

The Chorus effect gives an illusion of doubling up the instruments and results in a fuller, richer sound.

8 At the bottom of the settings for the Chorus effect, in the box for Output Level, click on the Wet slider and raise it to 60%. Click on the Dry slider above it and lower it to 40%.

Note: *This is not the Mix wet/dry slider found on the left, but the one which appears at the bottom of chorus settings in the frame for Output Level.*

In effect terminology, the original signal without any effects applied to it is known as the 'dry' signal. The signal to which the effect has already been applied is known as the 'wet' signal. The Rich Chorus preset initially had a combination of 50% wet and 50% dry signal. When you raised the amount of wet signal to 60%, the total level of the signal also rises to 110%. It is a good practice to maintain the level at which you had initially started working with a track. Excessive addition of the wet signal to the dry signal can raise the level of the track and cause clipping in extreme cases.

9 Near the bottom left of the Effects Rack window, click on the Mix slider and set it at a value of 80%. This slider controls the wet/dry balance of all the effects used in a rack, not just the Chorus effect—more on this later. If you see the level meters clipping, lower the track volume using the Volume knob in the track properties. If you just see clipping in the output meter above the mix slider, then set it to a lower level. For more information about clipping, see Adobe Audition Help.

10 Press the spacebar to stop playback and close the Effects Rack window by clicking on the red Close button (☒) at its top right.

Inserting more effects into the Effects Rack

You will often need to use multiple effects on the same track to get sound you are looking for. Audition lets you 'chain' several effects together by inserting them into the successive slots of a track's Effects Rack. Multiple real-time effects can be used together on the same track. The effects can be re-ordered to alter the sonic texture of a file or saved as a preset and used in another track. You will now add a Reverb effect in the second effect slot for the guitar track.

1 In the Multitrack View, double-click on the next empty slot in the Effects Rack for the guitar track to re-open its Effects Rack window.

2 Toward the left side of this window, click on the black triangle for the next empty slot in the rack and choose Delay Effects > Studio Reverb.

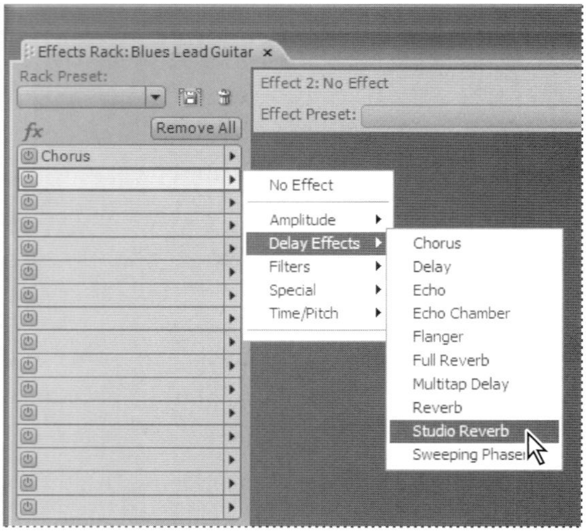

The Studio Reverb effect gets added to the rack as the second effect. Its Power button has been turned on and the settings pertaining to this effect appear on the right. Adding reverb to the track gives it a sense of space and makes it seem that the sound is occurring in a room or a hall.

3 Click on the Effect Preset menu in the settings for the Studio Reverb and, if necessary, choose the Guitar Amp Verb (stereo) preset. Press the spacebar to hear the result of the reverb. Press the spacebar again to stop the playback, then press the Home key. Drag the Wet slider to 100% and press the spacebar to hear how the sound is affected at this extreme setting. Press the spacebar to stop the playback, and press the Home key. Drag the Wet slider back and set it at 30%. Set the Dry slider above it to 70%.

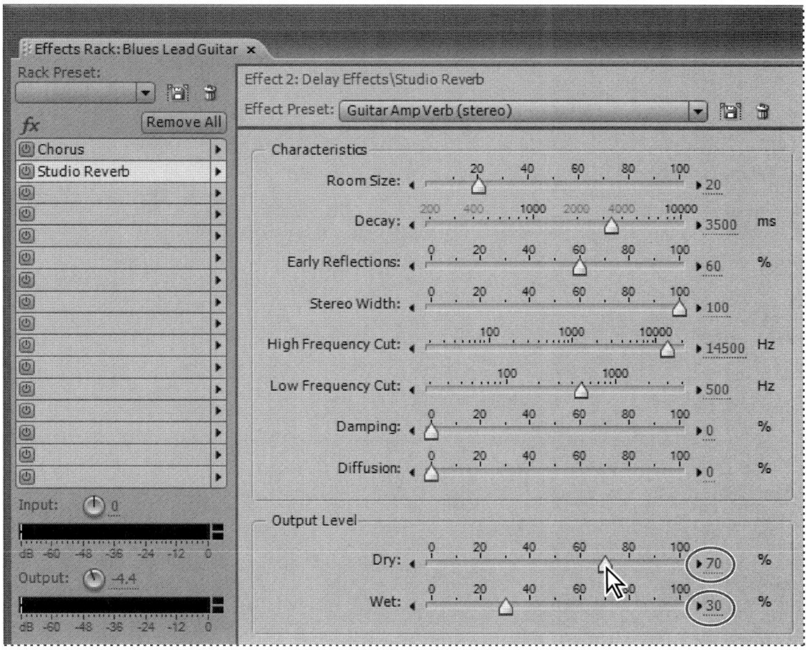

You can also click on the blue numbers that appear next to a slider or knob to type in an exact value. Within the Audition environment, wherever you see such numbers in blue font, you can actually scrub them by clicking and dragging to a desired value, or simply type in the value.

4 Click once on the slot for chorus in the rack. The right part of the screen switches to show you the settings of the chorus. Drag the slider for Delay Time to 10 ms. Click once on the number next to the Voices setting and enter **2**. Click on the Studio Reverb slot to see the settings for reverb again.

When you add another effect to the effect chain, settings of the previous one generally need to be modified. And when you go ahead and modify them, the other effect might need re-adjustment. Audition gives you the ability to quickly view the settings for any effect in the rack by just clicking on it. This is an extremely handy feature and can save you a lot of time while working with tracks that use multiple effects.

Saving effect presets and rack presets

You will now save the current settings of each of the Chorus and Reverb effects as new presets. Presets allow you to instantly recall desired settings for an effect just like you did when you chose the Rich Chorus and Guitar Amp Verb (stereo) presets for the two effects respectively. Now that you have made modifications to these presets, you will learn to save your modifications in the form of new presets.

1 Click on the Chorus slot to view its settings again. Toward the top right, press the Save a new preset button () to save your current settings of the Chorus effect as a new preset.

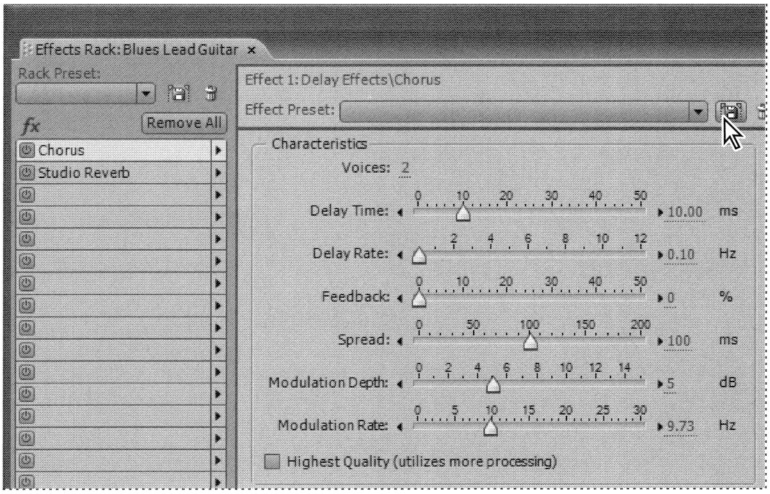

In the Add Preset dialog box that opens up, type **My Rich Chorus Preset** and press OK. Your new preset gets added to the list of available presets in the Effect Preset menu.

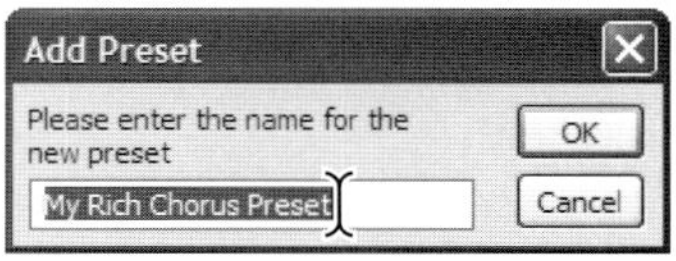

2 Click on the Studio Reverb slot to view its settings and similarly save its current state as a new preset called **My Guitar Amp Reverb Preset**.

3 Press the spacebar to start playback. Switch off the Chorus effect in the rack by clicking the Power button (⏻) to its left. This lets you hear just the Reverb effect applied to the track. Turn the Chorus effect back on by clicking on its Power button again.

4 Switch off the bigger Power button (⏻) at the bottom left of the rack to bypass all the effects simultaneously. When you do this, the individual Power buttons for all slots switch off automatically. Click on the main Power button to turn it on along with all effects within the rack.

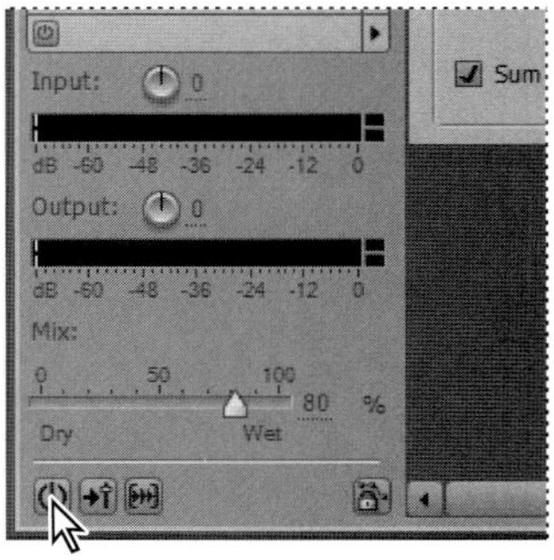

5 Just above the main Power button, click on the Mix Dry/Wet slider and drag it to the 75% level. This slider controls the overall balance between the original signal and the signal processed by the Effects Rack. When you lower this slider, the net effect of the chorus and the reverb is reduced together. Press the spacebar to stop playback.

Audition also lets you to save the entire rack as a preset that can later be used for other tracks. A rack preset saves all the effects that are being used in the rack, as well as their individual settings.

6 Click on the Save a new preset button (▣) directly above the rack in the Effects Rack window. In the following dialog box, type in **My Hall Rack Preset** and click OK. All the effects being used in the rack and their respective settings are saved when you save the rack preset. Now when you are working on other tracks or other sessions, you can instantly recall this specific combination of the Chorus and Reverb effects by choosing My Hall Rack Preset for that Effects Rack. Close the Effects Rack window.

Applying real-time effects using buses and sends

You could insert effects into the racks of the piano and drum tracks by following the same procedure described above. But when you need to use the same effect across many tracks, it becomes cumbersome to do so individually for each track. Moreover, it would be intensive for your computer to run multiple instances of the same effect.

You can instead choose to create a special type of a track called a bus, and insert the required effect(s) into it. Then you can send varying amounts of signal from other tracks to this bus. This way, when you hear the dry signal emerging from the track combined with the wet signal emerging from the bus, you would get similar results as you would have by inserting the effect individually. This method is much easier, faster, and requires just a single instance of that effect.

In the following steps, you will create a new bus and insert the My Hall Rack Preset into it. Then you will send different amounts of signal from the guitar, piano, and drum tracks to this bus.

1 If not already in the Main panel, click the Main tab. Make sure you can see the Effects Rack for the guitar track. In case you don't see it, use the FX button below the Main tab to view the effects settings. Adjust the height of the guitar track, if necessary, to make its Effects Rack visible.

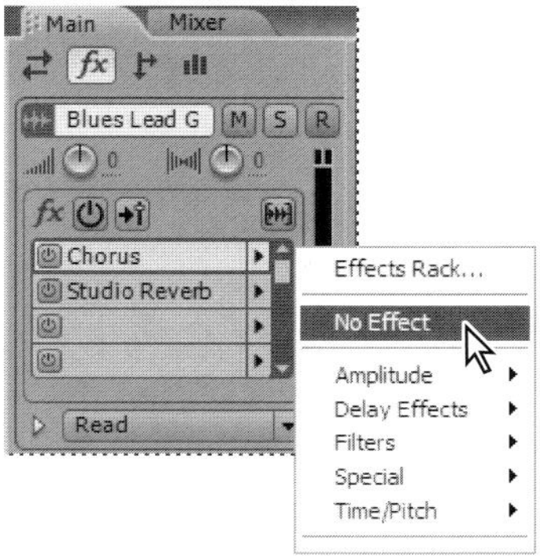

2 Remove the Chorus and Reverb effects that are currently inserted into this rack by clicking on the black triangle in their effect slots and choosing No Effect from the context menu.

When a lot of effects have been inserted into a track, you can quickly remove them all by right-clicking on an effect slot in the rack and choosing Remove All Effects from the context menu.

3 Press the Mixer tab to view the Mixer panel, or choose Window > Mixer. You will see the mixer strips for the guitar, piano, and drum tracks. Looking from top to bottom for each track, you find the sections for input, effects, sends, equalization, automation, pan, track status, volume, and output.

4 Click on an empty area within the Brush Kit track to bring it into focus. You can tell that a track is in focus when its color is lighter than the other tracks.

5 Choose Insert > Bus Track from the menu at the top of your screen to add a bus next to the focused track.

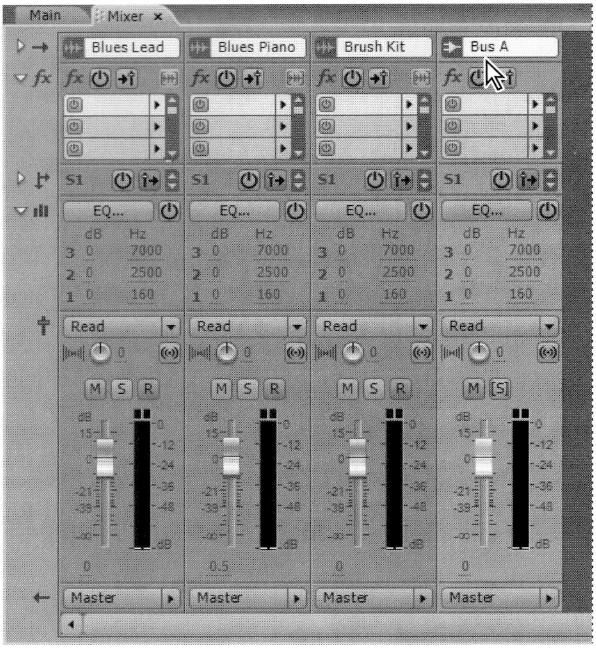

A new bus track called Bus A gets added to the right of the drum track. If some other track was in focus, this bus would have been inserted right next to it. You can always reorder the tracks in the Mixer by grabbing the ( ) or ( ) icon next to the track name at the top and dragging to the left or right. It is a common practice to keep all your tracks together on one side and your buses together on the other.

6 Click on the black triangle in the first effect slot in Bus A and choose Effects Rack from the context menu to open up the Effects Rack for this bus.

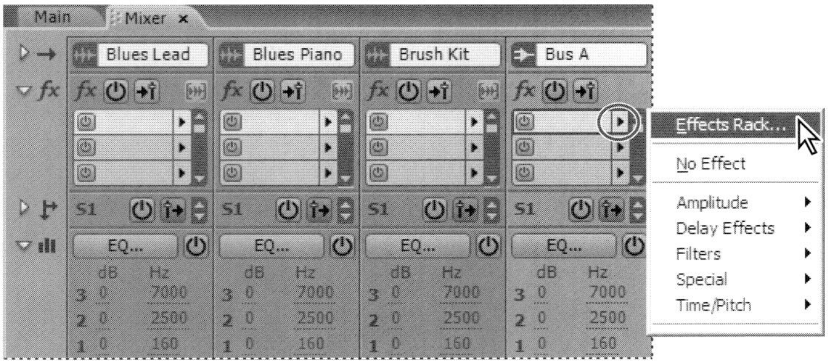

The Effects Rack window opens. Click on the Rack Preset menu at the top left of this window and choose My Hall Rack Preset from this menu. This is the same rack preset containing your custom Reverb and Chorus effect settings that you saved in the previous steps.

The My Hall Rack Preset gets loaded into the rack with its Chorus and Reverb effects. The Power buttons for these individual effects have been turned on for you and so is the main Power button for the Effects Rack.

7 Close the Effects Rack window to return to the Mixer panel.

8 Click on the Show/Hide Send Controls button (▷) found near the left edge of the Mixer. This gray triangle expands or collapses the Send controls in between the FX and EQ sections for the Mixer. If necessary, collapse the EQ section to make your Mixer look like the figure below for easy visibility of the effects and send sections.

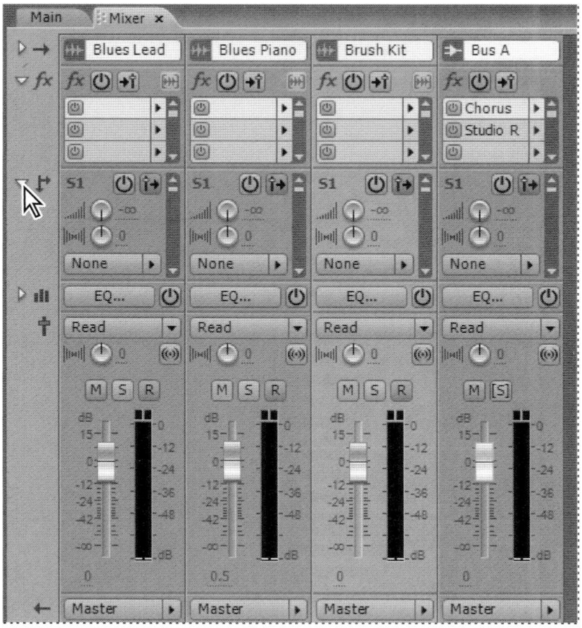

9 When expanded, the Send section shows a scrollable list of various sends you can assign for a track and the controls related to each such send. You can have as many as 16 sends per track.

10 Within the Blues Lead Guitar track, which is the first track on the left, press the Power button for Send 1 (S1) (⏻) to switch it on.

11 At the bottom of the S1 section for the guitar track, just below the S1 level and S1 Pan knobs, click on the menu for S1 output and choose Bus A.

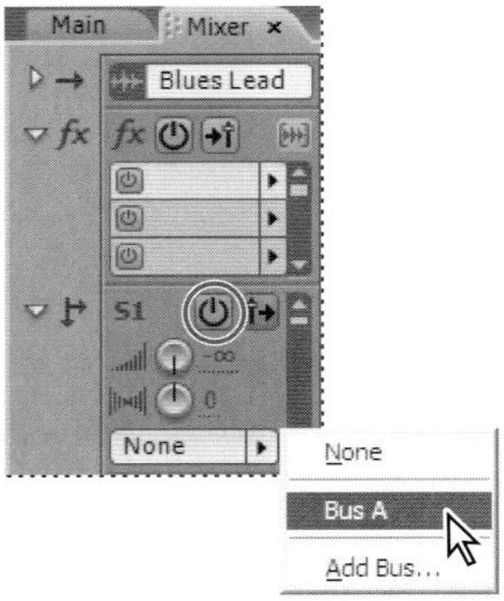

This routes the send S1 to Bus A. Sends are used to branch the signal from a track into buses. This is also suggested by the symbol used to represent for the sends section (↱). You decide where a send is to be routed by using the send's output menu. The send level knob controls how much signal is fed into the chosen bus. The higher setting this knob is at, the more signal goes to that bus.

12 Press the Home key on your keyboard, and then the spacebar, to begin playing the session from the beginning. The piano and drums tracks are currently muted, so you hear just the lead guitar track, which sounds dry because you've already removed the effects that were initially inserted into this track.

13 Press the spacebar to stop and then restart playback from the beginning. As the session plays, click on the S1 level knob, which is the upper of the two knobs for S1, for the guitar track and drag upwards to raise the send level to the -3 level. Release your mouse button.

You should now see activity in the level meters for Bus A as the session plays. The send level knob determines the amount of signal going to Bus A. Since Bus A already has the Chorus and Reverb effects inserted into it, turning up the send knob in the guitar track will determine how spacious and ambient this track sounds. The more signal that comes into a bus, the more will be the activity in the bus level meters and, accordingly, the more pronounced effect you will hear.

14 Un-mute the piano and drum tracks. Follow the same procedure you did for the guitar track in the previous steps, and assign the S1 for the piano and drum track to Bus A as well. Remember to turn on the Send 1 Power buttons () for these tracks. Set their S1 level knobs for piano and drum tracks to -6 and -20 respectively.

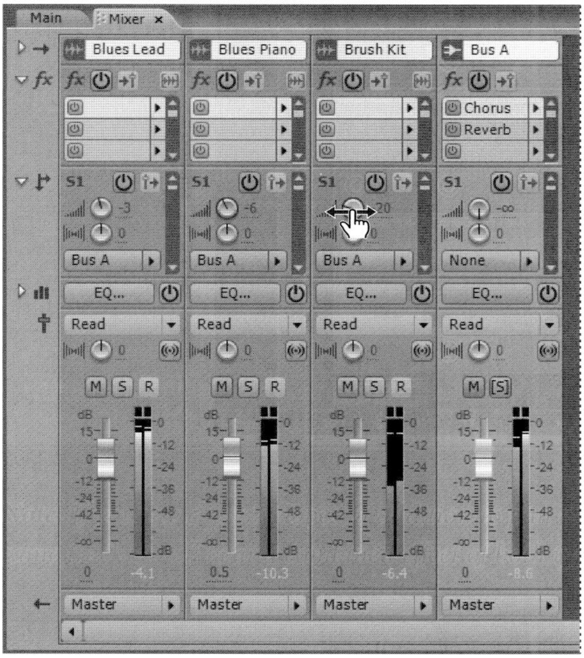

The volume fader for Bus A determines the overall level of 'wet' signal. When the wet output of Bus A mixes with the dry output of all the tracks, you can again hear as if the music is taking place in a live hall.

15 Click once on the name of Bus A at the top of the track and type in **Rev+Cho Bus**. As you become an advanced user of the Mixer and effects, you will generally have many buses in the session. It is helpful to rename the buses you create according to their purpose. This will make it easier for you to know where to route a send while working with complex sessions.

16 Choose File > Save Session to save your session.

Exploring on your own

1 Add another bus to your session and insert another effect into it. Use an effect which is easily perceivable, like a Delay Effects > Flanger, for example.

2 Rename this bus to an appropriate name, like **FlangeBus**.

3 Switch on the Send 2 Power buttons for the guitar, piano, and drum tracks. You may need to scroll down within the Sends to view Send 2 or additional Sends. Route this send (Send 2) in these tracks to FlangeBus. Set their Send 2 level knobs to different positions and study the results it has on the overall sound.

4 Try comparing the wet and dry sound by switching off the sends or muting the bus. Experiment with the volume fader for FlangeBus to create a different balance between wet and dry signal.

5 Solo each track one-by-one to hear how it sounds alone with the bus effects. Then mute the bus to hear the dry track itself.

6 Try panning the bus to the extreme right and the tracks to the extreme left to easily distinguish between the dry and wet signal.

Review

Review questions

1 What is the difference between non-destructive real-time effects and destructive effects?

2 What is the purpose of having sends in a track?

3 What is the advantage of using a bus effect as opposed to inserting the same effect into all tracks?

Review answers

1 You can apply effects to your tracks in the Multitrack View without worrying about changing the original audio files being used. Audition makes 'on-the-fly' calculations so that you can hear those effects. These are called non-destructive real-time effects. On the other hand, while working in the Edit View, the effects you apply to an audio file physically change the waveform. This is called destructive effects processing.

2 Sends are used to branch the signal from a track into buses. Sends allow you to create sub mixes, and manage effects more efficiently and quickly. You can route a send from a track to any bus being used in the session. This is done by using the send's output menu. A send can branch the signal either before or after the volume fader of the track. This is determined by the status of the Send Pre-Fader/Post-Fader button for that send.

3 You can insert effects into the Effects Rack for any track. The more real-time effects you insert, the harder your computer has to work to make the calculations necessary for you to hear those effects. So inserting a lot of effects into racks for various tracks is not a good idea. If you need to use the same effect for multiple tracks, then you can use the send and bus method. This implies that you first create a bus and insert the required effect into it. Then you set up your tracks to have sends into this bus and use their send level knobs to determine how much signal is passed to the bus. The more a track's send level to a bus, the more prominent the effect will be for that track.

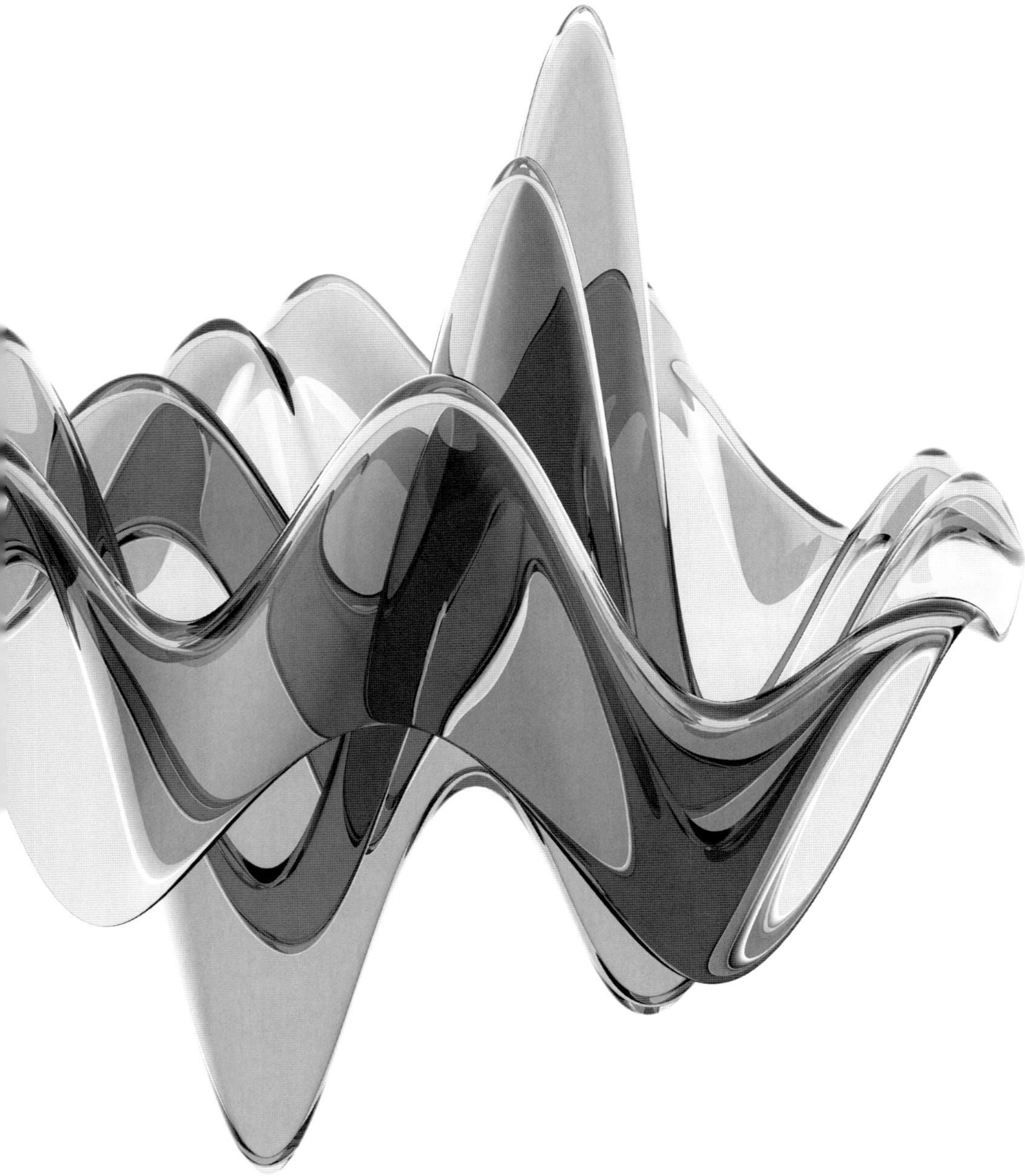

9 Using Audition's Equalization Tools

Audition provides a variety of methods for improving sound quality using equalization techniques. Audition's Track Equalizers and Graphic Equalizer effect provide these controls. Additional control over equalization levels is available using Automation techniques that you will learn in the next lesson.

In this lesson, you'll learn how to do the following:

- Use the Quick Filter.
- Use Track Equalizers in the Multitrack View.
- Use the Graphic Equalizer as an insert effect in the Multitrack View.

Getting started

Equalization, or EQ for short, is the art and science of emphasizing or reducing parts of the audio spectrum to produce a change in sonic texture. If you have ever adjusted the Bass and Treble control on a radio, you have used a very basic equalizer. More sophisticated equalizers allow you to precisely and selectively change the tone of a sound.

Note: *Working with equalization requires very careful listening, as changes made to sounds can be quite subtle. Frequent work with equalization trains your ear to notice small changes in a sound. All the exercises in this lesson involve making such changes to certain frequency ranges of audio tracks and clips. If you are using the built-in speakers on a laptop or other small computer speakers, the changes you apply may be less noticeable. If your computer speakers do not reproduce a wide range of sound frequencies, you may wish to use headphones for this lesson.*

1 Start Adobe Audition. Click on the Multitrack View button (■) if not already selected.

2 If you have not already copied the resource files for this lesson onto your hard disk from the AA_09 folder from the *Adobe Audition 2.0 Classroom in a Book* CD, do so now. See "Copying the Classroom in a Book files" on page 2.

3 To review the finished session file, choose File > Open Session. Navigate to the AA_CIB folder you created on your hard disk, and open the file 09_end.ses in the AA_09 folder. Click the Play button (▶) in the Transport panel or press the spacebar on your keyboard. The finished session is played for you.

4 When you have finished listening to the file, close the 09_end.ses file by choosing File > Close All.

5 Choose File > Open Session and open the file 09_start.ses and play this session. The announcer's voice in this session does not sound as deep, because equalization has not yet been applied to it. You will start this exercise by modifying the equalization for the announcer's voice.

Using the Quick Filter

Audition offers EQ tools for the Edit View (destructive) as well as the Multitrack View (non-destructive). The Quick Filter is one of the tools available in the Edit View to modify the equalization of a given waveform. It is an 8-band graphic equalizer that allows you to boost or reduce the amplitude within a specific frequency range.

Frequency Chart

The human ear is capable of hearing audio frequencies from approximately 20 Hz to 20 kHz. Sounds produced by any musical instrument, including the human voice, fall within a specific area within this range.

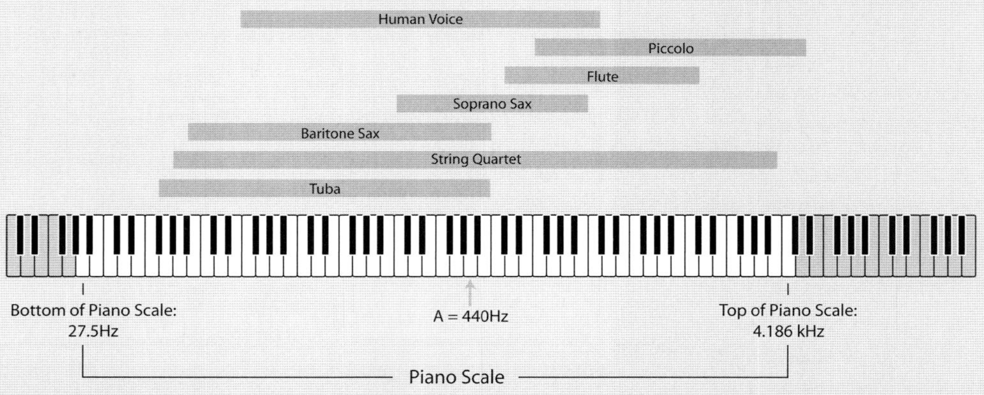

1 In the Multitrack View, double-click on the Announcer.wav clip to open it in the Edit View.

2 At the top of your display, choose Edit > Select Entire Wave. You can alternatively use the keyboard shortcut Ctrl+A. The entire waveform is selected and gets highlighted. Press the Play button () to play the clip, which is 8.5 seconds in length.

3 Choose Effects > Filters > Quick Filter (process) and the Quick Filter window opens. Look at the bottom of the Quick Filter window. The 8 bands span the range from 86 Hz, which is low end, or bass, to 22 kHz, which is high end, or treble.

4 In the Quick Filter window, click the Preset name Flat to reset the slider values of all the frequency bands to 0. You will now manually modify the amplitudes of certain bands to better understand how each band impacts the sound.

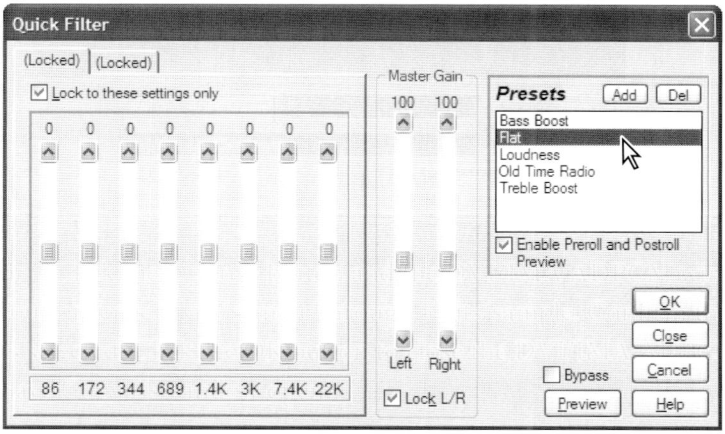

5 Click the Preview button to play the clip. As the voice is playing, click and drag the left-most frequency band slider, labeled 86, upwards. The value at the top of the slider changes as you push the slider up. This value represents the amplitude of this frequency band. This adjustment increases the low bass range of the announcer's voice.

6 Push the slider up to the 14 value and you should hear the voice become deeper. Click on the Bypass check box to temporarily disable the effect and to hear the original audio. Click on the Bypass check box again to uncheck it and restore the effect.

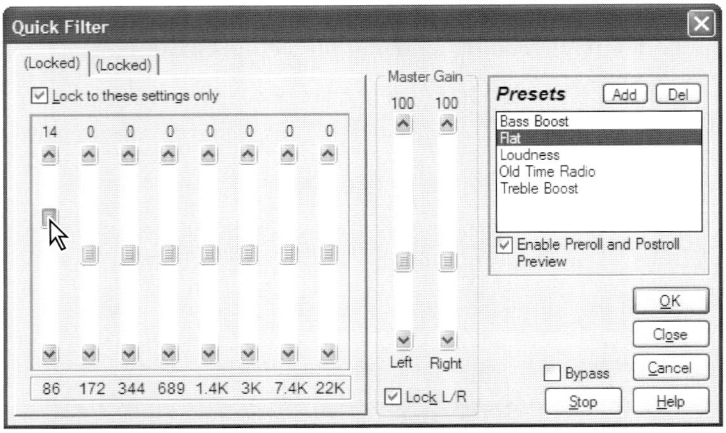

7 Press the Stop button to stop the preview of the effect. Click the Flat preset to reset the first slider, as you are going to try additional adjustments using the Quick Filter.

8 Click the Preview button to play the announcer clip. As the voice is playing, click and drag the right-most frequency band slider, labeled 22K, upwards. Change the amplitude value of this slider to 14.

This increases the treble, and causes the voice to sound brighter. Listen to the phrase "Most cell phones sound…" and note that this adjustment to the high-frequency range accentuates the "s" sounds in this sentence. The occurrence of "s" sounds is referred to as sibilance. The more you increase the amplitude of high frequency levels the more likely you are to increase sibilance. Heavy sibilance sounds harsh and should be avoided. Decreasing high frequency levels often minimizes distracting sibilance.

9 Press the Stop button to stop the preview of the effect. Click the Flat preset to reset the adjustments you had made, as you will continue to experiment with equalization adjustments.

10 Click and drag the sliders for all eights frequency bands individually upwards, changing all the amplitude values to 4.

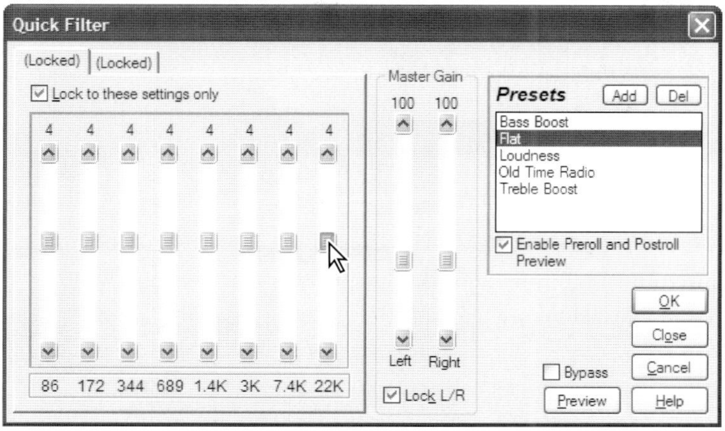

11 Click the Preview button. Increasing the amplitude values for all 8 bands equally raised the volume of the entire waveform. Click the Bypass check box in order to hear the original clip, which has a slightly lower volume level. Click the Bypass check box again to hear the effect of raising all 8 bands equally.

12 Click the OK button to apply the effect. The amplitude of the waveform increases. To compare the waveform before and after applying the effect, press Ctrl+Z to undo the Quick Filter. To reapply the effect, press Ctrl+Shift+Z. Note the visual change in the waveform. Press Ctrl+Z one final time to undo the effect.

Using the Quick Filter to boost frequency bands may push amplitude levels above 0 dB, causing clipping, and therefore should be avoided. Changing the levels of all frequency bands is not an efficient way to adjust volume. Instead, use the Amplify/Fade effect to increase or decrease volume levels.

13 Choose Edit > Repeat Last Command and the Quick Filter window opens. You can also use F2 as a keyboard shortcut to access this command.

14 Press the Flat preset to reset the sliders to zero. Move the slider for the 172 Hz frequency band to a level of 4. Increase the slider for the 344 Hz frequency band up to 5 and then set the slider for the 689 Hz frequency band to 4. Click the Preview button to play the clip. Boosting the range between 172 and 689 Hz generally makes sounds warmer.

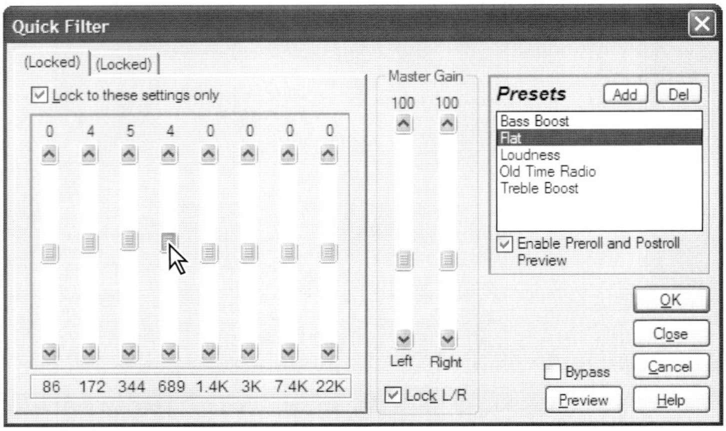

15 Click the Stop button to stop playing the clip. Click the Flat Preset to reset all the values. In addition to increasing frequency bands, you can also use the Quick Filter to reduce the frequency bands.

16 Click the Preview button to start playing the clip. Click and drag the 3K slider down until the amplitude value is -8. Then click and drag the 7.4 Hz slider down until its amplitude value is -9. Cutting the amplitude levels in the 3 to 7.4 kHz range reduces the higher frequencies, which emphasizes the lower frequency ranges. Because you reduced the amplitude levels, you have a quieter overall waveform. This results in a warmer sound, similar to the sound achieved in step 14, although not as loud.

17 Click the Stop button to stop playing the clip. Click the Flat Preset to reset all the values, and then click on the Bass Boost preset. This preset changes the frequency bands and Master Gain values are set to 91. Master Gain is equivalent to the overall volume and is set at a level of 100 by default.

18 If necessary, select the Lock L/R check box. Click and drag the master gain up to a level of 140 and then click the OK button. This increases the amplitude of the entire waveform, which makes the clip louder.

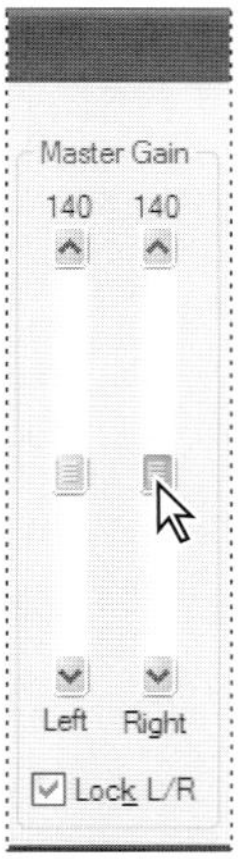

19 Choose File > Save As. Navigate to the AA_09 folder on your hard disk and enter the name **Announcer_Bass.wav** for this file. If you are prompted to overwrite an existing file by the same name, click Yes. Remember that all edits you make in the Edit View are destructive, and if you want to keep both an edited and original version of the audio, you need to rename the edited file when saving.

20 Click on the Multitrack View button (). Choose File > Save Session As. Rename this session **09_BassBoost.ses** and save into the AA_09 folder on your hard disk.

Using equalization in the multitrack

Using the Quick Filter in the Edit View is a good way to quickly modify the tone of an audio clip. However, the Quick Filter uses destructive editing and it is applied one single clip at a time. If you want to apply equalization effects to all the clips in an entire track, you can do so in the Multitrack View, using the equalization track controls.

1 Choose File > Close All to close the current session and unload its audio contents from the Files panel. Choose File > Open Session. Navigate to the AA_09 folder on your hard disk and click to select the multitrack_eq.ses file, and then click the Open button. This 4 track session file opens up. Press the spacebar on your keyboard to play the session. When the session ends, press the spacebar to stop playing.

2 Click the EQ button () at the top of the panel in the track controls. This is the fourth icon below the Main tab and its icon has three vertical bars on it. When you press the EQ button, you can see some of the EQ settings in the track properties.

3 Click the Zoom Out Full Both Axes button (), then click on the Solo button () in the Drums track to solo this track. Press the Play Looped button () in the Transport panel to begin playing the session.

4 Bring your cursor on the border between the Drums track controls and the Scratchin track controls. When it changes shape to the resizing cursor (), click and drag downwards so that you can see three rows of blue numbers representing three EQ bands for the Drums track.

Audition offers an independent 3 band parametric equalizer for each track. The blue numbers you see on the right are center frequencies of the three bands. The numbers on the left are for boosting or reducing those center frequencies.

In Adobe Audition 2.0, when you see a number that is blue in color and has a dotted underline below it, this means that you can scrub this number to raise or lower its value. In other words, you can click and drag on it to change the number. The center frequency for the second band in the Drums track is currently set at 2500 Hz and its gain is set at 0 dB.

You will now change the center frequency of this band and also boost this frequency area by changing its gain.

5 Press the EQ power button (⏻) below the Solo button for Drums track to turn it on. If the session is not playing, press the Home key and then the spacebar on your keyboard to start playback of the session from the beginning. As the session is playing, click on the 0 to the left of the 2500 Hz band and drag to the right to raise it to 6. Release your mouse button.

This boosts the middle frequencies (around 2500 Hz) for the Drums track by 6 dB. In this track, the middle frequency corresponds to the bandwidth of the snare drum. Boosting this region creates a more pronounced snare sound for the Drums track. Press the spacebar to stop playing the session.

6 Press the spacebar again to start playing the session from the beginning. To compare the original changes caused by equalization boost at 2500 Hz, switch off the EQ power button (⏻). This turns off the track EQ for the drum track. Play for a few seconds to hear how the track sounded without equalization. Press the EQ power button again to bring back the 6 dB boost at 2500 Hz and notice how this emphasizes the snare drum. Press the spacebar to stop playing the session. Click on the Solo button (S) for the Drums track to switch it off.

***Note:** EQ changes are generally subtle and require careful listening. As mentioned earlier, in case you don't have good quality speakers, to hear such equalization changes, you might want to use headphones for the exercises in this lesson.*

Now you will make some equalization changes for the Bass track using a similar procedure as above.

7 Just as you did for the Drums track in steps 2 thru 4, resize the height of the Bass track so that you can see its three rows of blue numbers representing the equalization bands for the Bass track. You might have to reduce the height of other tracks to be able to do this.

8 Select the Time Selection tool ( ), then click and drag over the two clips, ClavBasA03 and ClavBasA02 starting at Bar 3 beat 1. Continue to drag to the Bar 9 beat 1 mark, creating a selection that covers this range. Confirm your selection by looking at the Selection/View panel below the multitrack.

9 Click the Solo button (S) in the Bass track to solo this track. Turn on the EQ power button ( ) for this track by clicking on it. Click the Play Looped button ( ) to play the selection only. Playing a looped selection allows you to focus on changing the EQ values without having to reset the start-time indicator each time the clip ends.

10 Press the spacebar to stop playing the session. As was the case in the Drums track, the center frequencies of the three equalization bands for the Bass track are set at 7000 Hz, 2500 Hz and 160 Hz, by default. These are generally associated with the highs, mids, and lows in terms of equalization. Right now they are all set to 0 gain. You will now change the frequency of the 160 Hz band by typing instead of scrubbing.

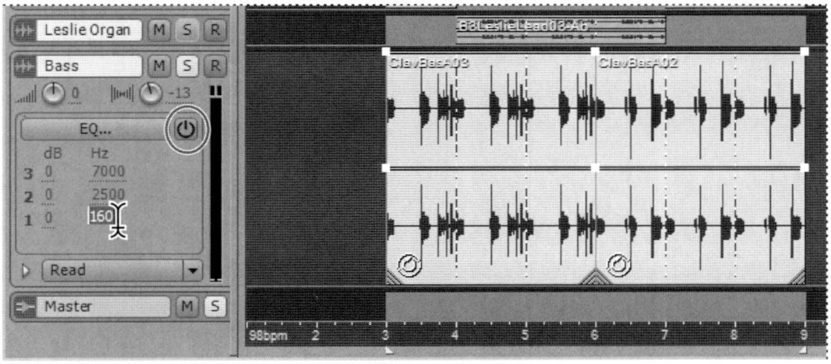

11 Click once where it says 160 and type **120** into this box. Press Enter on your keyboard to finalize your text entry. The center frequency for this band has now been set to 120 Hz. This is the frequency that will be affected when you change the gain setting on the left. Now click once where it says 0 to the left of 120 Hz and type in **8** as the new decibel value and press Enter. This raises the amplitude of the 120 Hz band by 8 dB.

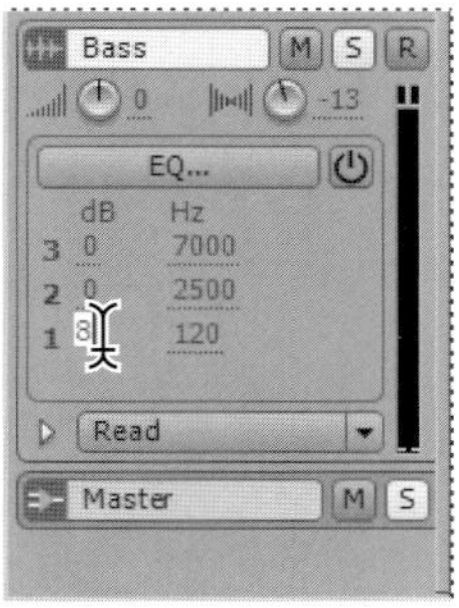

Note: *Be cautious about boosting the lower frequencies of instruments such as bass guitars, bass drums, or any electronic bass. Boosting the low frequency of a bass instrument may sound acceptable when using headphones or computer speakers, but the same effect may overwhelm the rest of the song when using a home or car stereo system. If you anticipate that audio will be played on a variety of devices, it is best to preview the audio using these different speaker systems before committing to a final mix.*

12 Press the Esc key, then press the Home key and then the spacebar to playback the session from the beginning. You hear the soloed bass guitar with the equalization applied to it. This is an 8 dB boost at 120 Hz. Switch off the EQ power to hear the track without the equalization. After listening for a few seconds, turn the EQ power back on. The boost you applied in the low frequency region of the bass creates a fuller sound for the bass guitar. If you see the level meters for the Bass track clipping, with the values exceeding the maximum, then type in a lower value instead of 8, or simply click and drag to a lower value.

Using the Track Equalizer window

As you work on sessions with multiple tracks, it will be quicker and more intuitive to use the graphical interface available for the 3-band parametric equalizer available for each of your tracks in the Multitrack View. Instead of typing-in or scrubbing various equalization parameters as you did in the previous steps, you will now use the Track Equalizer window.

1 Click on the long button labeled EQ (EQ...) in the Bass track to open the Track Equalizer window for this track.

A new window called EQ: Bass opens up, and it shows a graphical representation of the current equalization settings for the Bass track.

Notice how the 8 dB boost you had applied at 120 Hz in step 11 is apparent in the shape of the equalization curve and in the position of the sliders. You can see an 8 dB bump starting at 120 Hz. You can also see the horizontal slider for band 1 set at 120 Hz and the vertical slider for band 1 set at 8 dB. This reflects the equalization changes you made to the Bass track in the previous steps.

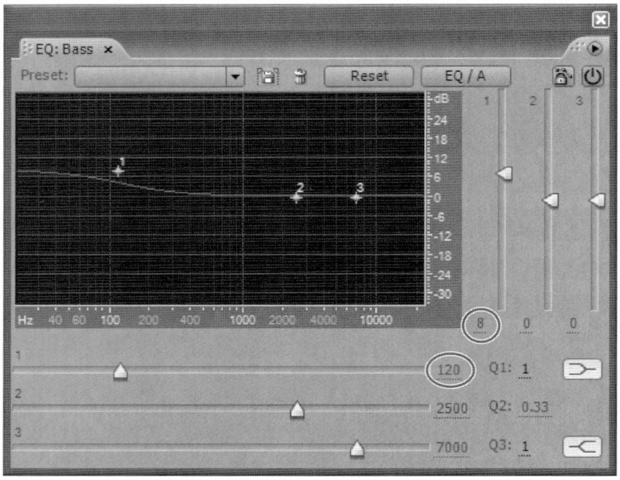

In this graph, x-axis (horizontal) represents frequency and y-axis represents amplitude. They are measured in Hertz (Hz) and decibels (dB) respectively. The three points available on the curve allow you to change it by clicking and dragging. You can also do the same using the sliders present on the right and the bottom of the graph.

2 Close this window by clicking the Close button (☒) on its top right. Click on the Solo button (S) for the Bass track to switch it off.

3 If necessary, choose the Time Selection tool ( ). Click and drag over the entire B3LeslieLead03-Ab clip located in the Leslie Organ track. The track is now selected. Click the Solo button ( ) in this track to hear just this track. Turn on the EQ power button ( ) below it. You might have to adjust the height of this track to be able to view this button. Click on the long EQ button next to it to open the Track Equalizer window for this track.

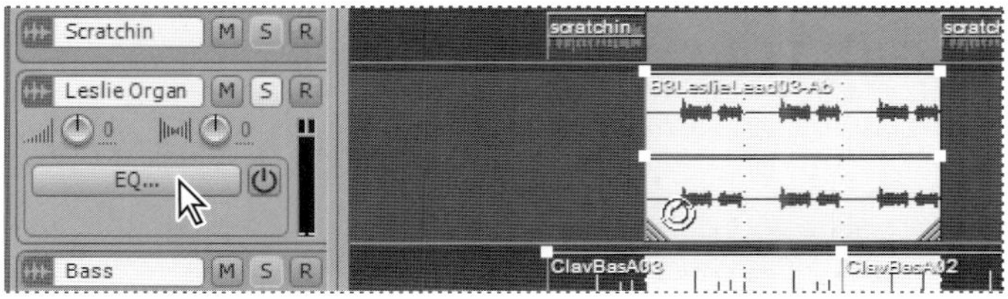

Note: *In case you don't see these buttons, confirm that you are actually viewing the equalization properties for your tracks by pressing the EQ button ( ) at the top of the Main panel.*

4 Confirm that the EQ power button has been turned on for the Leslie Organ track by looking at the Power button on the top right of this window. The equalization graph is currently a straight line because no boosts or cuts have yet been applied for any of the three available bands.

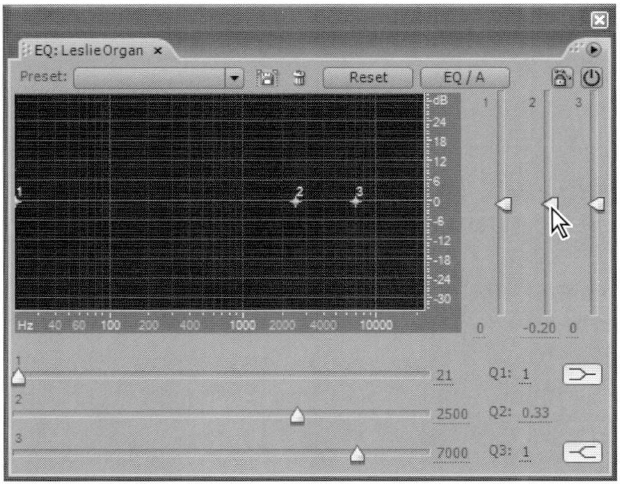

5 Press the spacebar to hear the organ play. To the right of the track equalizer graph, click and drag the middle slider toward the top, boosting the midrange value to 7.5 dB. As you push the slider, the green anchor point on the equalization curve moves up the graph, and the line becomes curved, increasing the midrange results in a brighter and louder organ tone. Press the spacebar to stop playback.

6 Press the spacebar to hear the organ again. As the sample is playing, click and drag the middle slider, located below the graph, to the left. Change its value from 2500 to 1000. The entire curve shifts to the left as you redefine the frequency for this band. This produces a different tone in the organ sample. Press the spacebar to stop playback.

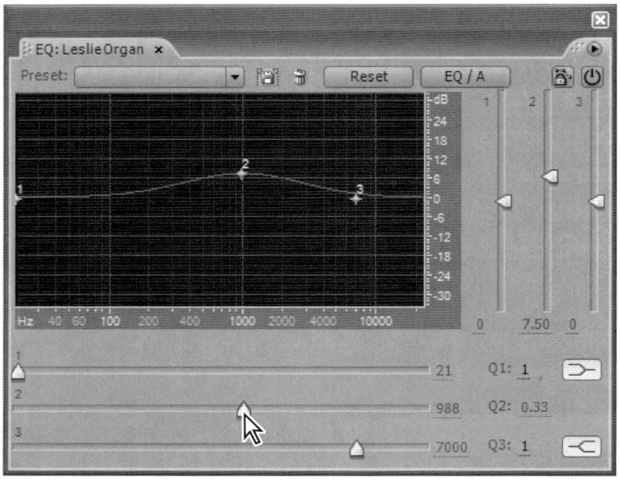

7 Play the organ sample again. As it plays, click the button labeled EQ/A above the graph. When you do so, its label changes to EQ/B and the Equalization Values are all set to zero, the default values for the track. Click on the EQ/B button to switch back to the first EQ setting. Switching between the EQ/A and EQ/B banks provides an excellent way to compare EQ values and preview EQ changes in real time.

8 Make sure that a bank is set to EQ/A, and then click on the Save a new preset button (💾) above the graph. In the dialog box that follows, type in **Leslie Eq** and click the OK button. This preset gets added to the Preset menu. Saving the EQ Presets makes it easy to use the same equalization adjustments on other tracks.

9 While this Track Equalizer window for the organ track is still open, click the long EQ button (EQ...) for the Drums track and the Bass track. The equalization windows for these two tracks get added to the currently open window as new tabs. You can click on these tabs to quickly view and modify the track equalization settings of different tracks.

To make very accurate changes in the Track Equalization window, you can resize it by clicking on one of the window edges and dragging outward when the cursor changes to a double ended arrow (↖↘).

10 Close the equalizer window by clicking on the Close button in the upper right corner. Choose File > Save Session to save your session. Then choose File > Close All to close the session and its associated media.

Using the Graphic Equalizer on a final mix

The Track Equalizers are excellent tools for changing the tonal qualities of individual instruments or groups of instruments. Once you have achieved a general balance with the Track Equalizers and have mixed down a session into a single waveform, you can apply the finishing touches using the Graphic Equalizer. In this exercise you will modify the equalization of a track using the graphic equalizer as an insert effect in the track's Effects Rack. Other changes, such as volume and pan settings, along with effects, have already been applied to the file.

1 Choose File > Open Session. If necessary, navigate to the AA_09 folder and select the graphic_equalizer.ses file and click the Open button.

2 Press the Home key to position the start-time indicator at the beginning of the timeline. Choose the Time Selection tool (I) and then click and drag over the entire disco_eq clip to select it. Press the spacebar to play the disco_eq clip. This clip is a mixed down version of a song with a number of different instruments, including drums, guitars, bass, and strings. There has been no equalization applied to the original tracks. When the clip is finished, press the spacebar to stop playback.

3 Click on the FX button () below the Main tab to view the track effect properties. Click on the border between Track 1 and the Master track and drag downwards to see the first effect slot for the Effects Rack for Track 1.

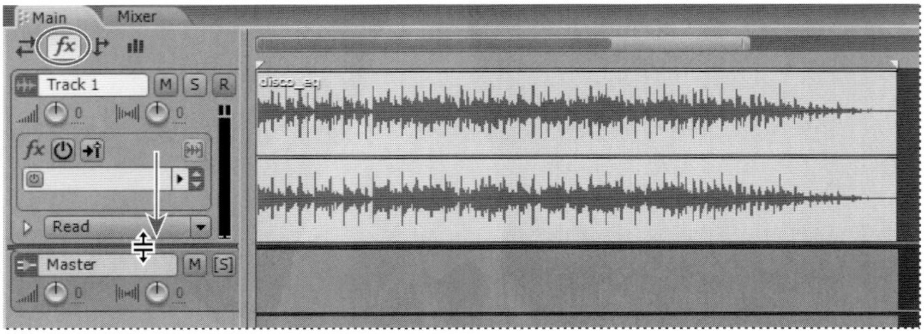

4 Click the black triangle on the first effect slot to open up a context menu of all the real-time effects that can be inserted into this effect slot.

5 From the categorized context menu of effects, choose Filters > Graphic Equalizer.

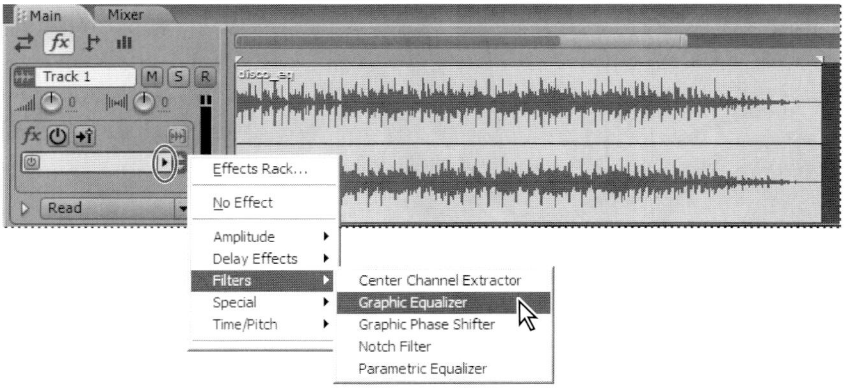

A new window called Effects Rack: Track 1 opens up and shows you that the requested effect has been inserted into the first slot. On the right side, you can see the settings pertaining to the Graphic Equalizer effect.

The Graphic Equalizer is similar to the 3-band parametric track equalizer you used in the previous exercise. Both equalizers provide control for boosting or cutting specific frequency bands, along with a visual representation of the process. In the Graphic Equalizer window however, there are a number of sliders that let you emphasize or attenuate the region around a certain frequency. The first slider controls the amplitude of frequencies at 31 Hz and below, while the last slider controls the frequencies above 16 kHz. The other sliders are labeled according to the frequencies to which they correspond.

6 Click on the Reset button at the bottom of the Graphic Equalizer window to make sure that all sliders are set to the 0 dB level.

7 Click on the 10 Bands button above the sliders, if it is not already selected.

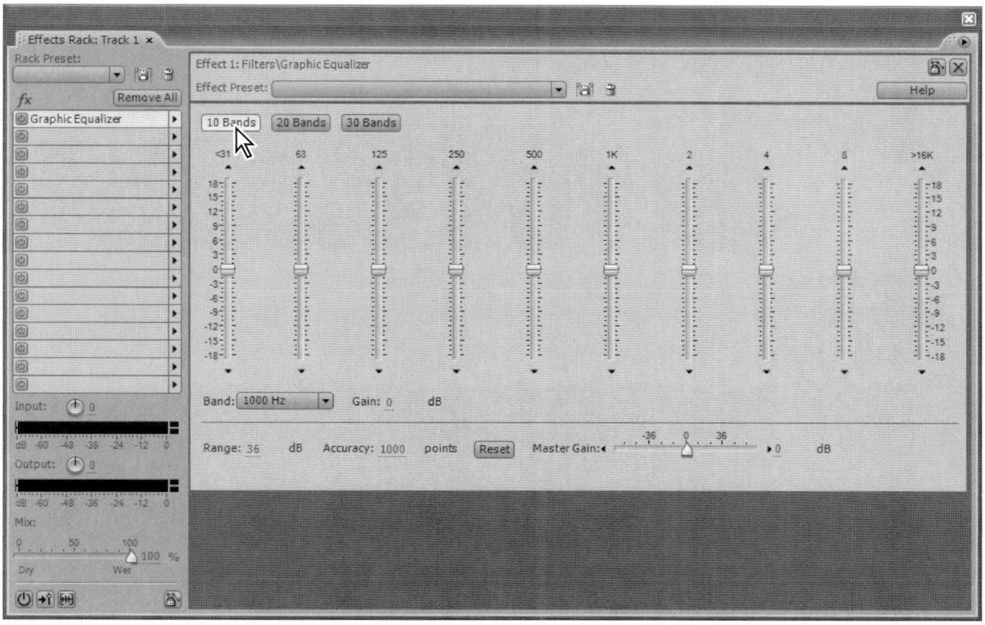

8 Press the spacebar to play the session. Click and drag the 125 Hz slider upwards to approximately 6 dB. As you move the slider, the Gain values change. Gain is represented in decibels, increasing the gain increases the amplitude of this frequency band. The 125 Hz range represents the low end, or bass range, of the frequency spectrum, and you should hear a corresponding boost in the bass guitar. Press the spacebar to stop playing the song.

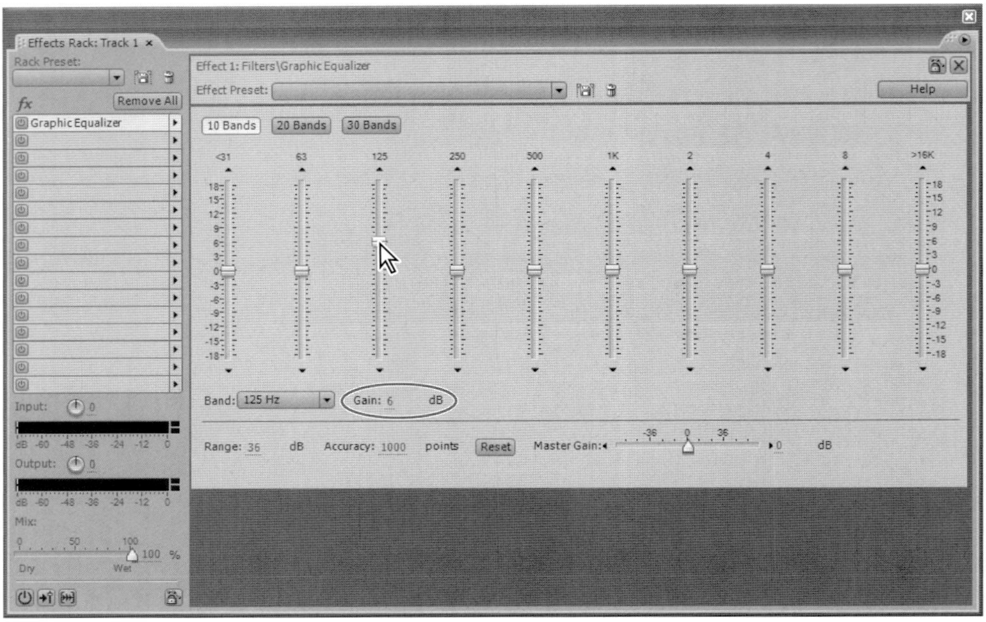

9 Click the button marked 20 Bands. This switches the view to show you 20 sliders between 31 Hz and 22 kHz, which allows you to have more precise control for adjustments to the frequency bands. The original 125 Hz range is now split into sliders for 88 Hz, 125 Hz, and 180 Hz.

10 Click the button marked 30 Bands. This provides further control beyond the 20 bands. The original 125 Hz range is now split into sliders for 80 Hz, 100 Hz, 125 Hz, 160 Hz, 200 Hz, and 250 Hz. Having access to more frequency bands results in finer control of the frequency values.

11 Click on the Effect Preset menu. This opens a drop-down menu, displaying a list of equalizer presets. Press the spacebar to play the session, and then choose the Classic V preset.

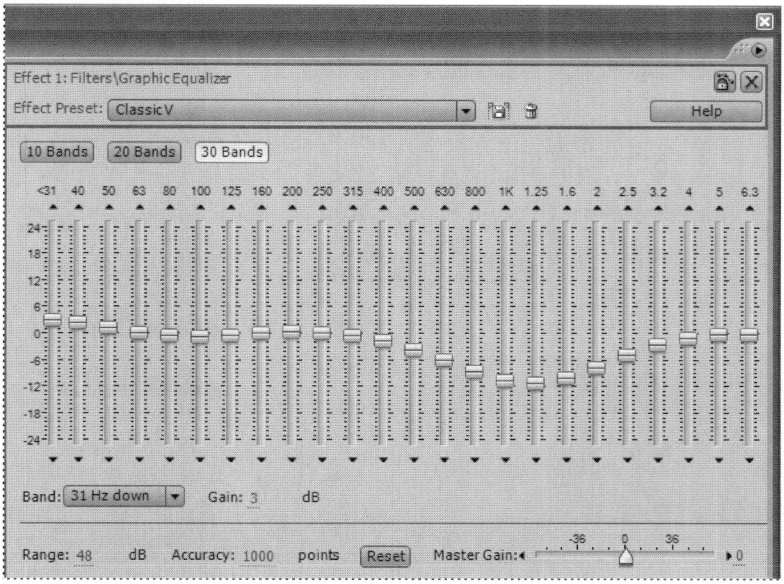

Choosing the preset changes the sliders to pre-determined values: the levels for the low and high frequencies have been boosted and the mids have been reduced a little. This results in a sound that emphasizes the crisp, high hat cymbals as well as the bass. Such equalization creates a pleasing sound for the ears by having a deeper bass as well as crisper highs.

12 Press the spacebar to stop playing the session, then close the equalizer window. Choose File > Save Session to save the current session.

Note: *Because every song is different, presets work best when used as the starting point for additional adjustments. For example, the Classic V equalizer preset could make an instrumental song sound brighter, while the same preset applied to a vocal track may create a dull-sounding voice.*

In the Multitrack View, the equalization settings for a track can be changed over the course of the song by using automation techniques. The next lesson teaches you how to use automation.

Exploring on your own

1 In the Edit View, open the file announcer.wav used in the first exercise. Choose Effects > Filters > Quick Filter (process) and preview the different presets. If you have access to both headphones and a speaker system, compare and contrast the sound of the equalization effects when played through the different monitors.

2 Open the multitrack_eq.ses file used in the second exercise and Save As **multitrack_eq_onyourown.ses**. Use the Track Equalizer controls to make a track which emphasizes the low frequency or bass levels of the song. Save the resulting song by choosing File > Export > Audio Mix Down. Return to the original session, and, using the Track Equalizer controls, now make a track which emphasizes the high frequency, or treble levels of the song. Export this track as well and compare the two. The process of equalization often involves making several versions of the same song and evaluating the benefits of one mix over another.

3 Open the graphic_equalizer.ses file from the AA_09 folder on your hard disk and apply the Graphic Equalizer effect. Click on the 30-band view and experiment with the various sliders, identifying the frequency bandwidths for the string section of the song. Once you identify those frequencies, note how raising and lowering these frequencies affects the sound of other instruments in the song.

Review

Review questions

1 What is the definition of equalization and when is it used?

2 What is the Quick Filter and what are the advantages and concerns in using it?

3 What are Track Equalizers and when are they used?

Review answers

1 Equalization is the process of emphasizing or de-emphasizing parts of the audio spectrum. Equalization is used to change the tone of a sound or a musical instrument. Equalization can be used to make the bass line of a dance song more prominent or a soloist's voice in a chorus recital more present.

2 The Quick Filter is an 8-band Graphic Equalizer effect that is applied using the Edit View. It offers a simple interface that allows you to quickly change, and experiment with, the frequency levels of a sound. It must be used cautiously, as changes made to one frequency band will affect nearby frequency bands. Additionally, the Quick Filter is a destructive effect used in the Edit View, so the effect is applied to only one clip at a time.

3 The Track Equalizer is a non-destructive, 3-band parametric equalizer available for every track in the Multitrack View. The three bands can be modified by clicking and dragging on the anchor points in the Track Equalizer window. You can use the Track Equalizer to shape the sound of each of your tracks by enhancing or reducing specific frequencies.

10 Using Audition's Automation Tools

Adobe Audition's automation features allow you to execute complicated mixes with great flexibility and accuracy. Most knobs, switches, faders, and other settings on the mixer can be automated to create a great sounding mix.

In this lesson, you'll learn how to:

- Use Audition's automation features.
- Draw automation data.
- Record automation data in real time.
- Edit, overdub, and fine-tune automation data.
- Use clip envelopes.

Getting started

It can be quite a task to make accurate and timely changes to mixer settings as the session plays. For example, while mixing a multitrack song, you might have to raise the volume fader for the synth track during the solo section, and then drop it back during the chorus. In the same breath, you might also have to mute a track, change panning for one, and raise the reverb for another.

Audition's automation features are a great help in such situations. They let you record your actions on the mixer and play them back. This frees you from constantly having to adjust faders, knobs, and other mixer settings as the session plays.

Audition's automation features work in the Multitrack View only, and are non-destructive in nature. In other words, your source audio files are not changed in any way when you use automation.

This lesson includes advanced concepts and features of Adobe Audition. Introductory users should make sure they have a solid understanding of the concepts covered in earlier chapters before starting this chapter.

1 If you have not already copied the resource files for this lesson onto your hard disk from AA_10 folder from the *Adobe Audition 2.0 Classroom in a Book* CD, do so now. See "Copying the Classroom in a Book files" on page 2.

2 Start Adobe Audition 2.0. In the Multitrack View, choose File > Open Session. Navigate to the AA_CIB folder you created on your hard disk, and open the 10_end.ses session file in the AA_10 folder.

3 Press the Home key to ensure that the playback cursor is at the beginning of the session. Press the spacebar to start playback. Try to hear the changes that take place in the settings for various tracks within this 30 second session.

4 Press the spacebar again to stop playback. If necessary, choose Windows > Mixer to bring up the Mixer panel. Play the session again from the beginning while looking at the Mixer. You'll notice that different mixer settings update themselves automatically as the session plays back.

These movements in the mixer settings are a result of automation data recorded into the various tracks of this session. Automation data for a setting controls how that setting behaves when the session is played back. You'll be learning how to create such automation data in the following exercises.

5 Click the Main tab to the left of the Mixer tab, and choose File > Close All.

Drawing automation data

The most basic way to use automation within Adobe Audition is to draw it manually. Then, when you playback the session, Audition reads what you have drawn, and makes the required changes as the session plays.

1 In the Multitrack View, choose File > Open Session. Locate and open 10_ start.ses present in the same folder you used in the previous exercise.

2 Save this session as **10_automation.ses** using File > Save Session As command.

3 Press the Solo button (S) for Lead Track, which is the second track from top. Notice that toward the bottom of the track controls area for Lead Track, the Automation Mode menu has been set to Read mode.

Note: *If you can't see this menu, increase the height of the track until this menu becomes visible.*

4 Click on the small gray triangle to the left of the Track Automation Mode menu in Lead Track. This triangle shows or hides the automation data for Lead Track. When you click on it, the track expands downwards, and an automation lane for the volume appears in between Lead Track and Bass Track.

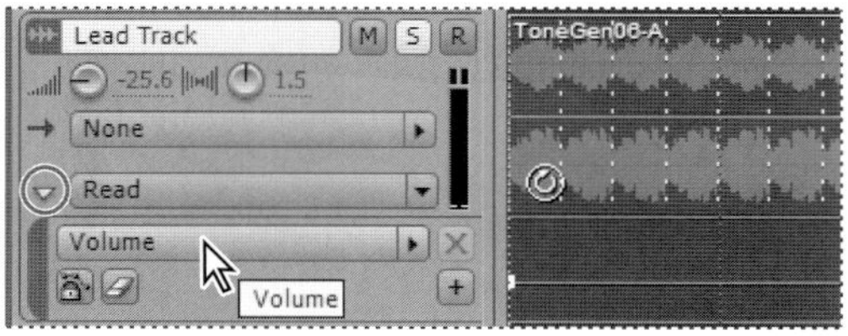

An automation lane contains a graph of the changes that happen in a track setting during the course of the session. Each automation lane is dedicated to a single setting. In this case, you are seeing the automation lane for volume for Lead Track.

The top edge of this lane represents the maximum possible volume for this track, and the bottom edge represents the minimum. As of now, there are no changes in volume for this track throughout the session; therefore, all you see is a straight blue line.

5 Bring your cursor near the thin blue line until the cursor changes into a pointing hand with a plus sign (☝). Click once on the blue line at Bar 5 beat 1, which is the Enter Drums marker noted at the top of the multitrack. A white edit point appears where you clicked, the cursor changes to a hand icon (☝), and a tooltip is displayed.

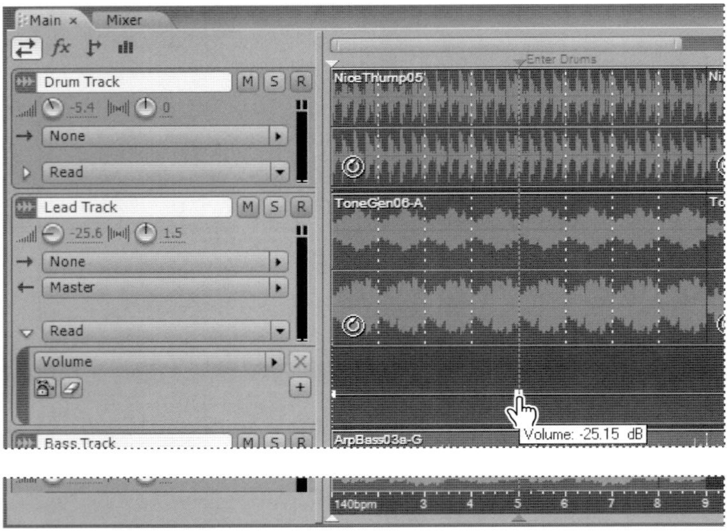

Click again on this edit point and drag it to Bar 9 beat 1 and set it near -10 dB. As you click and drag an edit point to another location, a gray vertical guide and tooltip appear.

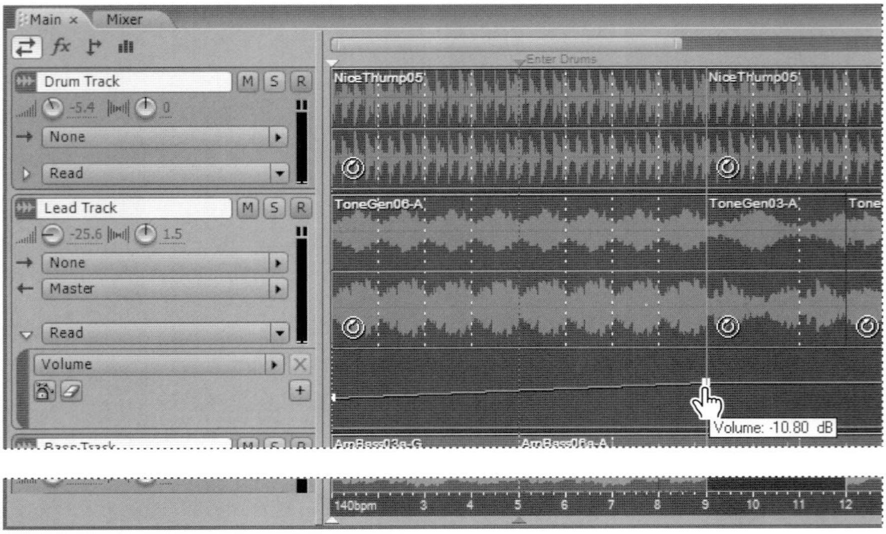

An edit point can be deleted by clicking and dragging it beyond the top or bottom edge of the automation lane.

6 Click on the edit point that's already present at the beginning of this volume lane, and drag it to the minimum position (-∞).

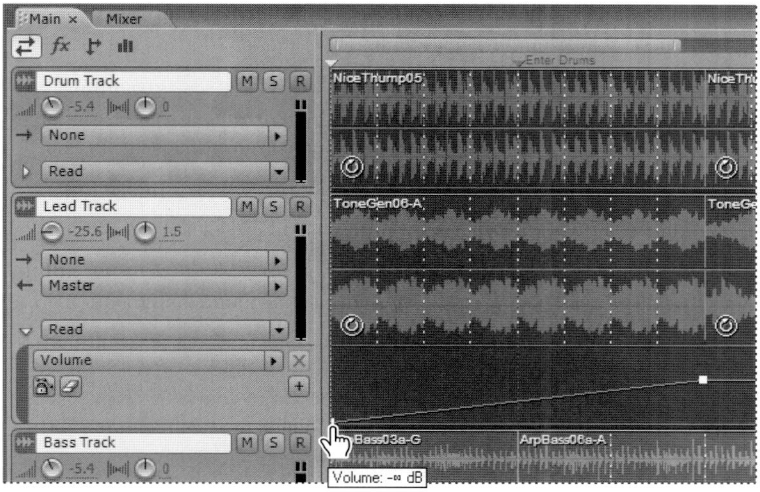

7 Play the session from the beginning. Due to the shape of the edit points you have drawn in the volume lane for Lead Track, you hear a gradual fade in over a period of 9 bars.

8 Stop playback. Press the Solo button (S) for Lead Track again to un-solo it.

9 Click on the Mixer tab to bring up the Mixer panel. At the top-right corner of the Mixer panel, click on the Palette menu button (▶) and choose Undock Panel. The Mixer panel becomes an independent window when you do so. Resize this Mixer window by clicking and dragging on its edges, and adjust its location so that you can simultaneously see the multitrack and the mixer, as shown on the next page. Zoom out horizontally and adjust the widths of the Files panel and the track controls to get a better view.

10 Play the session from the beginning.

See how the volume fader for the Lead Track in the Mixer moves according to the graph of the volume automation lane.

11 Stop the playback. In the mixer strip for Lead Track, find the Automation Mode menu just above the Pan knob. It is currently set to Read mode. Click on this drop-down menu and select Off as the automation mode.

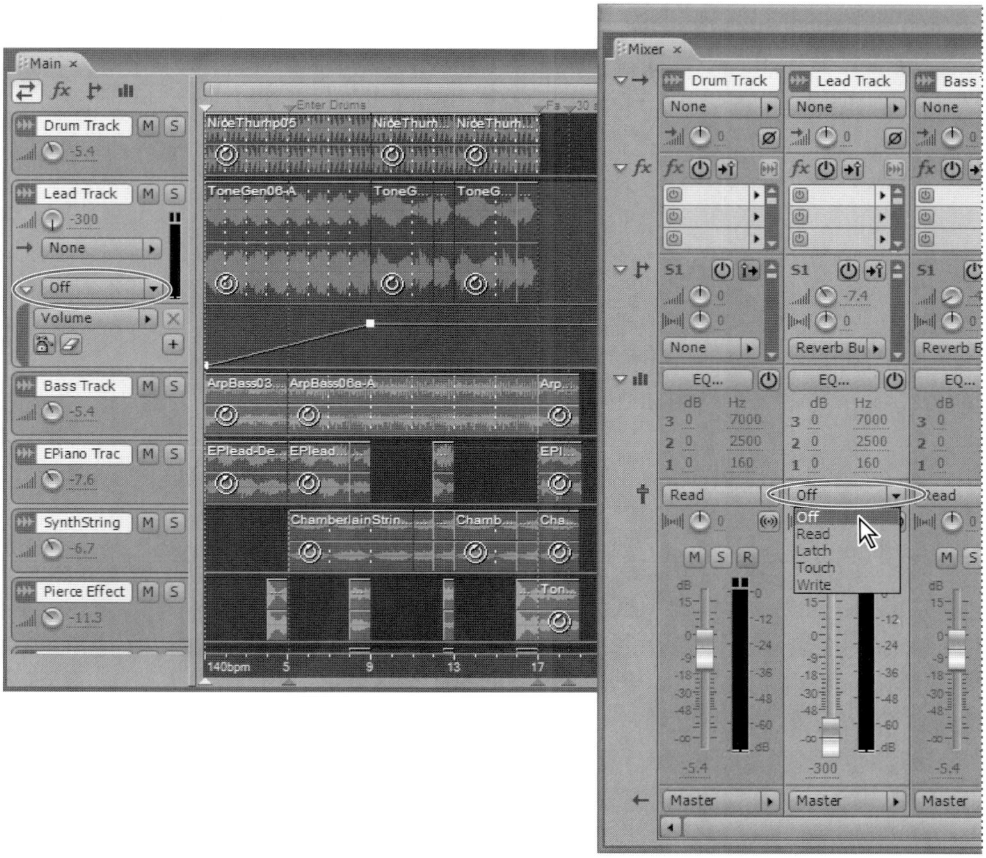

Notice that this change is also reflected in the track controls for Lead Track in the Main panel. If you can't see the menu there, resize the height of the track.

12 Play the session once again from the beginning. This time, you can hear and see that the volume automation is not read as the session plays back. The volume fader for Lead Track remains stationary.

Note: *The position at which the volume fader stays depends on where it was immediately before you changed the automation mode from Read to Off.*

Read and Off are two of the five automation modes available in Audition. The automation mode for a track determines how its automation data is read or written. Choosing Off ignores all information present in all the automation lanes of a track.

See sidebar, "Track Automation Mode options" on page 232.

13 Press the Clear Edit Points button () in the track controls for the volume lane. This erases all edit points in the volume lane except the first one. Click OK if a dialog box appears warning you about erasing all existing points in the automation lane.

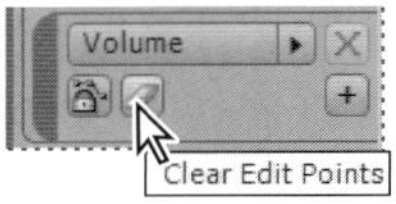

14 Click and drag the first edit point to the -15 dB position.

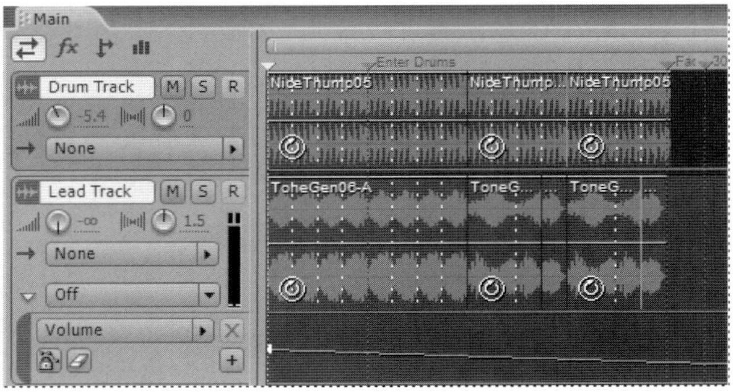

Recording automation data in real time

Audition allows you to record your actions on the mixer 'while' the session is playing. This is commonly known as on-the-fly automation, and is an extremely powerful and intuitive way to control your tracks. Depending on the automation mode you choose for a track, you can record, overdub, or touch-up previously recorded automation actions.

1 Arrange the multitrack and Mixer windows across your screen just like the previous exercise. Make sure that the volume automation lane for Lead Track is visible to you and a sloping blue line is visible within it.

2 In the Mixer window, within the strip for Lead Track, click on the Automation Mode drop-down menu and select Write as the automation mode. This change is reflected in the track controls for Lead Track in the Main panel.

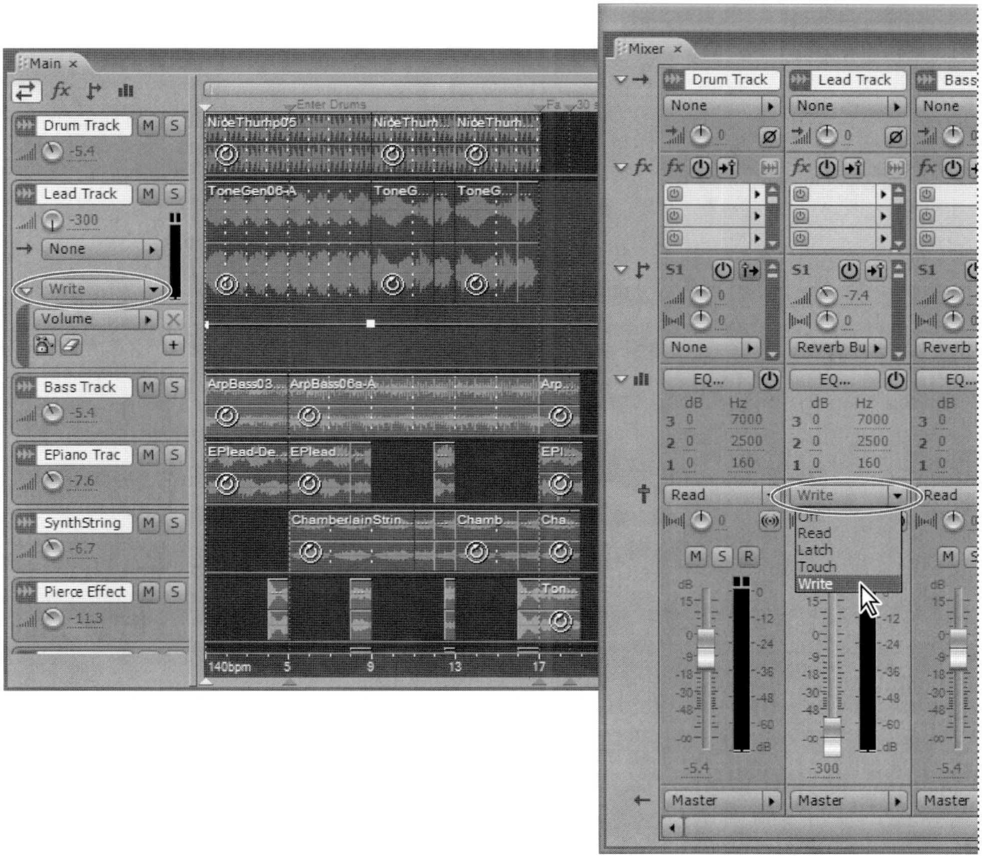

3 Press the Esc key, then press the Home key to return the start-time indicator to the beginning of the session. In the Mixer window, click on the volume fader for Lead Track and, if it is not already at the minimum, drag it down to its minimum position (-∞).

4 Begin playback. Click again on the volume fader for Lead Track. As the session approaches Bar 2 beat 1 (2:1.00), gradually raise your cursor to raise the fader. Create a fade in (crescendo) starting from the minimum position and ending at the -9 dB when the playback approaches Bar 9 beat 1 (9:1.00). Let the fader remain at this level until Bar 17 beat 1 (17:1.00). Stop playback. Your display may vary slightly from that shown below.

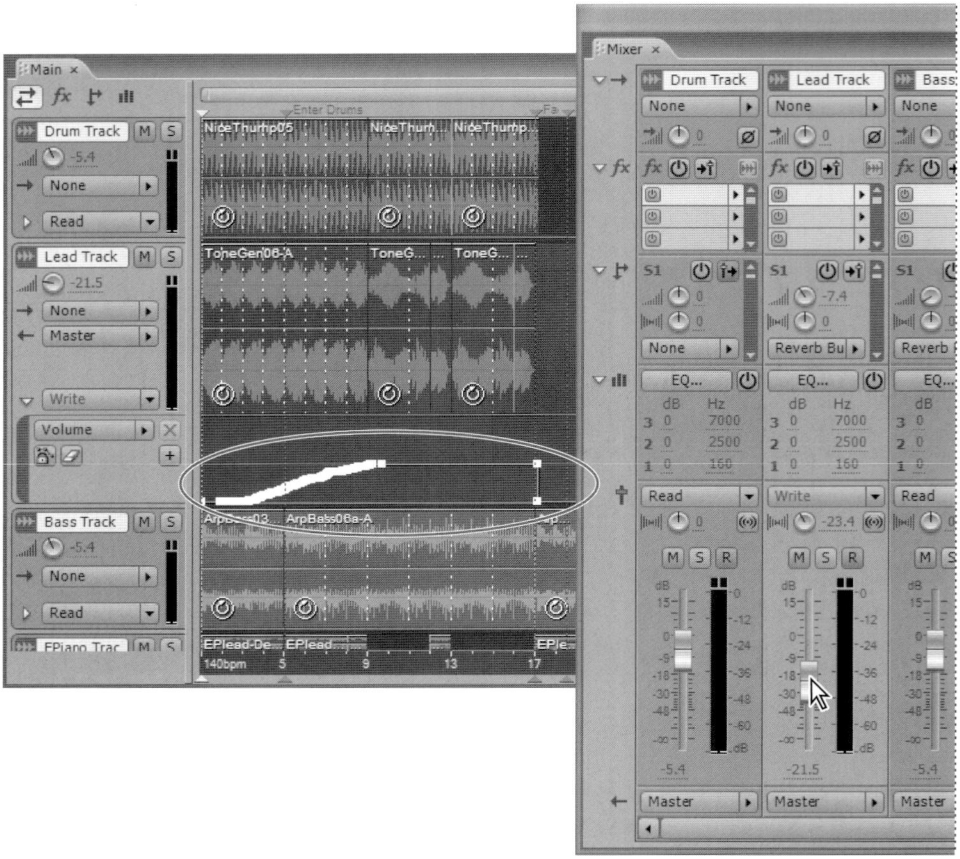

Take a look at the volume automation lane for Lead Track. The actions you performed on the volume fader have been captured as a graph in the lane. This graph is a series of edit points. Zoom in to see the edit points in more detail. These are exactly like the ones you drew manually in the previous exercise, and thus can be moved around or deleted by clicking and dragging. Zoom out to the previous zoom level.

5 Set the automation mode for Lead Track back to Read and play the session from the beginning. You'll see that the volume fader for Lead Track reproduces the actions you performed on it. Stop playback.

6 Press the Esc key, and then press the Home key. Now set the automation mode for Lead Track to Write again and set its volume fader at -9 dB. Hit the spacebar to start playback. Don't make any changes to the volume fader this time. Let the playback continue for the first 10 bars. Stop playback.

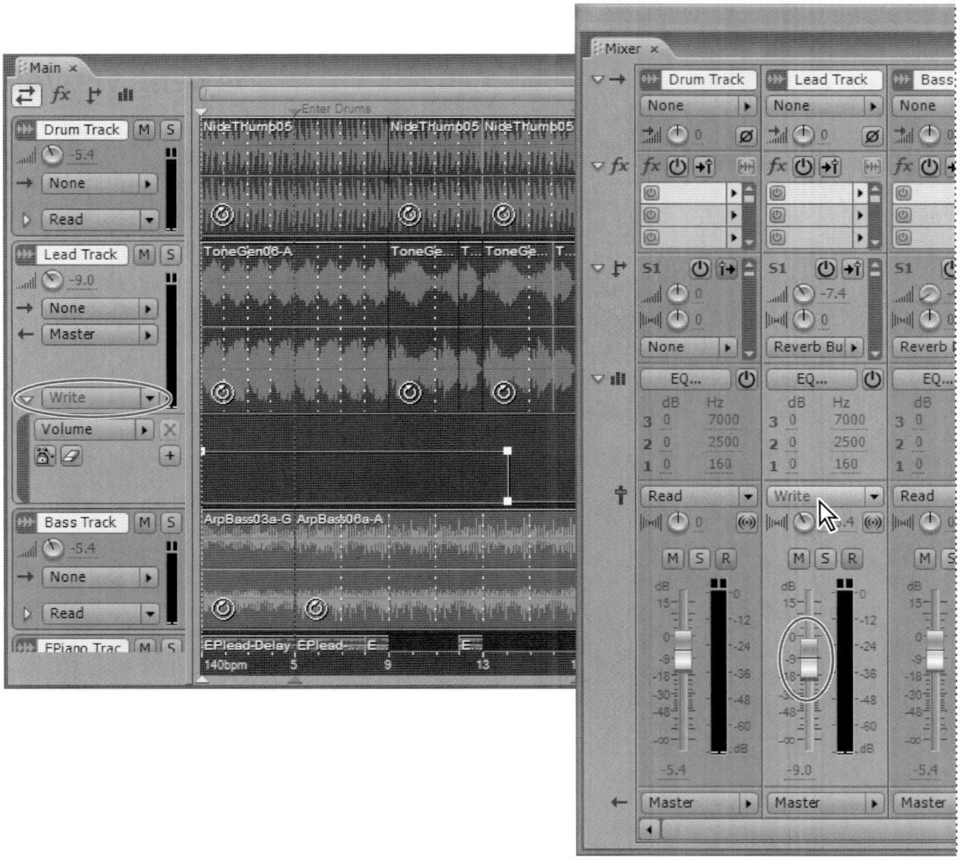

The 9-bar fade in that had been previously captured in the volume automation lane has been lost! This is because the write mode overwrites any data previously contained in an automation lane.

Note: *When a track's automation mode is set to Write, it starts recording as soon as playback is started. Since you kept the fader fixed at -9 dB level this time, this has been recorded as an 'action,' thereby overwriting the fade in you had created earlier. See sidebar, "Track Automation Mode options" on page 232 for further details about automation modes.*

7 Repeat steps 2, 3, and 4 to create the 9-bar fade in again and then go to step 8.

8 Engage the Safe During Write button (🔒) in the track controls for the volume automation lane for Lead Track. Choosing this option does not allow new data to be added to the volume lane. If you make changes to the volume fader now, they will not be recorded.

Note: *Making a lane 'write-safe' prevents accidental loss of information that's already present within the lane. It is a good habit to do this to protect a good recording or drawing of automation data.*

9 Change the automation mode for Lead Track back to Read and close its automation lane by clicking the Show/Hide Automation Lanes triangle (▶) in the track controls for the lane.

Automating additional track parameters

Most features present in the Audition Mixer can be automated in the same manner as volume automation. You'll carry out mute automation for Drum Track in this exercise.

1 Click on the Show/Hide Automation Lanes triangle for Drum Track to open its automation lane. A volume automation lane appears. It is much like the volume lane you saw in the previous exercise. But the important difference is that this one is dedicated to the volume of the Drum Track while the one in the last exercise was dedicated to Lead Track.

2 Click on the Show Additional Automation Lane button (⊞) in the volume automation lane for Drum Track.

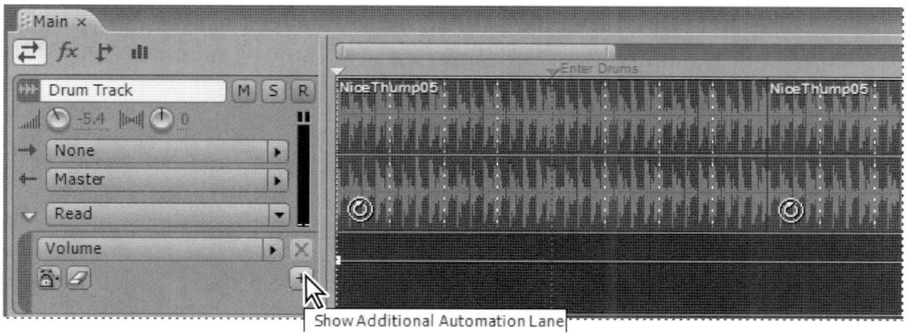

The track expands further and another lane for Mute automation appears just below the volume lane. For now, close the newly opened lane for mute automation by clicking the Close Automation Lane button (☒).

3 In the volume automation lane, click on the Volume drop-down menu. A menu of all the automatable parameters for Drum Track appears. Choose Mute On/Off.

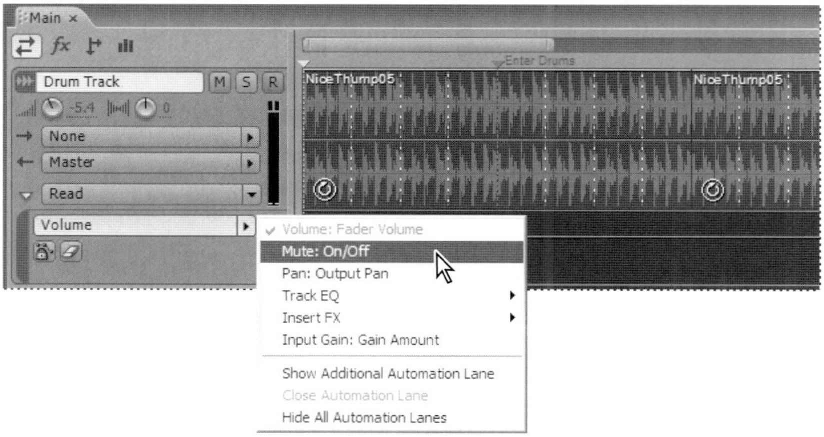

***Note:** This list of automatable parameters for a track changes as you add/remove effects, buses, EQ, etc., for a track. This means that the contents will be updated depending on the effects and buses a track uses. For example, when you activate a reverb as an insert effect for a track, all the automatable parameters for the reverb get added to this list, which can then be automated.*

4 In the mixer strip for Drum Track, press the Mute button (M) to mute the track. Set the automation mode to Write. Ensure that the Safe During Write button for Drum Track is not checked. Press the Home key and start playback.

5 The session starts playing with Drum Track muted. Just when the playback cursor approaches the cue, Enter Drums, at Bar 5 beat 1 (5:1.00), press the Mute button again to un-mute the Drum Track. Stop playback.

Your actions on the Mute button have been captured in the mute automation lane.

6 Set the automation mode for Drum Track to Read and engage the Safe During Write button for the mute lane. Rewind and playback the results.

Note: *While dealing with on/off type controls, as is the case with the Mute button, edit points that lie in the top half of the automation lane switch the control to 'off' and those that lie in the bottom half switch it to 'on.'*

Fine-tuning recorded automation data

Once the automation data has been captured within automation lanes, you might need to edit and touch-up some sections of captured automation data. While you could manually edit the points within an automation lane, it is much more efficient to just 'overdub' new actions over the previous ones. Audition offers two automation modes—Touch and Latch—for this purpose.

Using Touch Mode for editing automation data

Arrange your display just like in the previous exercises, with the Mixer window aligned alongside the multitrack, so that you can see both of them simultaneously.

1 Make the automation lane for EPiano Track visible.

Notice that volume automation data for this track already exists.

2 Playback the session.

The volume automation existing for EPiano Track has no effect on the playback of the track because the automation mode has been set to Off.

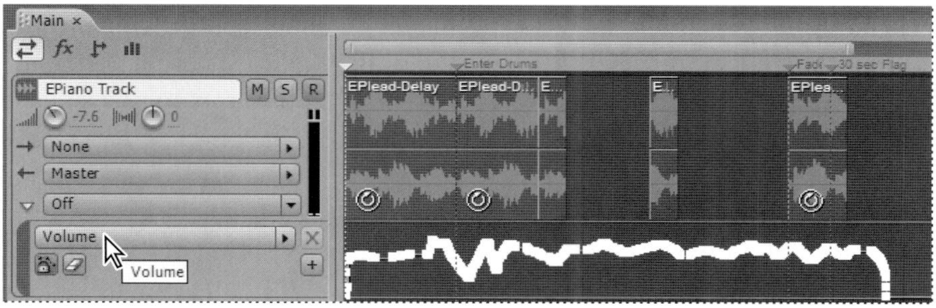

3 Set the automation mode for EPiano Track to Read and playback the session.

Hear the difference arising from enabling the automation data. The volume fader for EPiano Track in the mixer now moves according to the automation data present in the lane.

4 Stop playback. Switch off the Safe During Write button (icon) for the volume lane in EPiano Track. Set the automation mode for EPiano Track to Touch. Play back from the beginning. When the playback has ended, press the Home key to rewind the session.

Even after changing the mode to Touch, the volume changes in the EPiano Track still take place according to the automation data drawn in the volume lane, exactly as in step 3.

Note: *You cannot undo the changes you make to existing automation data. So it's advisable to save your session before attempting to make alterations to a good automation take. This way, if you make a wrong edit, you can easily revert to the saved version.*

5 Save the session using File > Save Session command or press Ctrl+S.

6 While playback is still stopped, click on the volume fader for EPiano Track and, if it is not already at the minimum, drag it down to its minimum position (-∞). Don't release the mouse button yet. While still holding it down, press the spacebar. The session starts to play with the volume fader still under the control of your mouse. Gradually raise the fader to create a fade in until Bar 2 beat 1. Release your mouse button. As soon as you do so, the fader jumps back to reading the graph contained in the automation lane.

This is a unique property of the Touch mode—the fader follows its automation lane unless you start moving the fader yourself. This is what you saw in step 4. When you do make changes to the fader in step 6, it begins to follow your mouse. When you let go, it reverts to reading the automation lane. This makes the Touch mode extremely useful for making minor edits (or punches) to previously existing automation data.

Using Latch Mode for editing automation data

1 Open the pan automation lane for SynthString Track by clicking the Show/Hide Automation Lanes button (▷) in the volume automation lane twice.

Take note of the triangular patterns in the graph of this lane. So far, this pan automation has had no effect on the playback of SynthString Track because its automation mode was set to Off. You may wish to increase the vertical zoom and increase the size of the SynthString track to see the lanes more clearly.

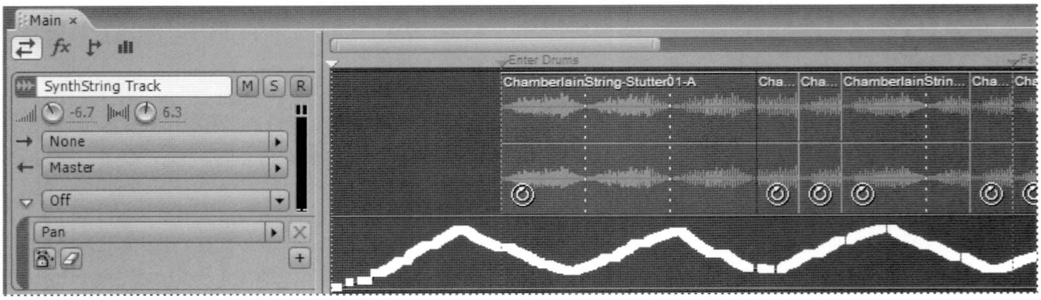

2 Change the automation mode to Latch and playback the session from the beginning. As the session plays, the panning knob in the mixer strip for SynthString Track starts to follow the cyclic graph contained in the pan automation lane.

3 Confirm that the Safe During Write (🔒) button for the pan automation lane for SynthString Track is off.

4 Start playback from the beginning. The Pan knob starts following its automation lane. At Bar 3 beat 1, turn the Pan knob to its extreme left position. Release your mouse button.

The Pan knob stays 'latched' to the position where you left it.

5 Stop the playback when you reach Bar 8 beat 1.

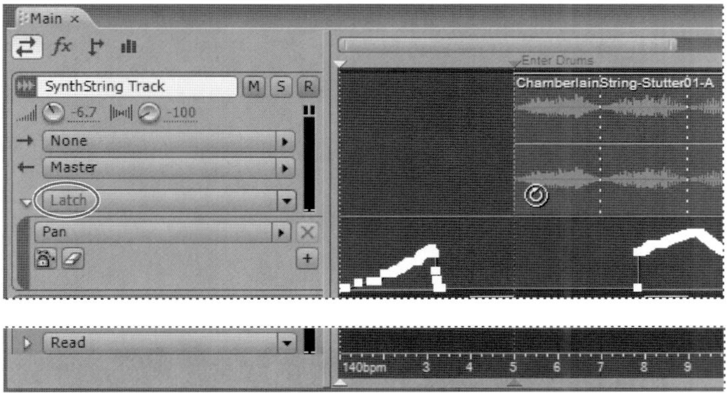

Study the changes made to the graph in the pan automation lane for SynthString Track while in the Latch automation mode. You can see that the Pan knob follows its automation lane as long as you don't start changing it yourself. This is what happens until Bar 3 beat 1. When you start changing it, the knob starts following your mouse instead. When you release the knob, it gets 'latched' to wherever you leave it. This position is maintained until you make another change to the knob.

If you did not stop the playback at Bar 8 beat 1, all the cyclic patterns after this point would have been overwritten.

Track Automation Mode options

When recording automation in the Main panel or Mixer, you can choose one of the following modes for each track:

Track Automation Mode menu.

Off Ignores track envelopes during playback and mix down, but continues to display envelopes so you can manually add or adjust edit points.

Read Applies track envelopes during playback and mix down, but doesn't record any changes you make to them. (You can preview such changes, but edit points return to recorded settings.)

Latch Records adjustments you make to settings and creates corresponding edit points on track envelopes. Begins recording when you first adjust a setting, and continues to record new settings until playback stops.

Touch Similar to Latch, but returns settings to previously recorded values when you stop adjusting them.

Write Similar to Latch, but records current settings as edit points when playback starts, without waiting for a setting to change.

—From Adobe Audition Help

Using clip envelopes for automation

Clip volume envelopes and clip pan envelopes are yet another powerful level of automation that work on a clip-by-clip basis. You can draw precise volume and pan curves for each clip, draw automatic fade ins, fade outs, etc.

Only volume and pan can be automated for a clip using this method. For automating other parameters, you'll have stick to using the automation lanes as shown in earlier exercises.

1 While changing the Automation Mode menu for Drum Track to Read, hold down the Ctrl and Shift keys. This sets the automation modes for all the tracks to Read.

You can use the Ctrl+Shift combination while changing many other track/mixer settings with your mouse to quickly make that setting across all tracks. The Ctrl+Shift combination does not apply to Bus Sends.

2 Close the Mixer window.

3 Choose View > Hide All Automation Lanes

4 Go to the View menu again and uncheck Show Clip Volume Envelopes.

This will hide the thin green line found at the top edge of each clip in the session.

5 Go to the View menu and uncheck Show Clip Pan Envelopes.

This hides the thin light blue line running through the center of each clip.

6 Finally, Choose View > Show Clip Volume Envelopes again and the thin green line reappears at the top edge of every clip.

This line represents the clip volume envelope that will be applied when this clip plays back.

Note: *The height of a clip represents the total range of a clip volume envelope. When the envelope line is at the top edge of the clip (which is the default), the clip plays back at its 100% volume (+0 dB). The bottom edge is the 0% (-∞ dB), and center is 50%.*

In the case of clip pan envelopes, the top edge is hard left panning, bottom is hard right, and middle (default) is center of the stereo field.

7 Select the Hybrid tool ( ) and click once on the clip ToneGen14-G which is the first clip in the Pierce Effects Track.

This clip becomes highlighted. Two white edit points appear on the ends of the volume envelope for this clip. Contents of this clip start rather abruptly right now. You'll fix this using this clip's volume envelope.

8 As you bring your cursor near the volume envelope of the clip, the appearance of the cursor changes to the familiar ( ) icon.

Note: *New edit points for the clip volume envelope can be added, moved, and deleted in the same manner as edit points for automation lanes. See "Drawing automation data" on page 216 for details on how edit points work.*

9 Drag the edit point at the beginning of the clip down to -6 dB (50%). Zoom in if required and create a new edit point at Bar 4 beat 2 and position it at -1 dB (89%).

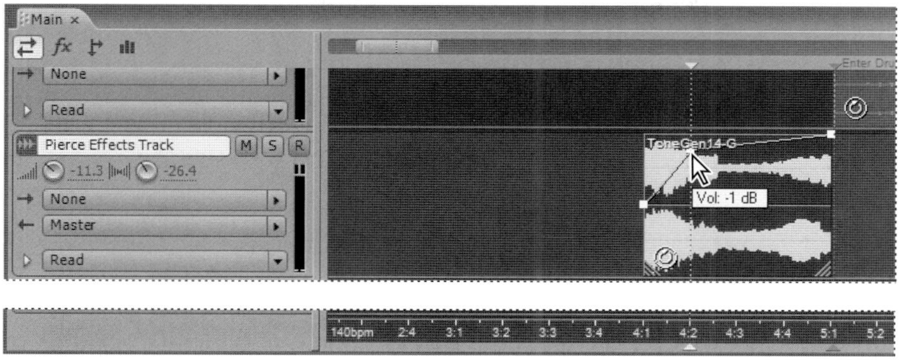

10 Right-click on this clip and, from the context menu that drops-down, choose Clip Envelopes > Volume and check Use Splines option.

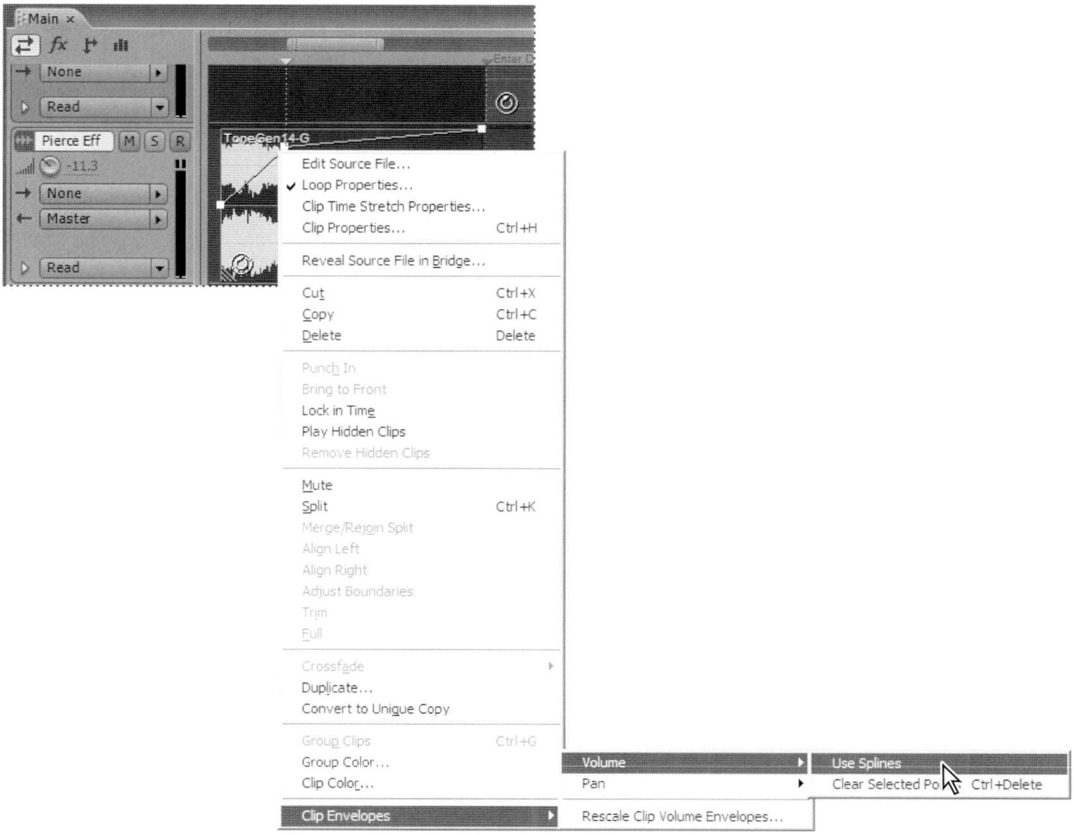

This will cause all the edit points within this clip to be connected with smooth curves. Try adding a new edit point on the clip volume envelope. Click and drag it to various locations within the envelope and note that the curves for the clip's volume envelope remain smooth.

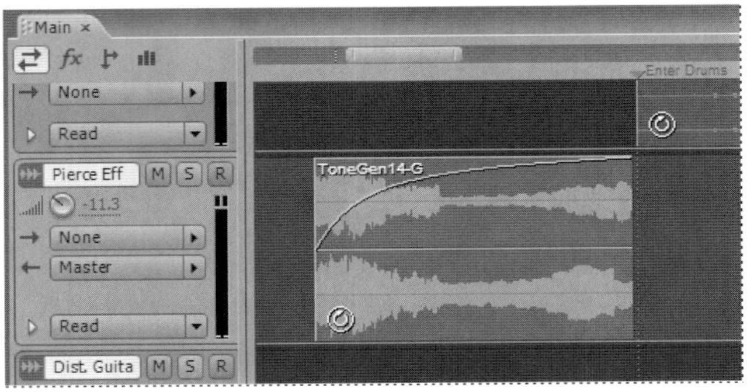

Note: *The clip envelopes for each clip within a track are independent, and you can have one clip set to have smooth curves and another clip to have angular connections between its edit points.*

11 Create similar curves for the starting portions of all clips within the Pierce Effects Track.

12 With the Hybrid tool (▶) still selected, make a time selection from Bar 18 beat 1 to Bar 19 beat 1 on the clip ToneGen17a-A which is the last clip in the Pierce Effects Track.

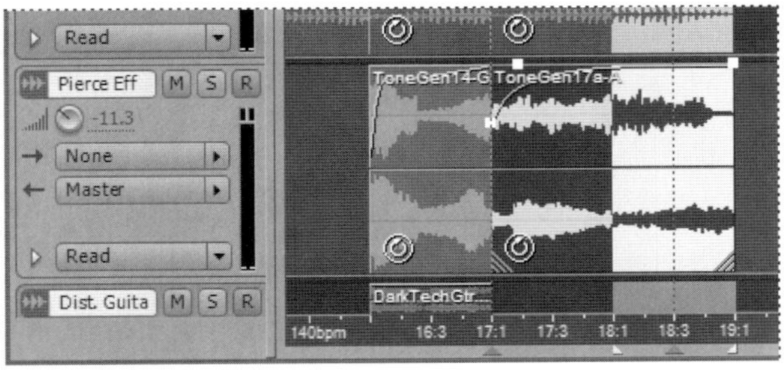

13 Right click on the clip and choose Crossfade > Logarithmic Out from the context menu. This creates a smooth fade out for this clip. While still maintaining the time selection, repeat this procedure for all the final clips near the 30 second Flag marker so that they fade out smoothly.

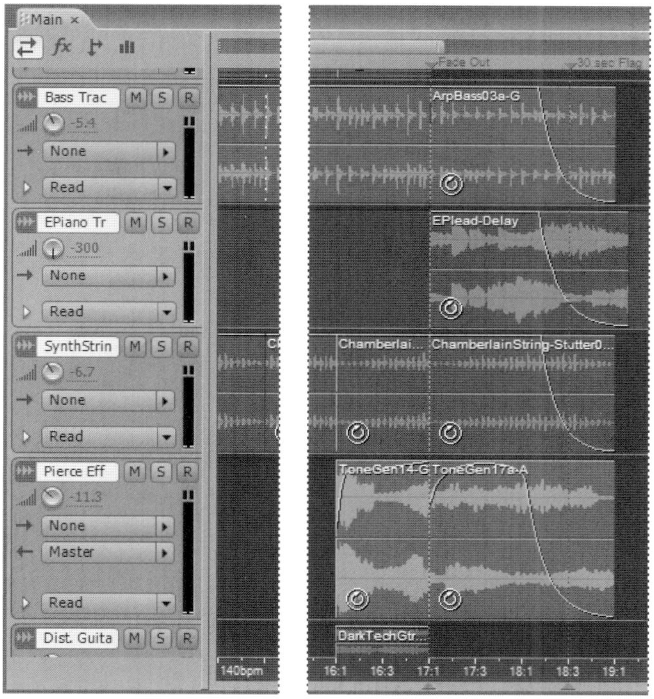

***Note:** If you use clip envelopes in addition to pan and volume lane automation for the same track, you'll hear a combined effect of both types of automation.*

Exploring on your own

1 Clip pan envelopes work in much the same way as clip volume envelopes. Draw a pan envelope on ArpBass03a-G, which is the first clip in Bass Track. Replace all other clips in this track with copies of ArpBass03a-G. You'll see that the pan envelope too gets copied each time. This is a helpful feature of clip envelopes that lets you create repetitive patterns in volume and pan.

2 Practice using automation without needing to look at automation lanes. Keep your track in touch mode most of the time, and whenever it's necessary to make an adjustment to existing automation data, just punch it in. With a little practice, you'll be able to automate an entire session without needing to look at automation lanes. However, remember to use the Write-safe feature so that you don't accidentally lose good takes of automation data.

Review

Review questions

1 What are the advantages of automation?

2 How many types of automation does Adobe Audition provide?

3 What are the five automation modes?

Review answers

1 As you mix a song, you might need to adjust various track and mixer settings while the session plays. Using automation, you can make Audition remember these changes for you and play them back along with the session. This gives you accurate and flexible control of your tracks, and helps you create better mixes.

2 Clip envelopes let you automate pan and volume on a clip-by-clip basis. The second type of automation is based on automation lanes. Track and mixer settings can be automated by either drawing into the appropriate automation lanes, or by recording into them.

3 Off, Read, Latch, Touch, and Write are the five automation modes. Off and Read disable and enable the reading of automation lanes for a track respectively. The last three modes are used to record and edit automation data into automation lanes.

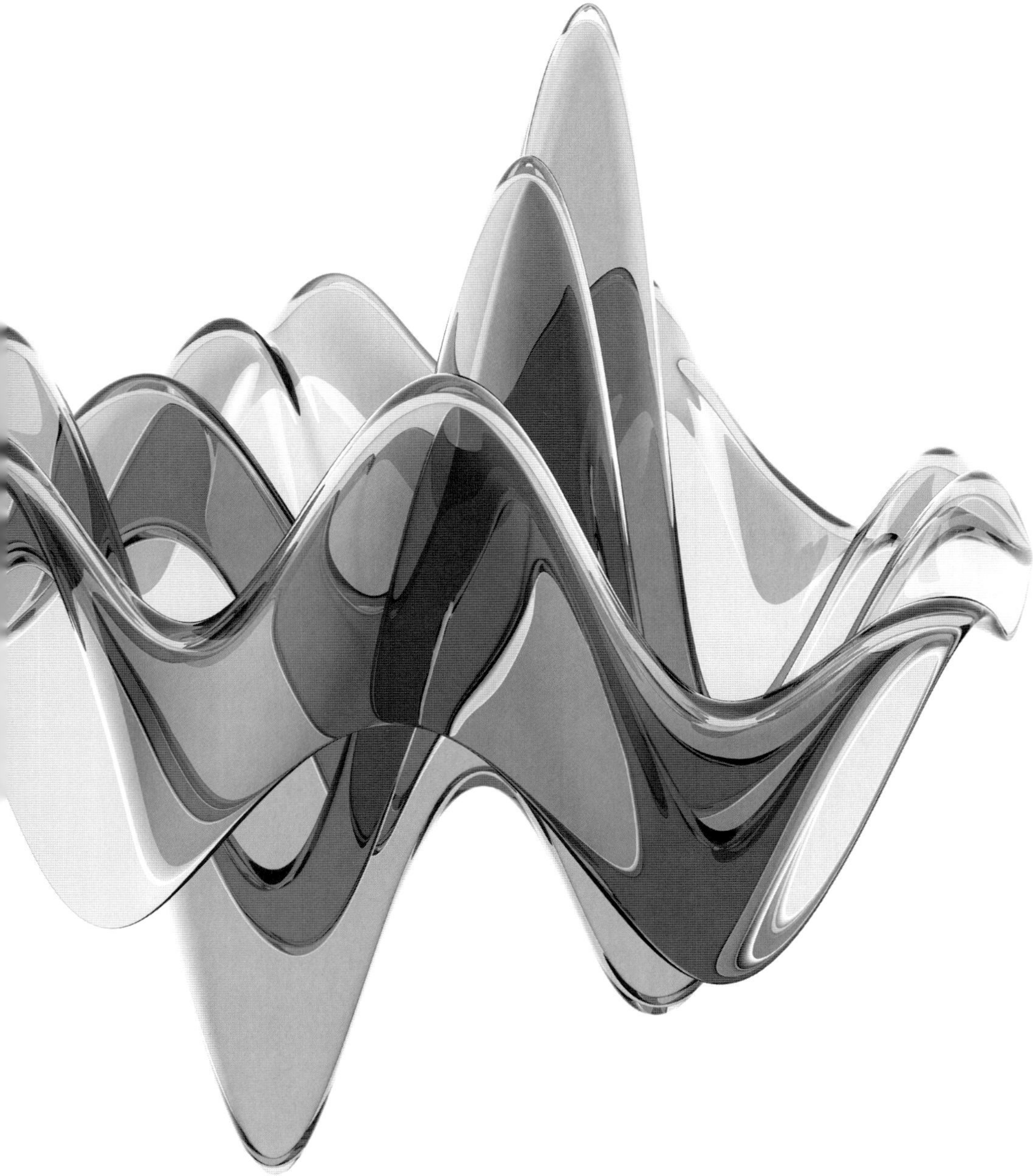

11 Optimizing Audio for the Internet

Distributing music files over the Internet requires special considerations. Audition allows you to effectively compress audio files based on the needs of your projects. Equalization, normalization, and hard limiting effects allow you to maximize the sound quality of your audio files that are delivered via the Internet.

In this lesson, you'll learn how to do the following:

- Apply data compression to reduce the size of files.
- Apply equalization, normalization, and hard limiting to optimize files.
- Batch Process files using mp3 compression.

Getting started

1 Start Adobe Audition. If you have not already copied the resource files for this lesson onto your hard disk from the AA_11 folder from the *Adobe Audition 2.0 Classroom in a Book* CD, do so now. See "Copying the Classroom in a Book files" on page 2.

2 If necessary, click on the Multitrack View button (▤) to switch to this view.

3 Open the session 11_start.ses by choosing File > Open Session.

Reducing file size for the Internet

One of the unique challenges when it comes to working with audio files is that the same music track may be played in different environments. The qualities of sound that are audible when listening through a pair of headphones are different than when listening using a basic car radio. In general, audio engineers attempt to mix tracks that sound acceptable in a variety of situations.

Creating audio files for distribution over the Internet provides another element of complexity: file size. A three-minute song saved in the .wav format may be 30 megabytes in size. Transferring files of this size is time-consuming and impractical. Fortunately, Audition provides methods to reduce file size while maintaining acceptable levels of fidelity.

In this lesson, you will examine some of the methods used to reduce file size, including changing the sample rate, reducing bit-depth, and applying compression. You will export a source file using a variety of methods to better understand how reductions in file size correlate to a reduction in quality.

1 In the Files panel, double-click on the ska.wav file to open the waveform into Edit View.

2 In the Edit View, choose File > File Info to open the File Info window. Using this window, you can add extra user-added information to an audio file as well as view important information about the file. Keep the File Info window open.

3 Click on the File Info tab on the right. Important information about the file is located in this window. You can see that this is a 44100 Hz, 16 Bit, Stereo .wav file. In addition, the file format is Windows PCM, which is a specific type of a .wav file. Audition uses the PCM format as its default method for saving .wav files because it is considered a lossless format, where sound quality is not affected. The uncompressed file size is displayed as 6.13 megabytes. The value for the size on disk is exactly the same, because there was no compression applied to this file. Compressed files may show a smaller size on disk than when they are uncompressed.

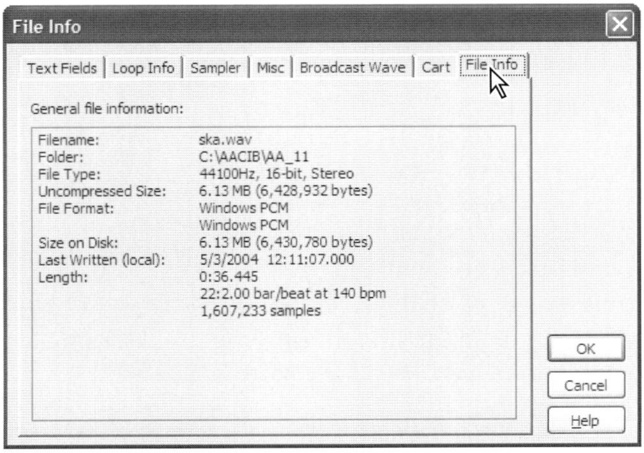

4 Click the OK button to close the File Info window. Choose File > Save Copy As. In the Save Copy As window, choose DVI/IMA ADPCM (*.wav) from the Save as type drop-down menu. Enter **ska_DVI_ADPCM.wav** in the File name field. Keep the window open.

5 Click the Options button and the DVI/IMA ADPCM window opens, presenting four options: 2 bits/sample through 5 bits/sample. Confirm that the 4 bits/sample option is selected. Click the OK button to close the DVI/IMA ADPCM window, but keep the Save Copy As window open.

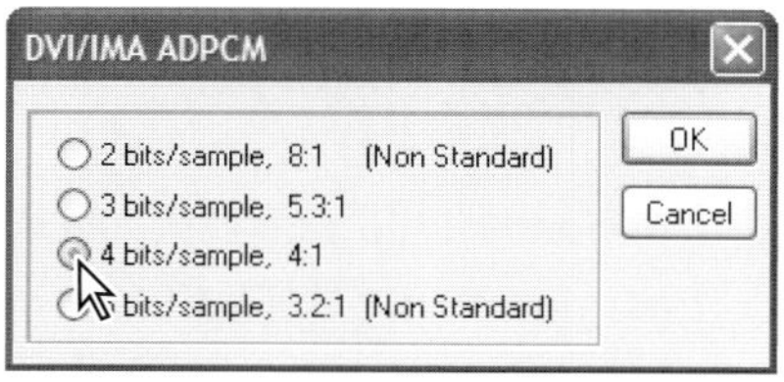

The DVI/IMA ADPCM window.

About bit depth

The bit depth of a file determines the amplitude resolution. A bit is a computer term meaning a single number that can have a value of either zero or one. A single bit can represent two states, such as on and off. Two bits together can represent four different states: zero/zero, one/zero, zero/one, or one/one. Each additional bit doubles the number of states that can be represented, so a third bit can represent eight states, a fourth 16, and so on.

Amplitude resolution is just as important as frequency resolution. Higher bit depth means greater dynamic range, a lower noise floor, and higher fidelity. When a waveform is sampled, each sample is assigned the amplitude value closest to the original analog wave. With a resolution of two bits, each sample can have one of only four possible amplitude positions. With three-bit resolution, each sample has eight possible amplitude values. CD-quality sound is 16-bit, which means that each sample has 65,536 possible amplitude values. DVD-quality sound is 24-bit, which means that each sample has 16,777,216 possible amplitude values.

—From Adobe Audition Help

6 Navigate to the AA_11 folder and open the Compressed_Export subfolder. Click the Save button. If a warning message appears indicating that you are saving to a lower fidelity format, click OK.

This window appears the first time you save a file at a lower compression rate. You can check the Don't display this message in the future option to prevent this window from opening. However, leaving it unchecked acts as a safeguard, ensuring you do not save compressed files unless you intentionally choose to do so.

7 Double-click in an empty area of the Files panel, opening the Import window. If necessary, navigate to the AA_11 folder and then select the ska_DVI_ADPCM.wav file you just exported, and then click the Open button. When the file ska_DVI_ADPCM.wav shows up in the Files panel, double-click on it to open it into the Edit View. In the Edit View, right-click on the waveform representing the file, and choose File Info from the context menu.

You can see in the File Info window under the File Info tab, that the value for the Uncompressed Size remains at 6.13 Mb, however the value for the Size on Disk has been reduced to 1.53 Mb. This is a result of the 4:1 compression applied to the file at the time it was saved. The uncompressed file is four times larger than the compressed file.

8 Click the OK button to close the File Info window. Press the spacebar on your keyboard to play the compressed ska file. After 5 seconds, press the spacebar again to stop playing the file. Double-click the original ska.wav in the Files panel to open its waveform and press the spacebar to listen to the file for five seconds. Return to the compressed file by double-clicking on ska_DVI_ADPCM.wav, and press the spacebar to hear the file.

You may not hear a significant difference in the two files, but the file size of the ska_DVI_ADPCM.wav file is approximately 75% smaller.

While in the Edit View, you should make it a habit to frequently look at the blue title bar at the top of your screen to make sure which file you are actually viewing and editing.

Compressing files in the mp3 format

The file you compressed in the previous exercise was only around 36 seconds in length. Songs and audio clips are often much longer, and would create a much larger file, even when using the ADPCM .wav compression method. To allow for the additional compression for big sound files, the mp3 and, more recently, the mp3PRO technologies were developed. These compression methods greatly reduce the file size while maintaining good quality levels. In this exercise, you will apply different compression modes using Audition's mp3 encoding tools.

1 In the Files panel, double-click the ska.wav file to see it in the Edit View.

2 Choose File > Save Copy As. From the Save as type drop-down menu, choose mp3PRO® (FhG) from the list of available file formats. In the File name field enter **ska_20_Kbps.mp3**. Click the Options button and the MP3/mp3PRO® Encoder Options window opens. If not already checked, select the radio button for the MP3 option and confirm that the Convert to Mono check box is not selected. Keep the MP3/mp3PRO® Encoder Options window open.

3 Choose 20 Kbps, 12000 Hz, Stereo (70.6:1) from the drop-down menu in the middle of the MP3/mp3PRO® Encoder Options window (**not** the Presets menu at the top).

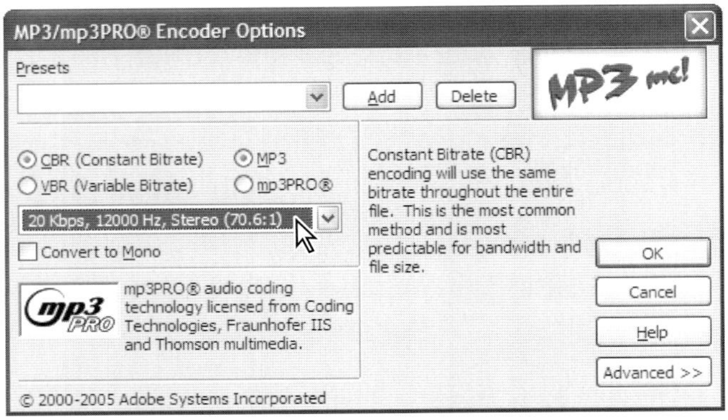

The MP3/mp3PRO® Encoder Options window.

The first value, 20 Kbps, refers to the bit rate, which is measured in Kilobits per second. Bit rate is the average number of bits that one second of audio data will consume. Higher bit rates produce larger file sizes and generally create better audio quality. The second value of 12,000 Hz refers to the sampling rate. The sampling rate of the original .wav file is 44,100 Hz.

4 Click OK in the MP3/mp3PRO® Encoder Options window. In the Save Copy As window, which is still open, navigate to the Compressed_Export folder located in the AA_11 folder on your hard disk. Click the Save button.

5 Double-click in an empty area of the Files panel, and the Import window opens. Select the ska_20_Kbps.mp3 file you just exported, and then click the Open button. In the Files panel, double-click the ska_20_Kbps.mp3 file to open it in Edit View. Look at the title bar at the top of your screen to check if you are looking at this file. Right-click on the waveform and choose File Info. Click on the File Info tab if it is not already chosen.

Note that the value for the Uncompressed Size is now 1.67 MB. The size is significantly smaller because the sample rate was reduced from 44,100 Hz to 12,000 Hz. Looking at the Size on Disk, note the size is approximately 90 KB, which is a result of setting the bit rate to 20 Kbps. This file is now 1/70th of the original file size. The size was first reduced by changing the sampling rate from 44,100 Hz to 12,000 Hz, and then further reduced by changing the bit rate to 20 Kbps.

What is sampling rate?

The sampling rate determines the frequency range of an audio file. The higher the sampling rate, the closer the shape of the digital waveform will be to that of the original analog waveform. Low sampling rates limit the range of frequencies that can be recorded, which can result in a recording that poorly represents the original sound.

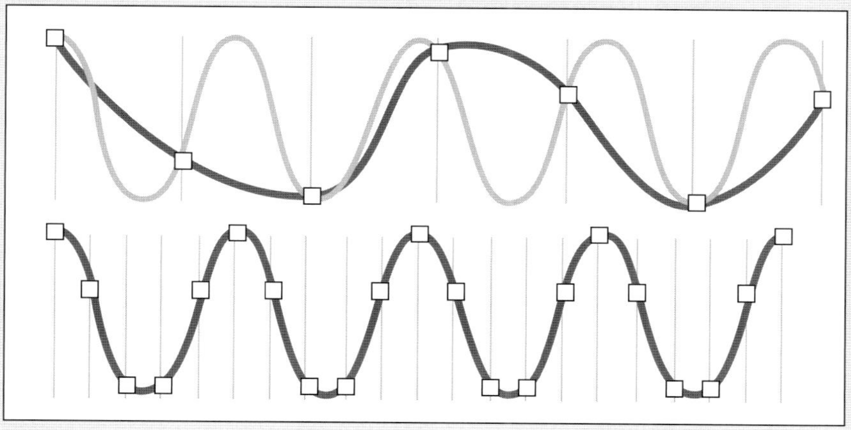

Two sample rates are displayed above. The top is an example of a low sample rate that distorts the original sound wave. The bottom shows a high sample rate that perfectly reproduces the original sound wave.

To reproduce a given frequency, the sampling rate must be at least twice that frequency. For example, if the audio contains audible frequencies as high as 8,000 Hz, you need a sample rate of 16,000 samples per second to represent this audio accurately in digital form. This calculation comes from the Nyquist Theorem, and the highest frequency that can be reproduced by a given sample rate is known as the Nyquist Frequency. CDs have a sample rate of 44,100 samples per second that allows sampling up to 22,050 Hz, which is higher than the upper limit of human hearing, 20,000 Hz.

6 Click OK to close the File Info window and then press the spacebar to play the ska_20_Kbps.mp3 file. The compression has adversely affected the audio quality of the file. The instruments have become muddy and indistinct, and the higher frequencies of the song, such as those in the drums, have deteriorated.

Using high-quality headphones when working with compression allows your ear to notice more of the artifacts and distortion created by data compression. You should listen to completed files through both headphones and speakers before distributing the completed track.

7 Double-click on the ska.wav file in the Files panel to open it into the Edit View. Choose File > Save Copy As. Enter the name **ska_50VBR.mp3**. Click the Options button to open the MP3/mp3PRO® Encoder Options window. Select the VBR (Variable Bit Rate) radio button option and choose 50 (105-140 Kbps), Average Quality from the drop-down menu. Make certain that the mp3 option is selected. Keep the MP3/mp3PRO® Encoder Options window open.

Variable Bit Rate

Variable Bit Rate or VBR is a technique which analyzes the audio file being encoded and uses higher bit rates for areas of higher complexity such as the crescendo of many instruments during a symphony. Conversely, areas of the same audio file which have less information, such as a trumpet solo, use lower bit rates. When you choose a level of compression, you are actually choosing a range of bit rates. Files encoded with VBR are less predictable in terms of file size than files encoded with Constant Bit Rate (CBR), this is because the file size is dependent on the type of music being encoded. In addition, not all mp3 players support files encoded with VBR. If you are planning on distributing .mp3 files to the widest possible audience, you should stick with CBR encoded files, which may be larger in size but are more compatible.

8 In the Preset section at the top of the MP3/mp3PRO® Encoder Options window, click on the Add button to open the Add Preset dialog box. In the Name field, type in **My VBR (50 Quality) mp3 format**. By adding this custom preset, you are adding to those that are included with Adobe Audition.

9 Click OK to close the Add Preset window and then click OK to close the mp3 Encoder window. Finally click the Save button to save the file into the Compressed_Export subfolder within the AA_11 folder on your hard disk.

10 Double-click in an empty area of the Files panel to open the Import window. Choose the ska_50VBR.mp3 file you just created, and then click the Open button. In the Files panel, double-click the ska_50VBR.mp3 file to open it in Edit View. Confirm that you are looking at this waveform by looking at the title bar at the top of the screen.

11 Click once on the waveform and then, using your keyboard, press Ctrl+P to open the File Info window. While the uncompressed size remains at 6.13 MB, the actual file size on disk has been compressed to approximately 480 KB.

12 Click OK to close the File Info window.

13 In the Files panel, double-click on the ska.wav to open the file into the Edit View. Choose File > Save Copy As. Enter the name for this file as **ska_pro96Kbps.mp3**. Click the Options button to open the MP3/mp3PRO® Encoder Options window. In the Presets field at the top of this window, choose the Pro 96 Kbps Stereo option from the drop-down menu. This preset uses the mp3Pro technology.

14 Click OK to close the MP3/mp3PRO® Encoder Options window. In the Save Copy As window, which is still open, click Save to save the ska_pro96Kbps.mp3 file into the Compressed_Export subfolder in the AA_11 folder.

mp3PRO technology

mp3PRO technology is a relatively new compression technique. Files encoded with mp3PRO use much lower bit rates than standard mp3 compression. The most common bit rates for standard .mp3 files are 192Kbps, 160Kbps, and 128Kbps. The latter is emerging as the de facto standard for files distributed on the Internet. mp3PRO on the other hand, generally uses bit rates no higher than 96Kbps, although 80Kbps and 64Kbps are popular as well. The technology behind mp3PRO is called spectral band replication (SBR), which splits the audio file into low and high frequencies. The low frequencies are compressed at low bit rates, high frequencies are not compressed at all but are reconstructed by the playback device.

mp3PRO files are backwards compatible with standard mp3 players, but there is a potential downside. mp3 Players which do not have mp3PRO capability will simply ignore the high frequency SBR data, which results in reduced sound quality. If you will be using mp3PRO technology you should check your software compatibility to make the most of this format.

15 Double-click in any empty area of the Files panel to open the Import window. In the Import window, select the ska_pro96Kbps.mp3 file and click Open. In the Files panel, double-click the ska_pro96Kbps.mp3 file to open it in the Edit View. Click once on the waveform and then press Ctrl+P to open the File Info window. The uncompressed file is approximately 6.15 MB and the file size is approximately 430 KB. This file, and the file ska_50VBR.mp3 that you created previously, have approximately the same file size, although they use two different forms of compression. Click OK to close the File Info window.

Optimizing sound quality

In the previous exercise, you used different types of data compression to reduce the size of a file. This makes the files more manageable for distribution on the Web. Regardless of the level of compression you use, a loss in quality always occurs when compressing the files. It is important to choose the compression technique that best suits the needs of your target audience. For example, an online news web site may sacrifice audio quality when compressing interviews, under the assumption that the benefits of the reduced file size outweighs the degradation to audio quality that occurs. Conversely, a band sending an .mp3 file to a talent agent may decide to compress at a higher bit rate to achieve higher audio quality. In this exercise, you'll use techniques that can improve the sound of audio files which will eventually be compressed. The three techniques you will be using are equalization, normalization, and hard limiting.

1 If you are not currently in the Edit View, click on the Edit View button ( ). Double-click in an empty area of the Files panel to open the Import window. Navigate to the pachebel_wedding.wav file located in your AA_11 folder and click the Open button to place the file into your Files panel. This is an uncompressed PCM .wav file. It takes a moment for Audition to load it up, as shown by the progress meter.

2 Double-click the pachebel_wedding.wav file to open it into Edit View. Press the spacebar and listen to this file for about 5 seconds to get an idea of how this file sounds. Choose Effects > Filters > Graphic Equalizer to open the Graphic Equalizer window. Since you had not made any time selection before opening the graphic equalizer, the entire file is selected and highlighted in the background.

Graphic EQ is extremely useful when optimizing files for the web. You can emphasize/reduce certain frequencies within an audio file to compensate for the losses that will occur once you compress the file. The process of compression generally introduces noise and unwanted artifacts in the higher frequencies.

3 Click on the Effect Preset menu at the top of the Graphic EQ window. A drop-down menu containing all the available presets appears. Scroll through the list of presets and choose Full Reset. Click on the 10 Bands button above the sliders to view a 10 band version of the Graphic Equalizer.

4 Click the last slider, labeled >16k, and drag it to the bottom, reducing the highest frequencies.

5 Click the first slider, labeled <31, and drag it to the bottom as well. As you drag the slider to the bottom, the values for the gain are updated.

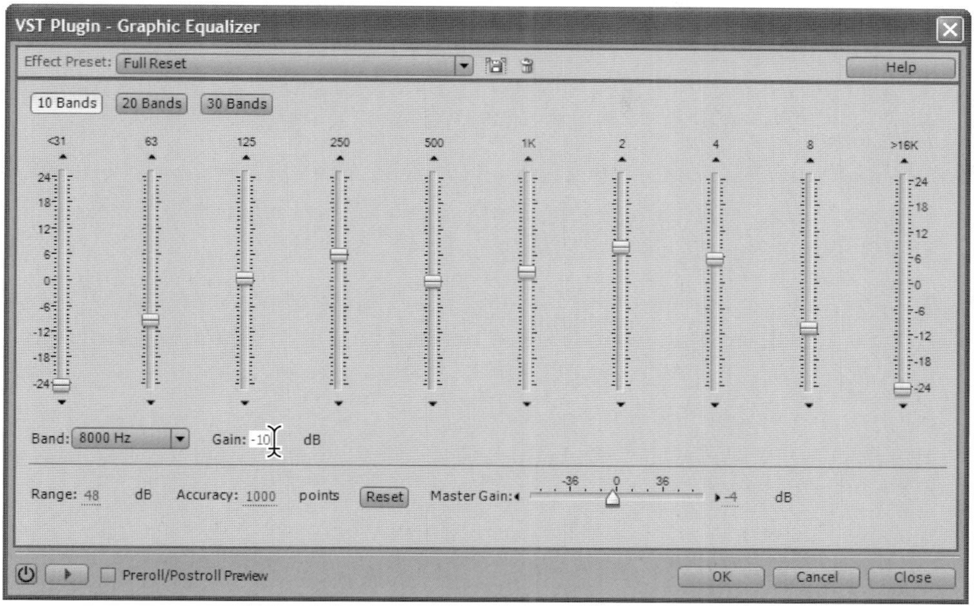

6 Set the following values for the remaining EQ bands by using the up or down arrows for each band or by typing in the Gain value:

- 63 Hz, -8.9 dB
- 125 Hz, 1.0 dB
- 250 Hz, 6.4 dB
- 500 Hz, 0.2 dB
- 1k, 2.6 dB
- 2k, 8.4 dB
- 4k, 5.59 dB
- 8k, -10 dB

7 Changing the EQ sliders affects the overall volume of the file. In the Master Gain text field, enter **-4**. This reduces the overall volume of the waveform by -4 dB while maintaining the EQ relationships.

Note: *For best results, experiment with these settings for different genres of music and for different songs. Settings that work well for one song may not work well for other songs.*

8 Press the Preview Play/Stop button ( ) at the bottom left of the Graphic EQ window to preview what your equalization changes sound like. While previewing, you can switch off the Power button ( ) to temporarily bypass the Graphic Equalizer effect. This lets you hear how the file sounded originally. Click on the Power button again to turn it on and continue previewing the file with the effect applied. When you are done, click the Preview Play/Stop button again to stop previewing the file.

Note: *Sometimes it is hard to hear the effect of equalization if you are using low-quality speakers. As suggested earlier, you might want to use headphones for these exercises, to be able to hear the results of equalization.*

9 Click the Save a new preset button ( ) in the Effects Preset section at the top of the Graphic Equalizer window. In the Add Preset dialog box that follows, enter **My Web Settings Classical** for the preset name, and then click OK. Your custom equalization settings are saved as this new preset.

10 Click OK in the Graphic Equalizer to apply these equalization settings to the file. The waveform changes slightly, due to the equalization changes you made.

11 Choose File > Save As and rename this file **pachebel_wedding_eq.wav**. This saves the modified version without changing the original file. Click the Save button. You should now see this file in the Edit View instead of the original pachebel_wedding.wav file. Press the spacebar to play this file.

You can see that level meters generally stay around the -9 dB area. You will now apply the Normalize effect to this file to raise its overall amplitude.

12 Choose Effects > Amplitude > Normalize (process) and enter **85%** in the Normalize to field. Confirm that the Normalize L/R Equally check box is checked. A normalization of 100% results in the maximum possible amplitude being applied to the file. For files destined for the web, be careful using high normalization values. Higher values may create clipping, which can sound very unpleasant to the human ear.

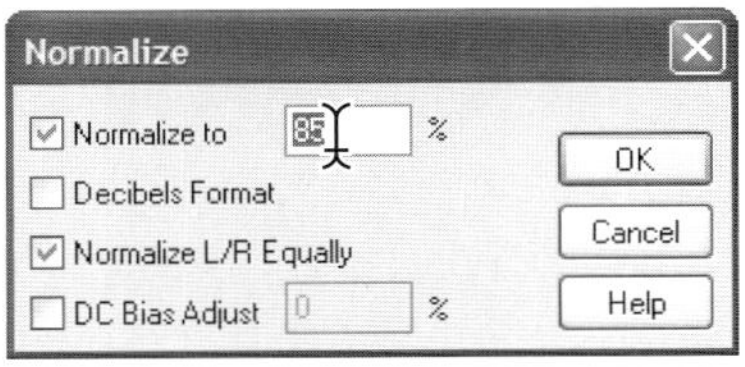

13 Click OK to apply the Normalize effect. The visual representation of the entire waveform displayed in the Edit View increases in height.

14 Choose Effects > Amplitude > Hard Limiting (process). The Hard Limiting window opens. In the Boost Input by field, type in **2**. Leave the other settings at their default values. Click OK and note the entire waveform increases in amplitude.

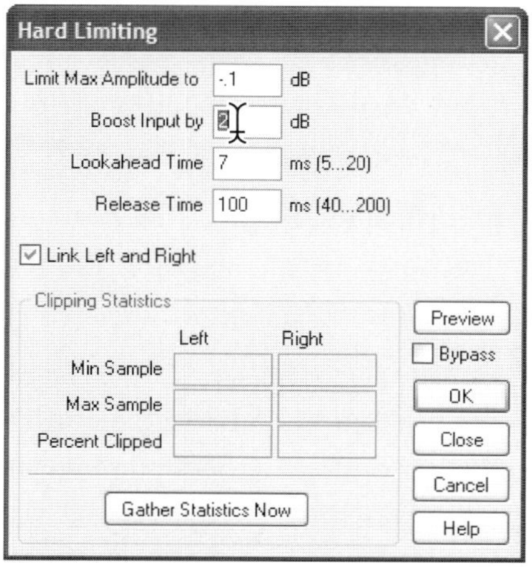

Hard limiting increases the perceived volume of an audio file by compressing the distance between the loudest sections of the waveform and the quietest sections. Even though the sound is louder, there will not be any clipping because the loudest sections are "limited" to a specified level.

15 Press the Play button to hear the file. Although it is louder, there is no distortion of the audio. Choose File > Save As and rename the filename to **pachebel_wedding_eq_NormLimited.wav**. Press the Save button to save this normalized and limited file as an independent file.

Compressing multiple files with the Batch Processor

Although individual files can be saved in the mp3 format as needed, you may need to convert a large number of files using the same settings. Adobe Audition's Batch Processor helps you accomplish this.

1 If necessary, switch to the Edit View. Choose File > Batch Processing and the Batch Processing window opens. You will be selecting a group of files to process.

2 At the bottom of the Batch Processing window, choose the Files tab. Click the Add Files button on the top right and navigate to the AA_11 folder on your hard disk. Click on the first file DanceCryTrance.wav, and then Ctrl+click on all the .wav files in the folder. Click the Add button. The names and paths of these files get added to the source files list.

3 In the Batch Processing window, click the New Format tab located at the bottom of the window.

4 From the Output Format menu, choose mp3Pro, and then click the Format Properties button to open the MP3/mp3PRO® Encoder Options window. From the drop-down Presets menu in the MP3/mp3PRO® Encoder Options window, choose 128 Kbps Stereo (Internet) and click OK.

5 In the Batch Processing window, click on the Destination tab located at the bottom. Select the radio button for Same as file's source folder option in the top left corner, and be certain the Overwrite existing files and Delete source file if converted OK options are deselected. Then, click the Run Batch button. Audition converts the four .wav files into .mp3 files using a bit rate of 128 Kbps and then places the files in the same folder from which the source files originated.

6 Click OK to close the Batch Processing progress window. You can navigate to the AA_11 folder on your hard disk to confirm that all the chosen files have been converted to .mp3 files.

Exploring on your own

1 Open the DanceCryTrance.wav file from the AA_11 folder and save a copy using the File > Save Copy As. Save the new copy as an .mp3 and experiment with changing the bit rate and the sample rate through the mp3 Encoder Options, determine which combination sounds the best to you.

2 Choose File > Batch Processing and select the music files located in your AA_11 folder. Output the files as Windows Media Audio, and be sure to click on the Format Properties button in the New Format tab.

Review

Review questions

1 How can you determine the compression used on any file?

2 What are sample rate and bit depth and how do they affect the size of a file?

3 What methods can you use to improve sound files which need to be heavily compressed, possibly for distribution via the Internet?

Review answers

1 Opening any file into the Edit View and choosing File > File Info will open the File Info window. Then, clicking on the File Info tab will show you information about the file, including the Uncompressed Size and the Size on Disk.

2 Sample rate is the number of samples per second and it determines the frequency range of a file. The limit of human hearing on the high end of the frequency range is approximately 20,000 Hz. Low sampling rates reduce the range of frequencies in a file. CDs have a sample rate of 44,100 Hz. Lower sample rates reduce the size of a file but also reduce the quality of the file. Bit depth is defined as the number of bits used to represent audio amplitude for each sample. Higher bit depth means greater dynamic range and higher fidelity. Audition uses 32 bit depth by default. Lower bit depths give you smaller file sizes, but also lower-quality files.

3 Equalization, normalization, and hard limiting are three methods you can use to optimize files destined for the Internet. Equalization can affect files in numerous ways. For Internet distribution, equalization allows you to manipulate the frequency content in the file. Higher frequencies are particularly affected by heavy compression. Normalization is the process of increasing the amplitude with respect to the highest peak in your file and all other samples are amplified by the same amount; which makes your file louder. Hard limiting increases perceived loudness, while ensuring that the file never clips.

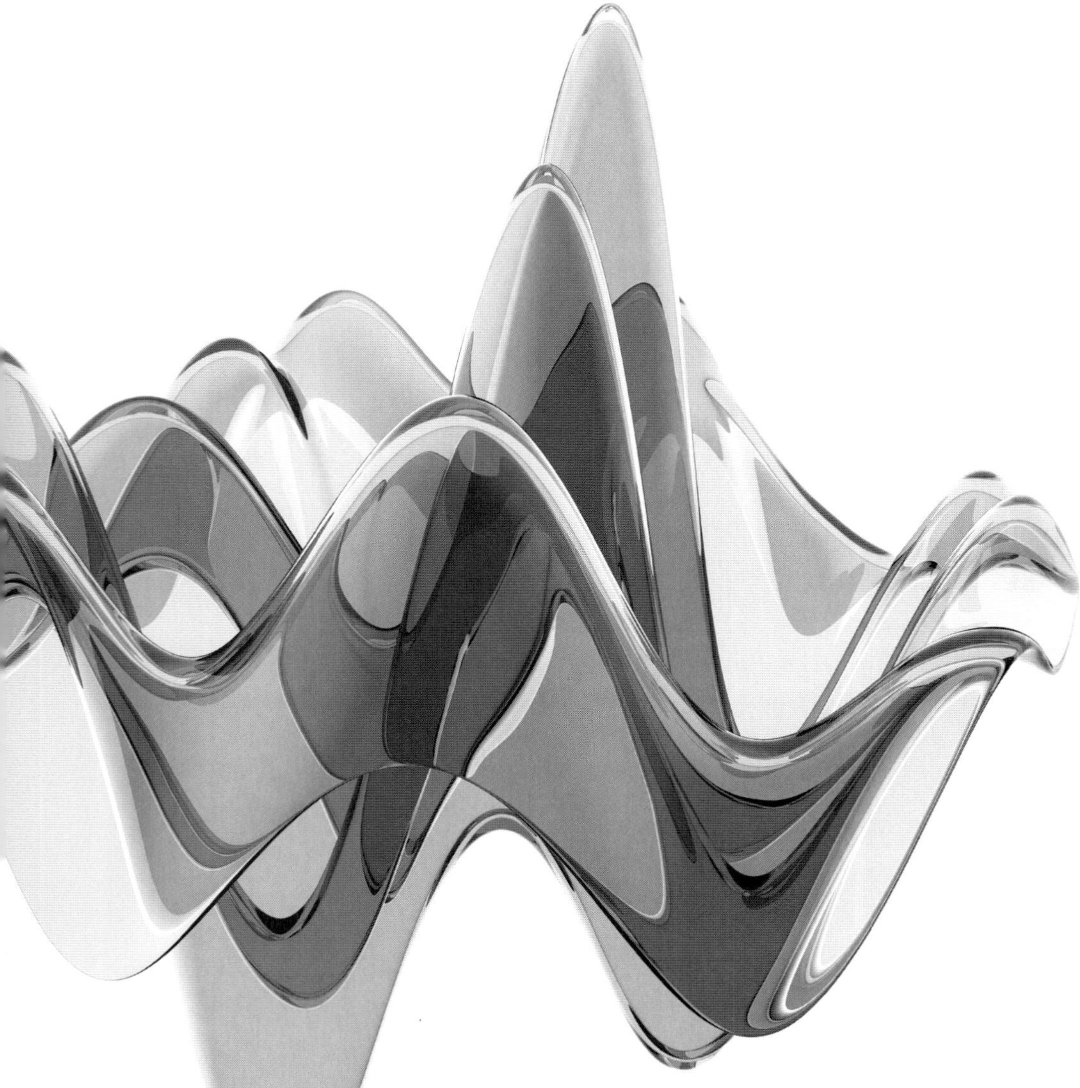

12 Using the CD View

Audition's advanced audio extraction features provide options for importing and extracting audio files. You can also add text labels and track information for your custom CD projects.

In this lesson, you'll learn how to do the following:

- Use the CD View.
- Extract audio tracks from CDs.
- Set track properties.
- Normalize a group of tracks.
- Burn a Red Book compliant audio CD.

Getting started

Using the CD View, you can engineer and create a professional quality audio CD from session files you've created, or from tracks you've extracted from your own CD library. You can also use Audition to extract pieces of audio tracks, or samples, which can be organized in the CD View.

Note: *There are no lesson files for this lesson in the data portion of the CD to copy for this lesson. The* Adobe Audition 2.0 Classroom in a Book *CD is a Mixed Media CD that includes both audio and data tracks. In this lesson, you will be working with the audio components of the CD. But you should still copy the empty folder called AA_12_no_files from the CD to your hard disk. This is where you'll be saving the files generating from this session.*

Some CD-Rom drives may not be able to display the contents of a Mixed Media CD properly. To complete the following exercises in Adobe Audition, it may be necessary to substitute any standard audio CD for the *Adobe Audition 2.0 Classroom in a Book* CD.

Extracting audio from a CD

The Extract Audio from CD command provides a refined control over what is extracted from an audio CD. You can use this method to extract all tracks, selected tracks, or a specific time selection from a CD. Once extracted, individual tracks can be used in your sessions just like the loops and waveforms you've been using in the previous lessons.

1 Start Adobe Audition. If necessary, insert the *Adobe Audition 2.0 Classroom in a Book* CD into the CD-ROM drive of your computer. If a window opens asking what action to take with the CD, click the Cancel button.

2 Click the CD View button ( ) at the top of your display, then choose File > Extract Audio from CD. A window opens for you to choose what you need to extract from the CD.

3 In the Extract Audio From CD window, choose the drive on your computer that contains the CD from the Device drop-down menu.

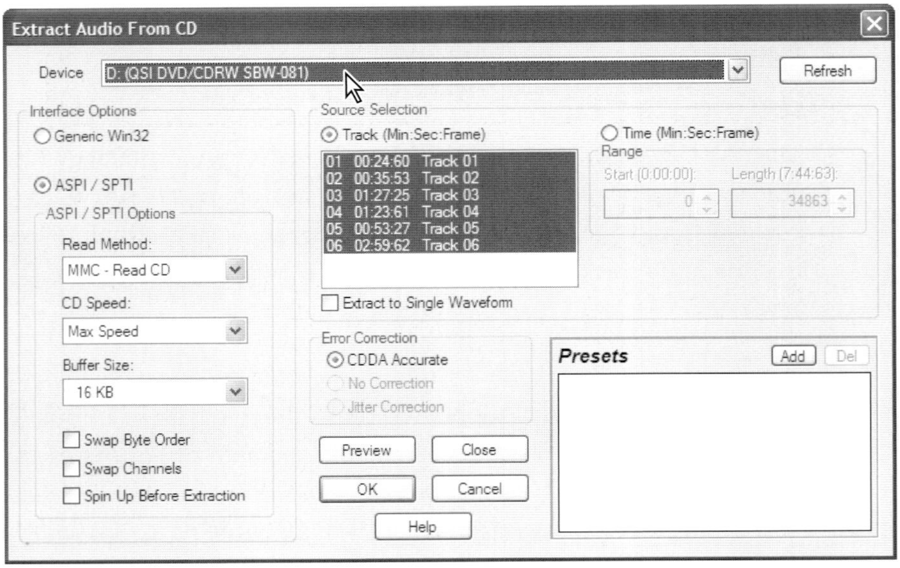

4 For Source Selection, choose the Time (Min: Sec: Frame) option to extract part of Track01. Input a Start value of **0** and a Length value of **475**. Notice the Length indicator above at 0:06:25 indicating a clip of 6.25 seconds in length will be extracted.

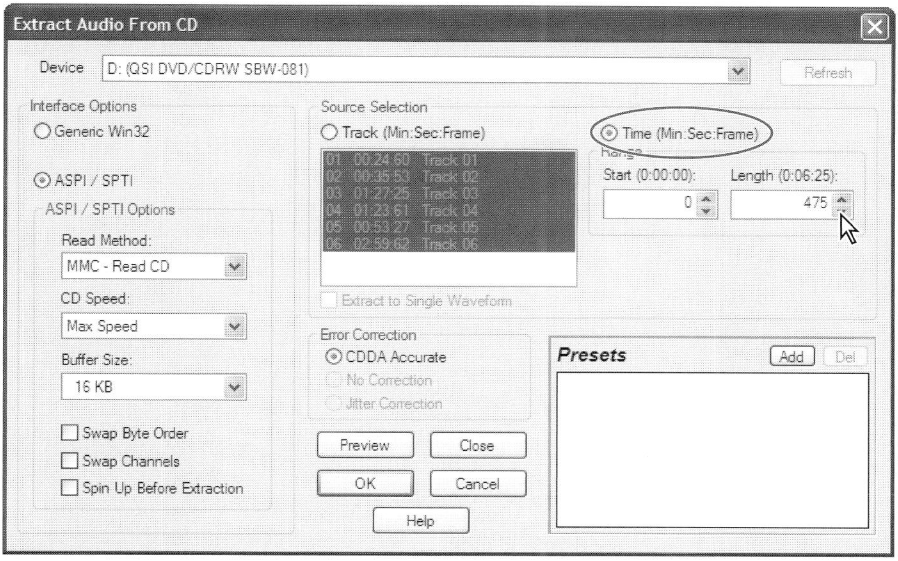

Selecting the Track option under Source Selection allows for the extraction of entire tracks from your audio CD. On the other hand, the Time option can be used for pulling hidden tracks from CDs, as well as for joining tracks that have been broken up by track indexes, such as performance track CDs and live albums.

5 The actual start and length times appear in Min: Sec: Frame format above their respective boxes. The beginning frame appears in the Start box, and the total number of frames you wish to extract in the Length box. Each second of CD audio has 75 frames.

6 In the Interface Options portion of the Extract Audio From CD window, confirm that the ASPI/SPTI option is selected. Leave the other fields in this section of the window unchanged.

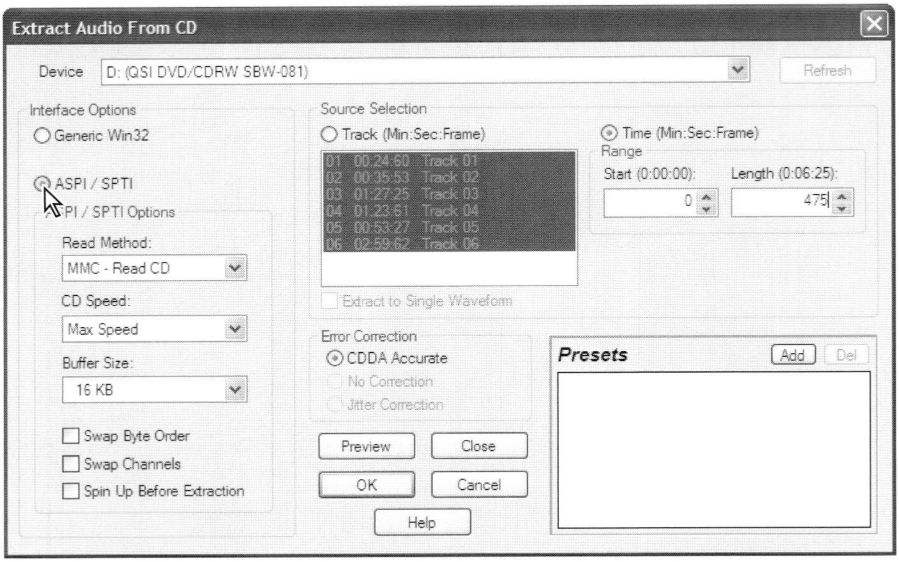

Note: *The default Read Method, MMC - Read CD, is a SCSI-3 compliant format and works with most modern CD drives.*

Error correction when ripping a CD

If the CD-ROM drive you are using has built-in ripping error correction, CDDA Accurate is automatically selected for Error Correction. For these types of drives, no error correction is needed, so you won't be able to select any options from this part of the Extract Audio from CD dialog box.

If your drive isn't CDDA Accurate, you can select the No Correction and Jitter Correction options. No Correction results in no error correction as the CD is ripping. Jitter Correction compensates for data reading problems that older drives may encounter when reading a CD.

7 Listen to the portion you have selected by clicking the Preview button.

8 Click OK to start extracting the selection from the CD. Once Audition has completed ripping your audio selection, the file is listed in the Files panel as Untitled. You can double-click on it to open it up in the Edit View, listen, edit, and save the file as a .cel file or any other audio file format.

9 Click on this file in the Files panel to select it, then delete it from your session file by pressing the Delete key on your keyboard. When a window opens asking if you want to save the file, click No.

10 In the CD View, choose File > Extract Audio from CD. The Extract Audio From CD window opens up again. Choose the drive that contains the CD from the Device drop-down menu.

11 Confirm the Track (Min: Sec: Frame) radio button is selected. Then select the following tracks for ripping, holding down the Ctrl key, if necessary:

- Track 01
- Track 02
- Track 03
- Track 04

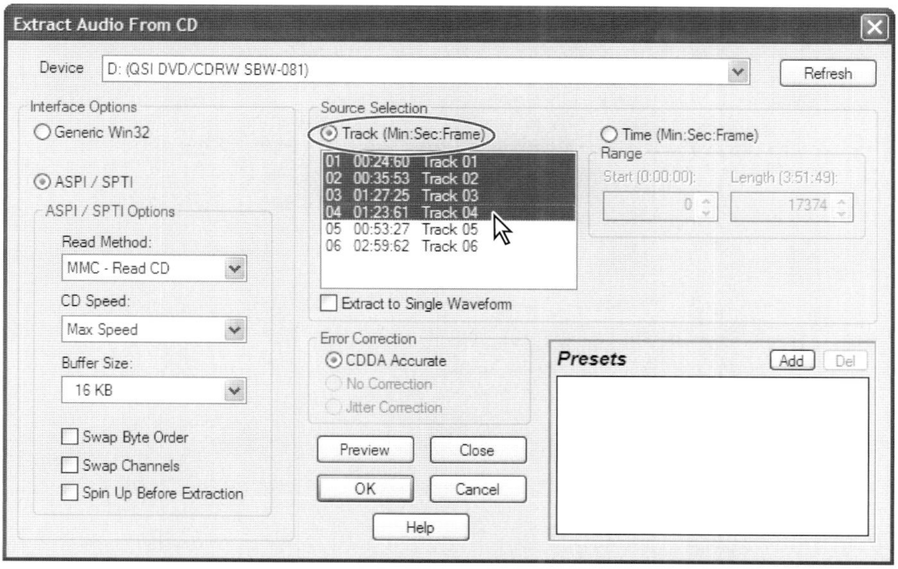

12 Click OK to extract the tracks from the CD into your project.

Audition takes a moment to extract the digital audio from the CD. Once the files are extracted, they are listed in the Files tab of the Organize window. The files have been converted into editable waveforms.

13 Choose File > Save All.

14 Double-click on the first extracted file, called Track 01*, in the Files panel to open it in the Edit View. An asterisk (*) after the filename means that this file has not yet been saved. In the Edit View, choose File > Save As. Choose the Windows PCM (*.wav) format in the Save as type menu. Navigate to the AA_12_no_files folder on your hard disk. Press the Save button. Once the file is saved, the asterisk sign disappears from the name of the file in the Files panel.

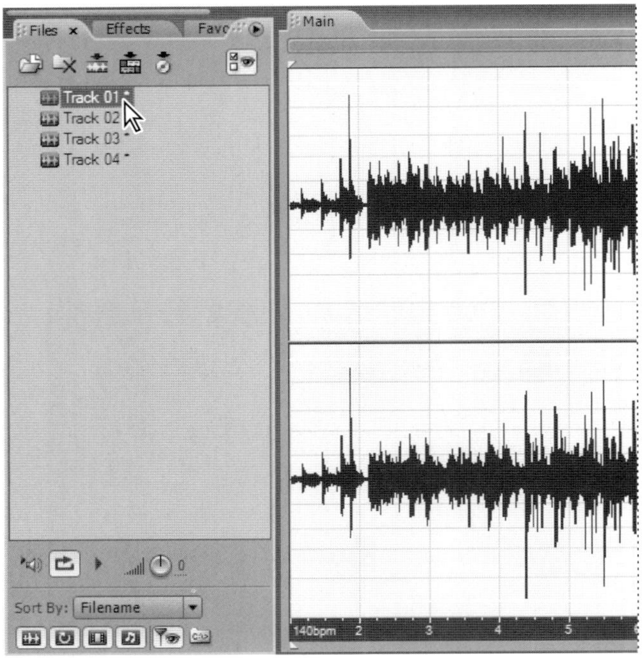

15 Repeat step 12 for the other files called Track 02*, Track 03* and Track 04* and save them onto your hard disk in the same folder. Now that these four tracks have been ripped from the CD and saved onto your hard disk, you can bring them into any other session just like the various loops and waveforms you've been working with in the previous lessons.

16 Click on the Multitrack View button () at the top of your screen to switch to the Multitrack View. Select File > Save Session. Navigate to the AA_12_no_files folder on your hard disk. Confirm that the Save copies of all associated files option is checked at the bottom of the window. Type in the name **extracted_files.ses** in the File name field. Press the Save button.

You don't necessarily have to be in the CD View to be able to extract audio from CDs. You can also do the same in the Edit View by choosing File > Extract Audio from CD.

Opening tracks from CDs

If your computer's CD-ROM drive supports audio digital extraction (also known as ripping), you can extract tracks from audio CDs. Extracting puts the audio into a waveform format which Adobe Audition can edit like any other waveform.

Adobe Audition provides two methods for ripping tracks from CDs: the Open command and the Extract Audio from CD command. The Open command is the fastest method and is preferred for ripping entire tracks. The Extract Audio from CD command provides more control, such as the ability to rip partial tracks and to specify the process used when extracting the file.

1 *Place an audio CD from your personal collection in the computer's CD-ROM drive.*

2 *Start Adobe Audition. Click the Edit View button ( ) and then choose File > Open.*

3 *Choose CD Digital Audio (*.cda) as the file type, and navigate to the computer's CD-ROM drive.*

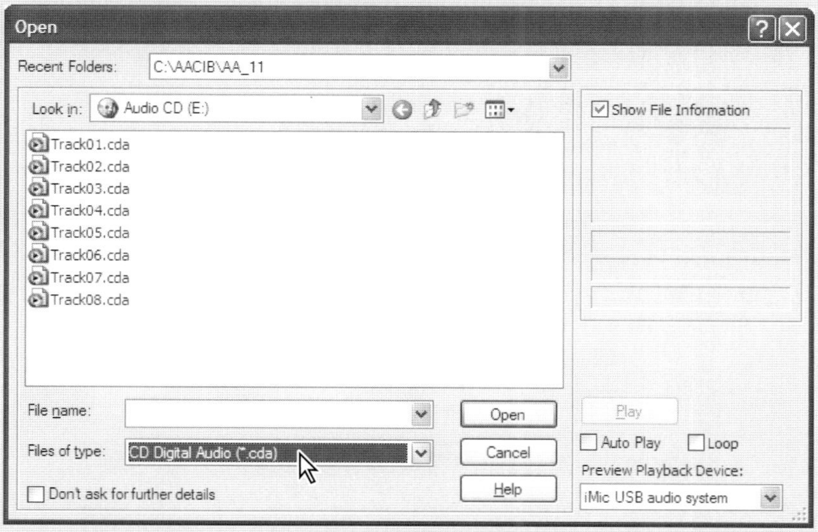

4 *Select the tracks to be ripped.*

5 *Click Open to extract the files into your CD project.*

Once the files are extracted, they are listed in the Files tab of the Organize Window. The files have been converted into editable waveforms. Just as you did in step 13 of the previous exercise, save the extracted files in to the AA_12_no_files folder on your hard disk.

6 *Choose File > Save As and save the files onto your hard disk.*

Inserting and removing tracks

You will now organize the files to be burned onto an audio CD by listing them in sequence in the CD View. The order in which these files are listed is the sequence in which they will be played by an audio device. Audition allows you to add, remove, or reorder files in the CD List.

There are a variety of ways to insert tracks into the CD View. Any file listed in the Files panel can be added to a CD project. If you have added track range markers in a waveform, you can also add them to the CD List as independent tracks.

1 If you don't already have it opened, open the extracted_files.ses by switching to the Multitrack View and choosing File > Open Session.

If for some reason you don't see the four files in the Files panel, then double-click on an empty space in the Files panel and import the four files (Track 01 thru Track 04) you saved in the AA_12_no_files folder in the previous exercise.

2 Press the CD View button (◉) at the top of the display to see the CD View. Here you will find that the Files panel is still on the left, and on the right is an empty track list where you can add and arrange tracks to be burned on a CD. Click one by one on the four files located in the Files panel (Track 01 through Track 04) and drag them into the Main panel or click the Insert Into CD List button (◉).

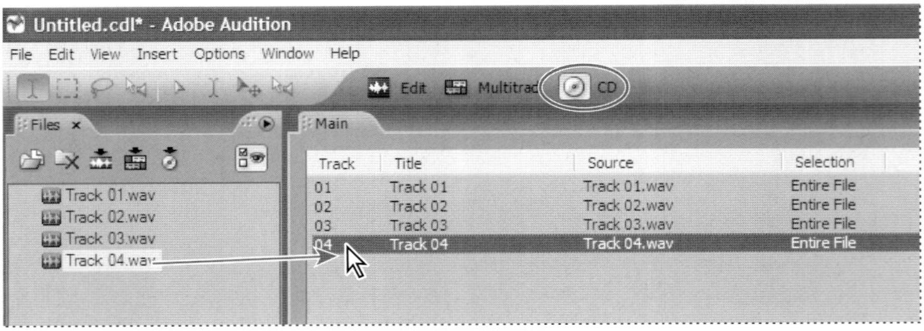

You can drag any supported audio file type from your Windows desktop, including My Computer or Windows Explorer, directly into the track list in CD View. The file first opens in Adobe Audition, and then is inserted into the track list. You should bear in mind that the standard file format for audio CDs is uncompressed audio at 44.1 kHz, 16 bits. When you add a file to the track list that has a different format, Audition automatically makes the necessary conversions for you so that you can burn that file onto a standard audio CD.

3 By using the Move Up and Move Down buttons on the right side of the CD View, or by simple drag and drop, reorganize your files to play in the following order of your new audio CD:

- Track 04
- Track 03
- Track 02
- Track 01

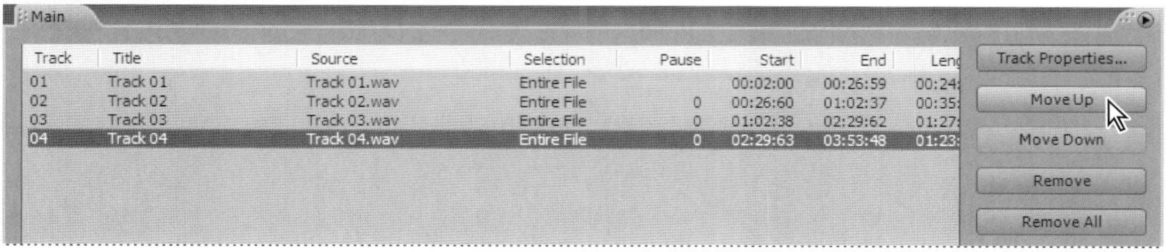

4 Delete Track 04 from your CD Project by selecting it in the CD View window, then clicking the Remove button. You can also remove a track from the track list by highlighting it and pressing the Delete key on your keyboard.

Investigating the CD project size

The CD Size section at the bottom right of the CD View window displays the overall length of the tracks included in your CD project, including the amount of space they will take on the CD. The amount of free space still available on the CD can be found in the taskbar at the bottom of the screen. Depending on whether you are using a 74 minute or an 80 minute CD, you can choose the appropriate option from the View > Free space based on option.

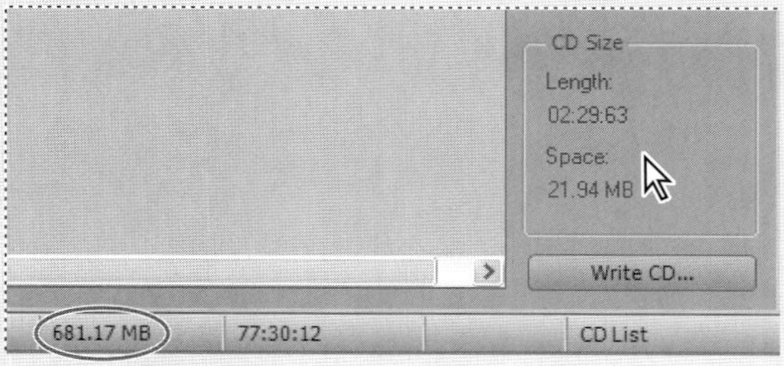

CD Size info.

Setting track properties

Using Track properties, you can change the length of pauses between tracks, enable or disable copy protection and pre-emphasis features, and add an ISRC (International Standard Recording Code) number to your project. You can also specify a title and artist for each track for devices which support CD text display.

1 In CD View, select song title Track 01 in the Main panel and click the Track Properties button. The Track Properties window opens.

2 In the Track Properties window, enter a Track Title of **Song 1**, and **Adobe Audition** in the Artist field of the window.

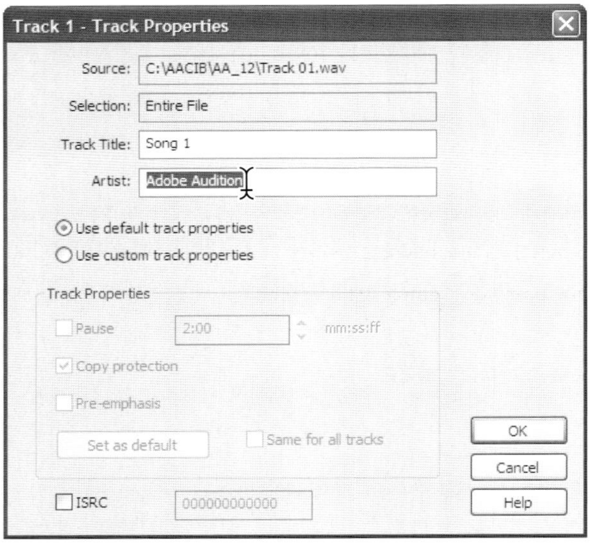

Note: *For Adobe Audition to write text to a CD, the Write CD-Text option must be selected before burning the CD. This option appears in the Write CD window which you will see in the end of this lesson.*

3 Click OK to close the Track Properties window.

Additional track properties

If you want to set additional properties for the track, select Use Custom Track Properties. Set any of the following options, and click OK:

Pause Adds a pause of the specified length before the track. By default, Adobe Audition assigns a 2-second pause to the beginning of each track.

Copy Protection Sets the copy protection flag (as defined by the Red Book specification) for the track. In order for copy protection to work, the CD player must support the copy protection flag.

Pre-Emphasis Sets the pre-emphasis flag (as defined by the Red Book specification) for the track. Pre-emphasis is a basic noise reduction process that is implemented by a CD player. For pre-emphasis to occur, the CD player must support the pre-emphasis flag.

Set As Default Uses the current settings as the default track properties.

Same For All Tracks Applies all settings, except the ISRC code, to all tracks in the track list.

ISRC Specifies an ISRC (International Standard Recording Code). This code is used only on CDs that are destined for commercial distribution.

ISRC codes have 12 characters and use the following format:

- ISO Country: 2-digit code (for example, US for USA).
- Registrant code: 3-digit alpha-numeric, unique reference.
- Year of reference: last 2 digits of the year (for example, 04 for 2004).
- Designation code: a 5-digit, unique number.

—From Adobe Audition Help

Normalizing groups of files for mastering

When you assemble audio for a CD, you may want to fine-tune the individual tracks so that they are consistent with each other. Normalizing is a step in the overall process known as mastering. Mastering may also involve cropping, adjusting dynamics, levels, and EQ.

When you normalize a waveform, the loudest part of the waveform is modified to a specific amplitude, raising or lowering all other parts of the same waveform by the same amount. In this section, you will use Group Waveform Normalize to normalize the volume of multiple open waveforms. Audition uses a three-screen batch process, providing control over statistical analysis, amount of normalization, and the files to which normalization is applied.

You will use Group Waveform Normalize to make sure that all tracks on the CD have a consistent volume.

1 While in CD View, choose Edit > Group Waveform Normalize.

2 Select the Choose Files tab at the bottom of the Group Waveform Normalize window. Select each of the individual waveforms while holding the Shift key from the Source Files portion of the window. All the waveforms become selected.

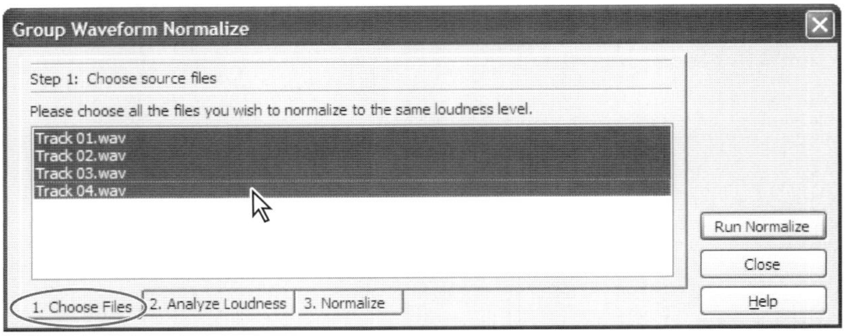

3 Click the Analyze Loudness tab at the bottom of the window, and then click the Analyze Statistical Information button. In the Analyze Loudness tab of the Group Waveform Normalize window, double-click on each filename to display amplitude statistics in the Advanced Statistical Report window.

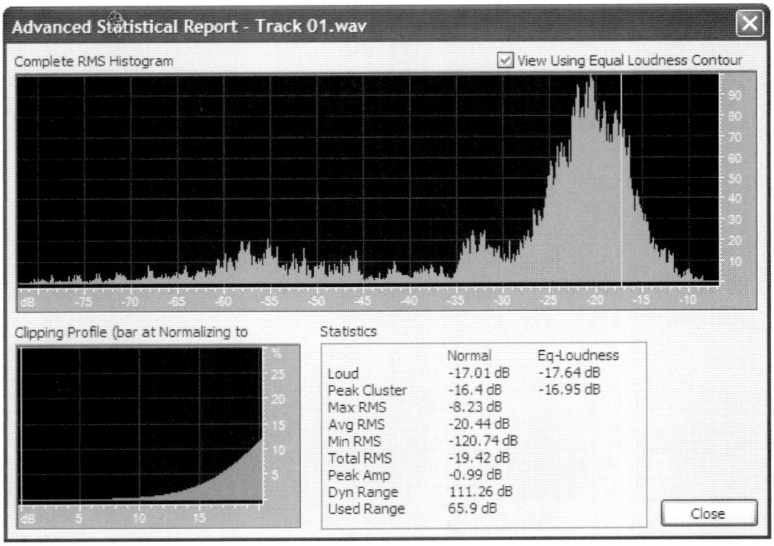

In the Analyze Loudness tab, double-clicking a file in this list provides more detailed statistics, including an RMS histogram and a clipping profile. Root Mean Square (RMS) is an average of continuous power, measured in watts, which a wave source produces.

4 Press the Close button to close the Statistical Report window. At the bottom of the Group Waveform Normalize window, click the Normalize tab. Confirm that the Normalize to Average Level of Source Files (-14.7 dB) option is selected and that the Use Limiting option is also selected.

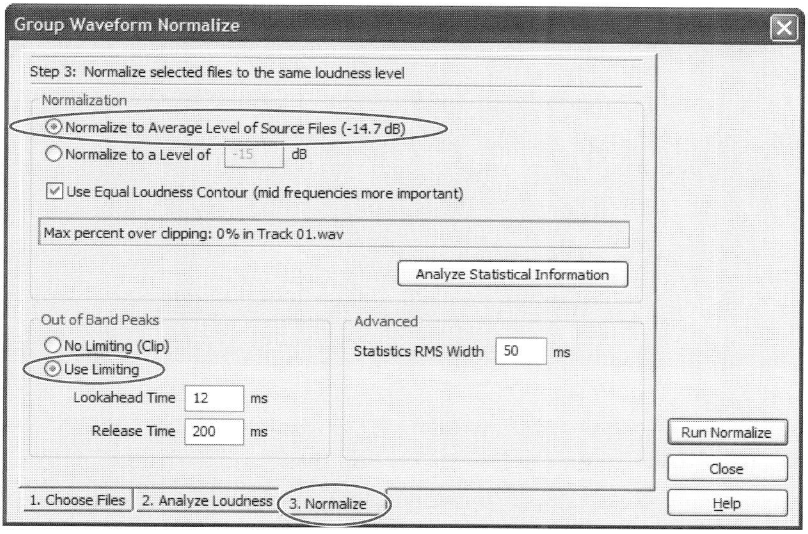

***Note:** The option to Use Equal Loudness Contour reduces the apparent volume of frequencies that might otherwise be perceived as being louder than others. Because the human ear is much more sensitive to frequencies between 2 kHz and 4 kHz, two different pieces of audio with the same RMS amplitude but with different frequencies will appear to have different volumes. This option ensures that audio has the same perceived loudness, regardless of the frequencies that are included in the recording.*

5 Click the Run Normalize button on the right. The original files are normalized, resulting in a more uniform and consistent group of waveforms ready for CD burning.

In the CD View, you can save your current CD List and settings by choosing File > Save CD List. This allows you to save your layout for future use and burn a CD at a later stage. You must be careful, however, to not move, rename or delete the files that constitute that CD List. Otherwise, when you re-open the CD List from File > Open CD List, it would not be able to locate the files that are pointed to by the track list.

Writing a CD

Before writing a CD, you will verify that your CD burning device is set up correctly, set CD options and then write the CD. If you do not have a CD writer on your computer you can move ahead to the Review questions.

As mentioned earlier, audio on CDs must be 44.1 kHz, 16 bit, stereo. If you insert a track with a different sample type, Adobe Audition automatically converts the audio for you.

1 Insert a blank, writable CD into the CD drive of your computer.

2 In CD View, click the Write CD button found at the bottom right corner of your screen or choose File > Write CD. The Write CD window opens.

3 Select the device you want to use to write the CD from the drop-down menu of available drives.

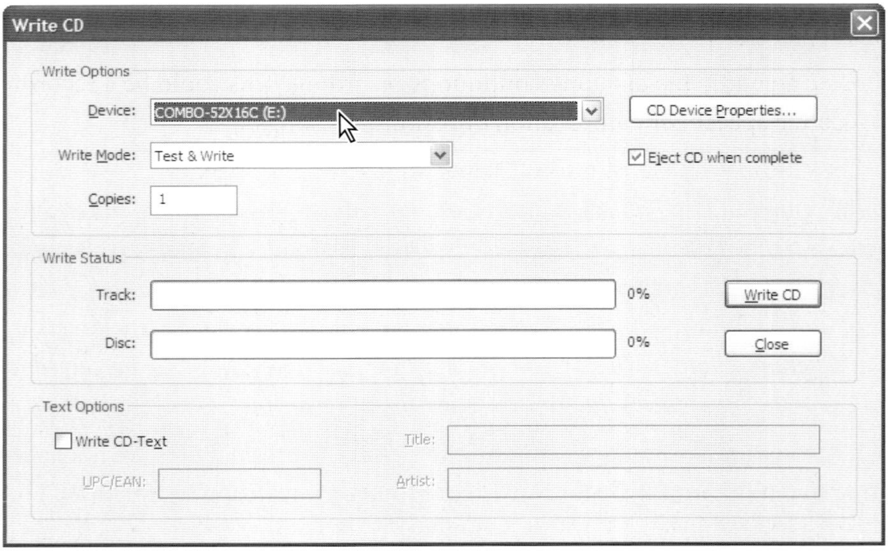

4 In the Write CD window, you have the option of selecting a setting from the Write Mode drop-down menu:

- Write writes the CD without testing for buffer underruns.
- Test only tests if the CD can be written without the occurrence of buffer underruns. No audio is written to the CD.
- Test & Write tests for buffer underruns and then proceeds with the actual write process if the test is successful.

5 From the Write Mode drop-down menu, select the Write option, then check the Eject CD when complete check box option.

6 Check the Write CD-Text option to write the track title and artist for each track to the CD.

If you have a UPC/EAN number, you can enter it here. The UPC/EAN is a 13-digit code that is used to uniquely identify merchandise and communicate product information between a vendor and retailer.

7 Click the Write CD button to write your tracks to CD. The Track and Disk progress meters show you the progress of the write process.

8 Once completed, close the Write CD window and test your CD in an audio CD player, or re-insert it into the CD drive of your computer and play the files using Windows Media Player or another similar program.

Exploring on your own

1 Locate an audio file of a long continuous recording. This could be a recording of a live concert, a speech, or combination of continuous songs.

2 Click on the Edit View button () and choose File > Open.

3 Navigate to the file and import into Adobe Audition. Double-click on the filename in the Files panel to see it in the Edit View.

4 If not already pressed, click on the Show Markers button () at the bottom of the Files panel. If this button is not visible to you, confirm that the Show options button () at the top of the Files panel has been pressed too.

5 Choose Window > Marker List, or use the Alt+8 shortcut from your keyboard.

6 Play the file by pressing the spacebar, making note of the points at which you would like to create separate CD tracks. You can separate sections from within a larger file using markers. The smaller waveforms included in markers can be independently used in a CD List.

7 With the Marker List window still open, click and drag in the waveform to highlight a subsection which you would like to be an independent track in the CD List.

8 Click the Add Marker button () in the Marker List window. Then select the Edit Marker Info button (), making the Marker Info visible on the right.

9 Change the Marker Type from Cue to Track from the drop-down menu, then label the marker in the Description field.

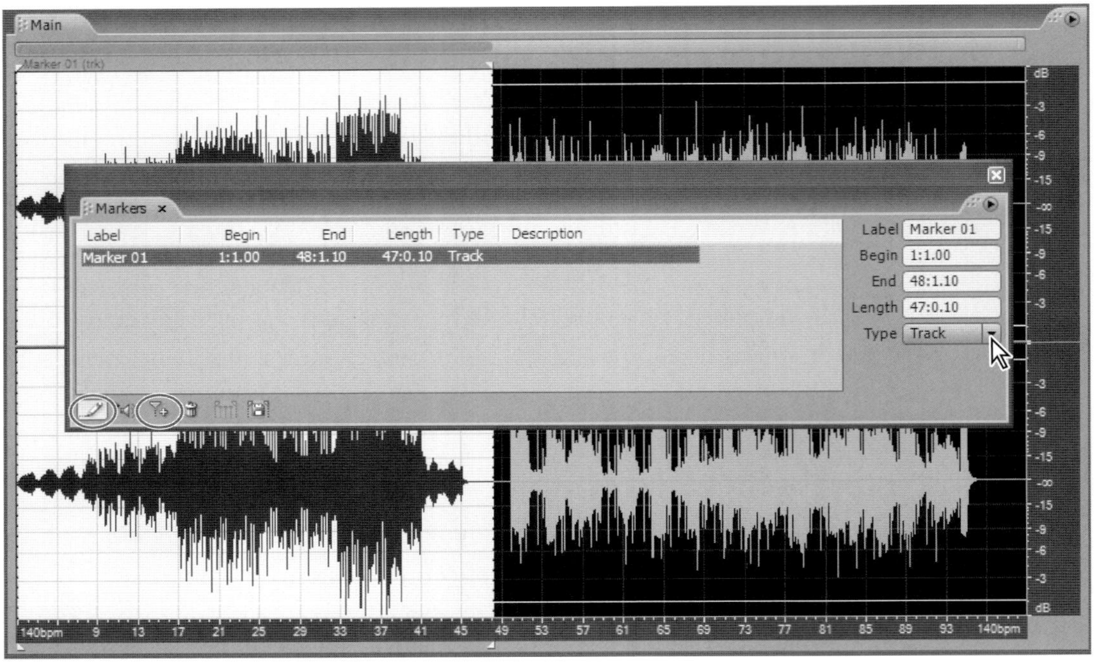

10 Using the same process, insert markers throughout the rest of the waveform, naming each region according to its content. Once you are finished inserting markers into your waveform, close the Markers window and select the CD View.

11 Click on the plus sign (+) next to the original file listed in the Files panel, revealing all the labeled markers you've just created for it.

12 Click and drag each marker into the CD track list. You can also highlight the name of the marker in the Files panel and press the Insert Into CD List button () at the top of the Files panel. If a marker does not represent a selection range and is not a track marker, Audition prompts you to consolidate two markers into a track range that can then be used in the CD List.

13 Reorganize the markers in the CD List in the order you wish them to be listed in your audio CD. Click the Write CD button and follow the same instructions as in the previous exercise to burn a CD.

Review

Review questions

1 What file format is used for most audio CD files?

2 What step ensures consistent amplitude across all audio tracks?

3 How can you ensure a consistent pause between tracks?

Review answers

1 CD audio (.cda) is the standard file format for audio CDs.

2 Audition's Group Waveform Normalize function allows several files to be processed so that relative amplitude is set to an average amount.

3 Using Custom Track Properties in the Track Properties window in CD View, you can specify an exact time pause between each track.

13 Integrating Adobe Audition and Adobe Premiere Pro

You can import high-quality audio files from Adobe Audition for use in Adobe Premiere Pro and easily modify audio files used in Adobe Premiere Pro by opening original multitrack sessions in Adobe Audition. You can also use noise reduction effects to clean up video soundtracks using Adobe Audition.

In this lesson, you'll learn how to do the following:

- Insert video files into Audition.
- Create a soundtrack to a video clip.
- Use the Edit in Adobe Audition command in Multitrack View.
- Use the Edit in Adobe Audition command in Edit View.

Getting started

Adobe Audition and Adobe Premiere Pro provide complementary tools for editing audio and video. In this lesson, you will use Audition's Multitrack View to create a soundtrack to a video clip. Additionally, you will use tools in Audition's Edit View to clean up and work with source audio files from Adobe Premiere Pro. Although Premiere Pro offers some mixing and effect capabilities, Audition's specialized audio tools allow you to extend your audio editing beyond the capabilities of Adobe Premiere.

Note: *The first two sections of this lesson use Adobe Audition, while the remaining sections require Adobe Premiere Pro. If you do not have Adobe Premiere Pro, you can download the trial version, which is available online at http://www.adobe.com/products/tryadobe/main.jsp at no charge.*

1 Start Adobe Audition. Click the Multitrack View button if it's not already selected.

Note: *If you have not already copied the resource files for this lesson onto your hard disk from the AA_13 folder from the* Adobe Audition 2.0 Classroom in a Book *CD, do so now. See "Copying the Classroom in a Book files" on page 2.*

2 To review the finished session file from this lesson, choose File > Open Session while in Multitrack View. Navigate to the AA_CIB folder you created on your hard disk, and open the file AA_13end.ses in the AA_13 folder. Click the Play from Cursor to End of View button (▶) in the Transport panel or press the spacebar on your keyboard. The completed file is played for you.

3 Close the AA_13end.ses file by choosing File > Close All.

4 In Multitrack View, choose File > New Session. In the New Session window, choose 48000 for the sample rate and then click the OK button. Choose File > Save Session As and name this session **AA_13start.ses**. Click Save.

In this lesson, you will be working with Premiere Pro. Premiere Pro uses the DV Playback mode and 48,000 Hz is the standard audio sample rate used in digital video projects. Using this sample rate allows for maximum compatibility with Premiere Pro.

Inserting video into Audition

Audition can import a variety of video file formats, including AVI, native DV, MPEG, and WMV files. You can also view the video component of movie files while in the Multitrack View. Using the Edit View, you can import only the audio portion of a movie file. Only one video file is displayed in the multitrack at a time.

1 Click on the Files tab and then click the Import File button. Navigate to the AA_13 folder on your hard disk and click to select the file supercar.avi. Click the Open button.

2 In the File panel, click to select the supercar.avi file, then click the Insert Into Multitrack Session button. The video file is added to the multitrack.

***Note:** If Audition did not automatically open a Video window, choose Window > Video from the main menu. Based on the previous workspace you were using, Audition may insert the Video window into another area of the interface.*

3 Click the Video tab or choose Window > Video. The video file is a full screen AVI file with a resolution of 720 pixels by 480 pixels.

4 To expand the viewing area of the Video panel, place your cursor over the bottom or right edge of the panel until it changes to the double arrows with parallel lines cursor, then click and drag to expand the panel.

5 Press the spacebar and the movie clip plays in the Video panel. The video clip is approximately 15 seconds long and includes no audio track. When the video finishes, press the spacebar to stop the playback cursor.

Note: *Although this AVI video clip has no audio track, Audition will import both the video and audio portion of any compatible video file.*

6 If necessary, press the Home key to return the start-time indicator to the beginning of the timeline. Right-click on the timeline and from the context menu confirm that Display Time Format > SMPTE 29.97 fps is selected. This changes Audition's time display to SMPTE timecode, a timing reference used to synchronize a camera with another device. SMPTE timecode is divided into hours, minutes, seconds, and frames, a standard method for measuring time for film and video.

7 Click on the Zoom to Selection tool () to increase the magnification of the timeline. The time display changes as well. Audition displays image thumbnails of the video content. Click the Zoom to Selection tool again, and the number of thumbnails increases as you increase the magnification.

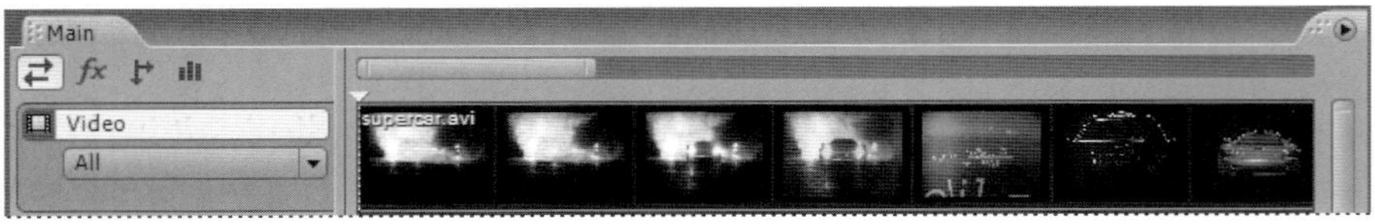

8 Click the Zoom Out Full Both Axes button () to display the complete video file from start to finish. Press the spacebar to play the movie clip. As the file plays, the Video panel display does not correspond to the exact position of the playback cursor. These thumbnails serve as a general guideline for positioning, and are not accurate to the specific frame of video being played.

9 Click the Files tab to bring the Files panel forward. Choose File > Import and navigate to the AA_13 folder on your hard disk. Select the trance05.cel file and the SnareRoll02.cel file by Ctrl+clicking them, and click Open to import the files into the Files panel. In the Files panel, click to select the trance05.cel clip and drag it into Track 2.

10 If necessary, select the Move/Copy Clip tool (), and click and drag the clip to align it with the beginning of the track. Choose Edit > Snapping and if the option for Snap to Clips is not checked, select it now. Click the handle at the bottom right hand corner of the trance05 clip and drag to extend the loop to the right and align the end with the video clip.

11 Click and drag the start-time indicator to the 4 second 12 frame mark.

12 From the Files panel, click and drag the loop SnareRoll02.cel into Track 3 and align the beginning of the clip with the start-time indicator.

13 In the Files panel, double-click the SnareRoll02.cel file to display it in the Edit View. If necessary, press the Home key on your keyboard to move the playback cursor to the start of the clip. In the Transport panel, press the Play from Cursor to End of View button to play the file.

14 Choose Effects > Reverse (process) in the main menu. Press the spacebar to hear the reversed sound effect. Playing a sound effect backwards is a simple and fast way to give it a distinctive sound.

15 Choose File > Save As and name this new file **BackwardsSnare.cel**. Navigate to the AA_13 folder on your hard disk, then click the Save button. Click Yes to overwrite the existing file and then click OK to bypass the lossy format warning. After the file has been saved, click on the Multitrack View button. Renaming the snare drum file after adding the Reverse effect is necessary in order to leave the original file untouched. The reverse snare drum is automatically updated in Track 3.

16 Press the Home key on your keyboard to return the playback cursor to the start of the timeline, and then press the spacebar to play the session file. Synchronizing the reverse snare drum clip with the animated equation sequence creates a pleasing effect, but the snare drum clip is currently shorter than the middle section of the video. You will use Audition's Clip Time Stretching feature to correct that.

17 Click the Video tab to bring the Video panel forward. Click and drag the start-time indicator to the right. Observe the Video panel while moving the start-time indicator. Move the start-time indicator to the 7 second 15 frame point, which is the location where the animated equation starts to fade.

18 In the multitrack, click on the BackwardsSnare clip to make sure it is selected, then choose Clip > Clip Time Stretch Properties. In the Clip Time Stretch Properties window, select Enable Time Stretching, enter **168%** in the Time Stretch text box, and click OK. The BackwardsSnare clip stretches to the start-time indicator.

Clip Time Stretching expands the length of the clip, which has the effect of slowing down the sound of the clip without changing the pitch. The time stretch icon appears in the bottom left of the clip, indicating that the clip has been stretched.

19 Click and drag the start-time indicator back to the 3 second mark in the timeline. Press the spacebar to play the file and listen to the effect of the time stretch. The backwards snare drum is now synchronized with the animated equation video sequence.

Inserting only the audio track into Audition

In the previous exercise you imported an AVI file into Audition. Audition is also capable of importing only the audio component of a video file.

You can use this feature to extract the audio portion of a recorded musical performance, or import the dialog from a video or film recording that needs to be improved. Because importing digital video and audio require more system resources than importing the audio alone, it is often more efficient to work exclusively with the audio. In this exercise, you will import the audio track from a racing car video clip, and then use it as a sound effect in your session file. You will also use Audition's effects tools to alter the shape of the sound.

1 Click on Track 4 to select it. Press the Home key to place the start-time indicator at the beginning of the session and then choose Insert > Audio from Video.

2 In the Insert Audio from Video window, navigate to the AA_13 folder and click to select the file racecar.avi, then click the Open button. The Extract Audio progress window appears as Audition extracts the audio portion of the AVI file and imports the file as racecar in the Multitrack View.

3 Click the Solo button (S) in Track 4 and press the spacebar on your keyboard to hear the sound of the racing car that was extracted from the video clip. Later you will match the sound effect of the racing car to the final section of the movie clip.

4 Click and drag the start-time indicator to the 9 second mark. You should still have the Video panel open from the last exercise. If not, click on the Video tab to reopen it. At the 9 second mark, the image of the car racing through the tunnel starts to appear.

5 If necessary, click to select the Multitrack View button (). Then click and drag the beginning of the racecar sound clip so it is positioned at the start-time indicator. Press the Play from Cursor to End of View button () to hear the sound clip and watch the video.

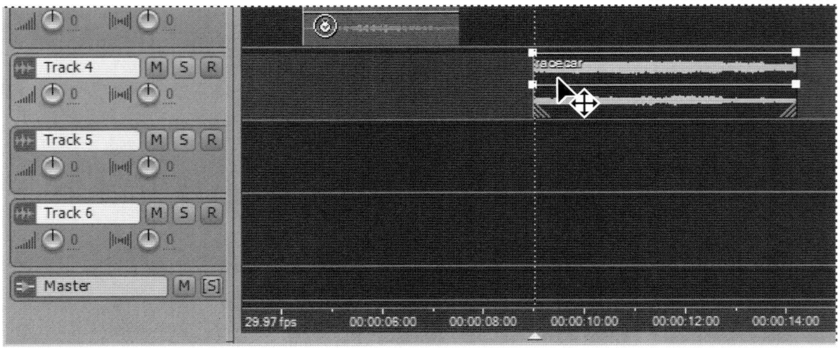

The position of the sound clip is synchronized with the video, but you will now fix the pan from the audio file.

6 In the multitrack, double-click the racecar clip in Track 4 to open it into the Edit View. Choose Edit > Convert Sample Type. Click to select the Mono option and then click OK. The left and right channels of the stereo file are converted to a single mono channel.

7 Choose File > Save As and navigate to the AA_13 folder on your hard disk. Name the file **racecar.cel** and click Save. Click OK to close any warnings relating to possibly saving a lower fidelity file format.

8 Click on the Multitrack View button to return to the Multitrack View. Now that the racecar has been converted to a mono file, you will be manipulating the pan properties to correspond with the video of the car exiting to the right side of the screen.

9 Click on the racecar.cel file to select it. Choose View and make sure Show Clip Pan Envelopes is checked; if not, select it now. The pan envelope line appears along the center of the clip, indicating that the sound is located stereo center.

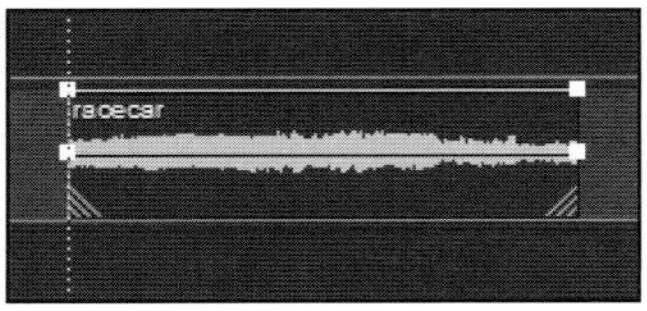

Clip with pan and volume envelopes selected.

10 Click and drag the start-time indicator to the 12 second mark in the timeline. At this point in the video, the car starts to race off-screen. You will match the racecar sound effect to the video.

11 Add an anchor point by clicking the pan envelope line at the 12 second mark when the cursor changes to the pointing finger with a plus sign ( ).

12 Click the pan envelope anchor point at the end of the clip and drag it to the bottom of the clip. This positions the sound of the car to stereo right.

13 Click the pan envelope line halfway between the two anchor points, adding another anchor point. Click and drag the new anchor point down and to the left. As you drag, the pan values appear in a small window. Use a value of approximately 60. This creates a Pan effect that accelerates the transition to stereo right. To hear the effect of the pan, click and drag the start-time indicator to the beginning of the racecar.cel clip and press the spacebar.

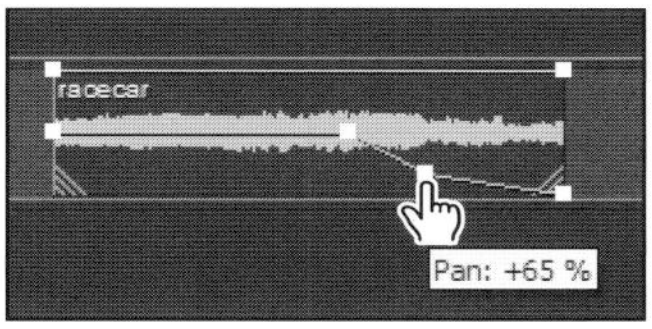

14 Track 4 should still be soloed. To hear the music track in addition to the racecar effect, click the Solo button in Track 4 to hear all of the tracks, then press the spacebar to play.

15 You will now fade in and out the sound of the racecar to make it even more realistic. If necessary, choose View > Show Clip Volume Envelopes to enable them. The volume envelope line appears at the top of the racecar.cel clip. Choose View > Show Clip Pan Envelopes to uncheck that option and hide the line from your clip. The racecar clip should still be selected from the previous step. If it is not, simply click on it. Place your cursor over the anchor point on the top left corner of the clip. Click and drag this anchor point all the way to the bottom. This creates a gradual fade in from the beginning of the clip to the end.

16 Place your cursor on the volume envelope line and using the ruler as a guide, click on the volume envelope at the 10 second mark to add an anchor point. Then click and drag this anchor point to the top of the clip. This creates a fade in.

17 To create a fade out, click on the volume envelope line at the 13 second mark to add an anchor point. Then click and drag the last anchor point at the end of the clip all the way to the bottom.

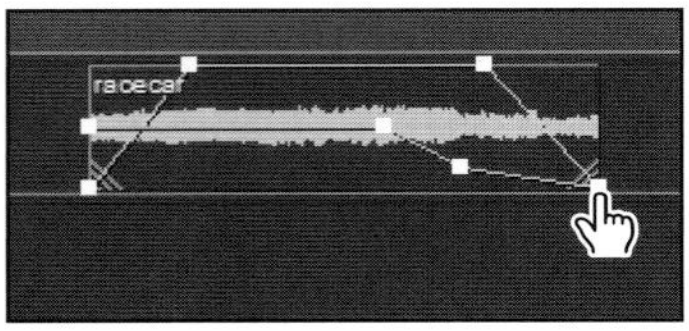

18 Press the Home key on your keyboard to place the start-time indicator at the start of the timeline. Press the spacebar to play the session from beginning to end.

19 Choose File > Save Session As. Name the file **AA13_mixdown.ses** and click Save.

Linking a Premiere audio clip to an Audition multitrack session

In this exercise you will switch between Adobe Audition and Adobe Premiere Pro. You will need to have Premiere Pro installed on your computer to perform the remaining portions of this lesson. You will use the Edit in Adobe Audition command, which links Audition session files to the corresponding .wav files used by Premiere Pro.

1 If you do not have the AA13_mixdown.ses file open from the last exercise, choose File > Open Session and open it now.

2 Choose File > Export > Audio Mix Down. The Export Audio Mix Down window opens.

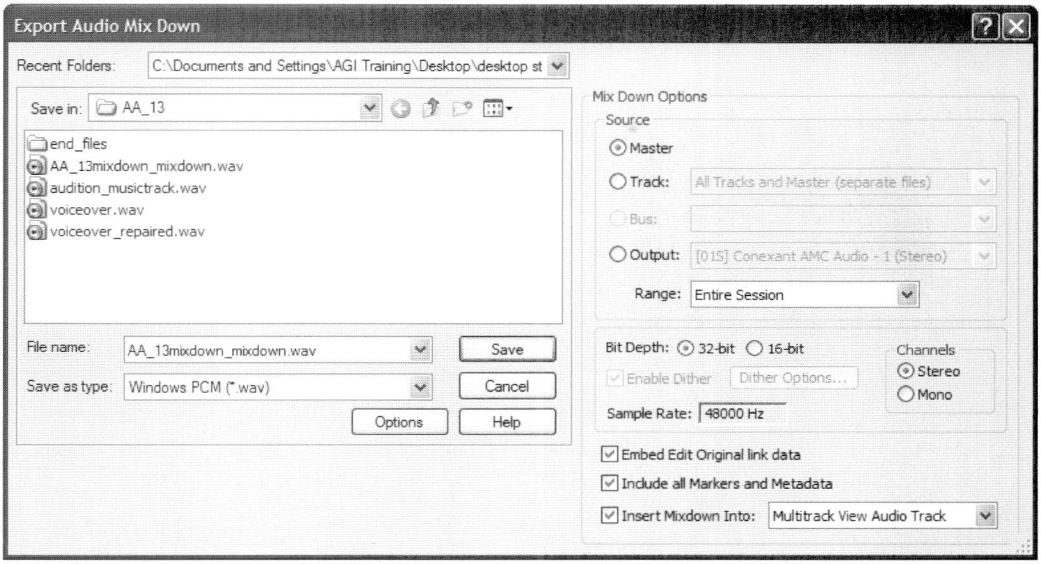

3 In the bottom right of the Export Audio Mix Down window, make sure Embed Edit Original link data is checked; if not, do so now. This ensures that Premiere Pro links your mixdown files to Audition.

4 Enter the name **audition_musictrack.wav** for this file. Keep the Export Audio Mix Down window open. By default, Audition saves exported music tracks as Windows PCM .wav files. If necessary, pull down the Save as type menu and choose Windows PCM from the list.

5 If necessary, navigate to your AA_13 folder on your hard disk and click the Save button. If necessary, click Yes to overwrite the existing file. Audition mixes down the tracks as a .wav file and saves it to your hard disk.

6 Launch Adobe Premiere Pro 2.0. Click the Open Project folder option in the window that displays when you start the program. Navigate to your AA_13 folder and choose the Premiere project file Saleen_Edit_Original.prproj and then click Open. The Premiere Pro workspace opens, and the file supercar.avi is displayed in the Video 1 track.

7 Double-click in an empty area of the Project panel, to open the Import window. In the Import window, navigate to the AA_13 folder and select the audition_musictrack .wav file you just exported from Audition. Click the Open button to import the file into the Project window.

8 Click and drag the audition_musictrack clip from the Project window into the Audio 1 track. Click and drag the clip to the left, so the start of the audio clip is aligned with the start of the supercar video clip.

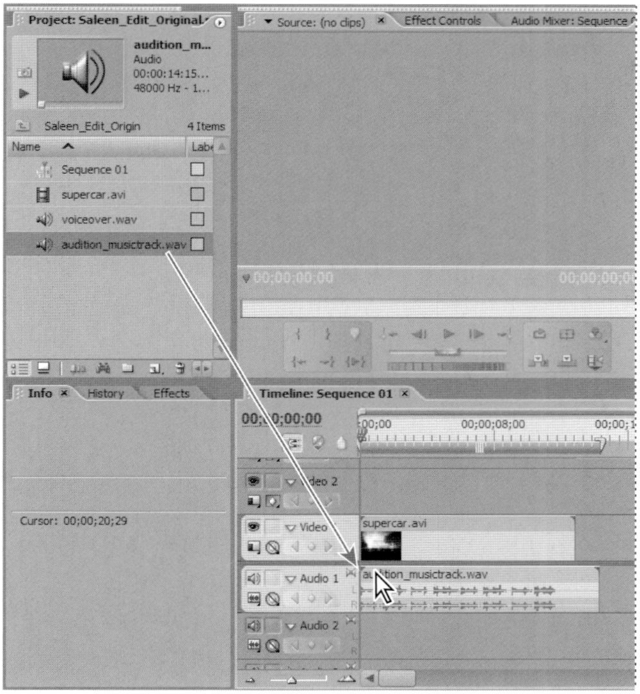

9 Click in the Timeline panel to make it active. Press the Home key on your keyboard to move the start-time indicator to the start of the timeline. Press the spacebar to play the sequence. The soundtrack you created in Audition is synchronized with the racecar. avi file.

10 Choose File > Save Session.

Opening a Premiere audio clip into Audition's Edit View

You can also use the Edit in Adobe Audition feature to open a .wav file directly into Audition's Edit View. Working with a file in Edit View allows you to make use of many Audition features, including Noise Reduction, Studio Reverb, parametric equalization, and more. In this exercise you will open a voiceover file which was originally recorded in Audition, and remove an imperfection.

1 If you do not have the project from the last exercise still open in Premiere Pro, choose File > Open. Navigate to the AA_13 lesson files folder and choose the Saleen_Edit_Original.prproj.

2 In the Project panel, double-click the file voiceover.wav. The voiceover.wav file opens in Premiere's Source Monitor panel as a waveform. Press the Play button in the Source window to listen to the voiceover file. At approximately the 5 second mark, there is a small click in the file, perhaps from the narrator's chair or from another source in the studio. While Premiere may allow for editing this file, Audition's tool set makes the process much easier.

3 In the Project panel, right-click the audio file voiceover.wav. From the context menu choose Edit in Adobe Audition. Choose the option to insert the file into Audition's Edit View.

4 Place your cursor at the 5 second mark in the top half of the timeline. Click and drag across the waveform to make a selection of approximately 15 frames. Use the Selection/View panel controls in the bottom right corner to help measure the selection. Press the spacebar on your keyboard to play the selection. You should be able to hear the click, and the beginning of the narrator's next phrase following the click.

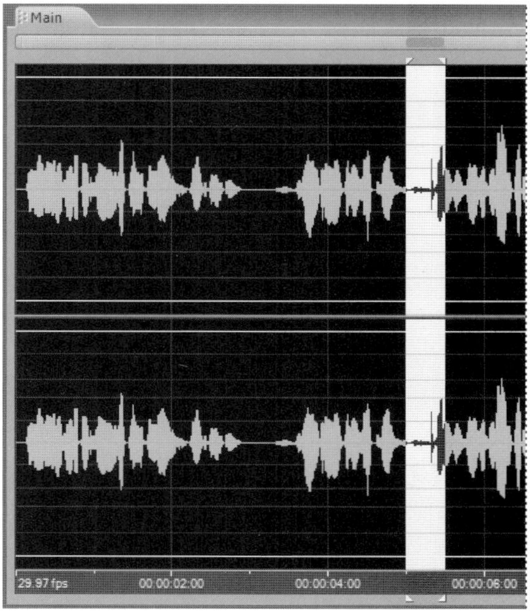

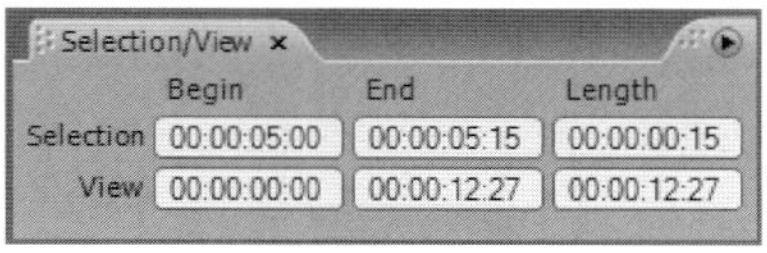

5 Click the Zoom to Selection button () and the selection is magnified in the display window. The click in the audio is visible as a peak in the waveform. Press the spacebar and the selection plays. You can visually match the sound of the click with its location in the waveform.

6 Choose View > Spectral Frequency Display to see the audio in Spectral View. The Spectral View displays the waveform based upon its frequency components: the x-axis (horizontal axis) represents time, and the y-axis (vertical axis) measures frequency.

7 Choose the Marquee Selection tool ().

8 Press the spacebar to play the selection. Note how the click is represented by the red-colored frequency band at the 5 second 10 frame mark. Place your cursor at the top left of the frequency band and drag down to the right to draw a selection around the frequency band that represents the click sound.

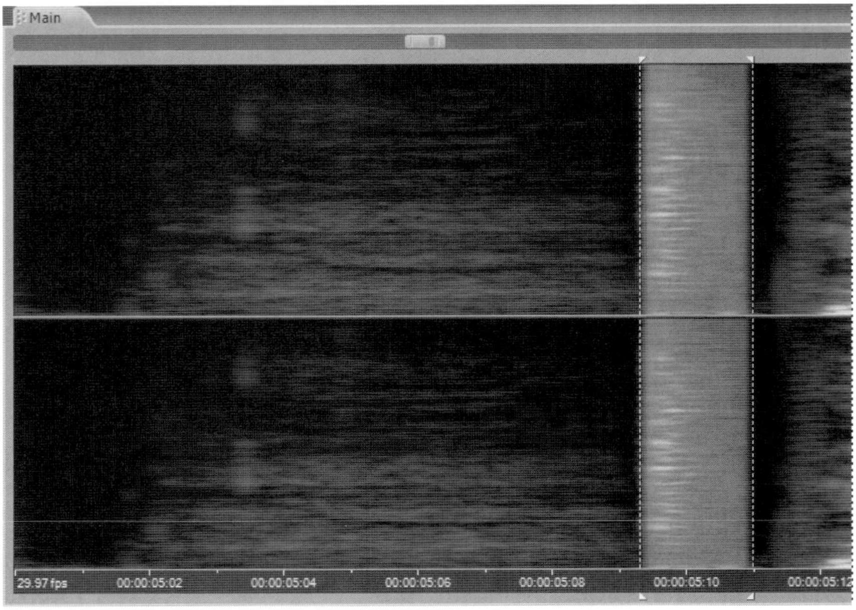

9 Press the spacebar on your keyboard to hear your selection. You should clearly hear the click as the selection plays.

10 Press the Delete key on your keyboard and the audio information in this frequency range is deleted. Press the spacebar and the click has been removed.

The overall length of the original waveform has not changed.

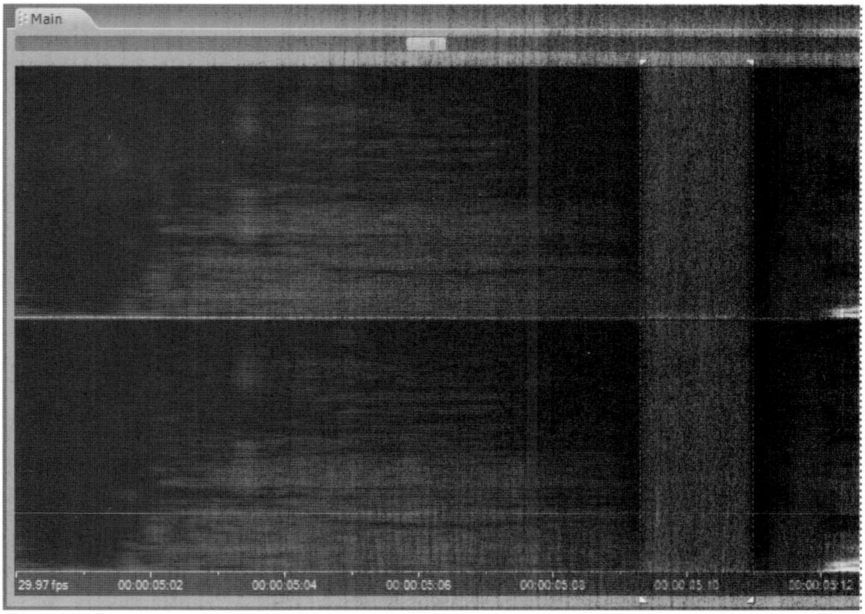

11 Choose View > Waveform Display to return to the waveform view. Note the waveform reflects the removal of the click. Click the Zoom Out Full Both Axis button () to view the entire waveform, click once at the 4 second mark to place your start-time indicator there, and then press the spacebar on your keyboard to play the audio clip. The click from the original file has been removed.

12 Choose File > Save As. Enter the name **voiceover_repaired.wav** for this file and then click the Save button. Work performed in the Edit View is destructive. By renaming files that you have modified, you ensure that a backup remains available. If necessary, click Yes to overwrite.

13 Choose File > Exit to quit Adobe Audition.

14 Switch to Premiere Pro. In the Project panel, click to select the voiceover.wav file. Click the trash can icon () to remove the file from the Project panel. This removes the original file with the click from the Project.

15 Double-click in the empty area of the Project panel below the file list. The Import window opens. Navigate to the AA_13 folder and click to select the voiceover_repaired .wav file. Click the Open button to import the file into the Project window. In the Project window, double-click the file to load it into the Source Monitor panel.

16 Press the spacebar to play the file. This file is the edited file, and the click has been removed.

17 Click and drag the voiceover_repaired.wav file from the Source Monitor View directly into Audio Track 2. Make certain that the clip is aligned at the beginning of the track. Press the Home key to return to the beginning of the timeline, and then press the spacebar to play the completed movie.

18 Save the Premiere project and exit Premiere Pro.

Exploring on your own

1 In the AA13_mixdown.ses file from the last exercise, practice using the volume envelopes you learned how to use in Lesson 4, "Working in the Multitrack View" to create a fade out on the clips you used in this lesson. Additionally, you can explore how Audition can create an automatic fade in and fade out, create a selection in the RhodesOrgan clip and right-click on the clip to choose Crossfade. Explore the differences between applying the Linear, Sinusoidal, and Logarithmic crossfades.

2 Create a new session at 48,000 Hz sample rate and using the racecar.avi clip, create a new soundtrack using the methods in the first exercise. Use at least three tracks with the clips provided for you on the Adobe Audition Loopology DVD. The Loopology DVD provides thousands of musical samples from all genres of music. When you are done creating the new soundtrack, choose Export > Audio to export the session as a .wav file. If you do not have Premiere, you have the option of choosing Export > Video in order to view your results.

Review

Review questions

1 What are the two methods of incorporating video into Audition?

2 What necessary step ensures that exported .wav files used in Premiere Pro or After Effects are linked to Audition session files?

3 How can you access Audition files while in Premiere Pro or After Effects?

Review answers

1 The first method of incorporating video into Audition is by inserting a video track into the Multitrack View. The following video formats are supported: AVI, native DV, MPEG, and WMV files. You can preview video in the Multitrack View, improve audio quality and create original soundtracks with Audition's real-time looping and mixing capabilities. The second method is to import only the audio data from a video file, which is useful when the video data is not necessarily needed.

2 When the session file is exported as a .wav file, select Embed Edit Original link data in the Export Audio dialog box in order for the program to use the Edit in Adobe Audition command.

3 Both Premiere Pro and After Effects will open .wav files created in Audition through the Edit in Adobe Audition command. The user then has the choice to open the original session file in the Multitrack View of Audition, or alternatively, to open the exported audio file into the Edit View as a single waveform.

Index

A

B

C

T

U

V

W

Y

Z

Production Notes

The *Adobe Audition 2.0 Classroom in a Book* was created electronically using Adobe InDesign CS2. Additional art was produced using Adobe Illustrator CS2, and Adobe Photoshop CS2.

Team credits

The following individuals contributed to the development of new and updated lessons for this edition of the *Adobe Audition Classroom in a Book*:

Project Manager: Christopher Smith

Technical writing: Gautam, based on work by Jeremy Osborn and Luis Mendes

Production and artwork: AGI Training: Elizabeth Chambers, Luis Mendes

Proofreading: Jay Donahue

Technical Editors: Cathy Auclair, Eric Rowse, Sean McKnight, Greg Heald

Original compositions: Gautam, Jason Levine

Thanks to Ken Gordon and Tad Lemire—Chapter 6; Tad Lemire and Amy Ryan of WCTK 98.1—Chapter 7; and Jason Levine—Lesson 12 CD audio tracks.

Typefaces used

Set in the Adobe Minion Pro and Adobe Myriad Pro OpenType families of typefaces. More information about OpenType and Adobe fonts is available at Adobe.com.

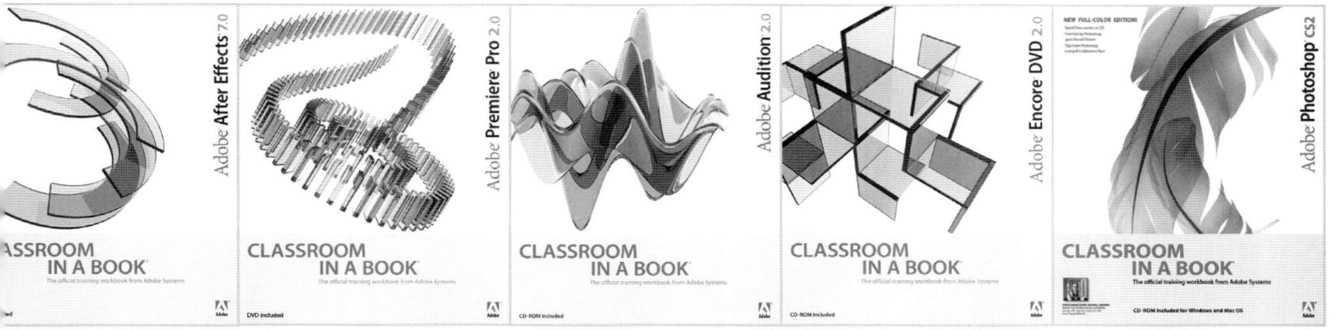
Adobe After Effects 7.0
ASSROOM IN A BOOK
Adobe Premiere Pro 2.0
CLASSROOM IN A BOOK
DVD included
Adobe Audition 2.0
CLASSROOM IN A BOOK
CD-ROM included
Adobe Encore DVD 2.0
CLASSROOM IN A BOOK
CD-ROM included
NEW FULL-COLOR EDITION!
Adobe Photoshop CS2
CLASSROOM IN A BOOK
The official training workbook from Adobe Systems
CD-ROM included for Windows and Mac OS